ERASMUS AND THE MIDDLE AGES

BRILL'S STUDIES IN INTELLECTUAL HISTORY

ERASMUS AND THE MIDDLE AGES

The Historical Consciousness of a Christian Humanist

BY

ISTVÁN BEJCZY

BRILL

LEIDEN · BOSTON · KÖLN

2001

This book is printed on acid-free paper.

On the cover:
Portrait of Erasmus on his death-bed by an anonymous artist. Drawing in black chalk on grey paper, 138 x 127 mm. Teylers Museum, Haarlem, The Netherlands.

Library of Congress Cataloging-in-Publication Data

Bejczy, István Pieter, 1965-
  Erasmus and the Middle Ages : the historical consciousness of a Christian humanist / by István Bejczy.
    p. cm. — (Brill's studies in intellectual history, ISSN 0920-8607 ; v. 106)
  Includes bibliographical references and index.
  ISBN 9004122184 (alk.paper)
    1. Erasmus, Desiderius, d. 1536. 2. Middle Ages—Historiography. 3. History—Philosophy—History—16th century. 4. History—Religious aspects—Christianity—History of doctrines—16th century. I. Title. II. Series.

B785.E64 B45   2001
199'.492—dc21

2001037777

Die Deutsche Bibliothek - CIP-Einheitsaufnahme

Bejczy, István:
Erasmus and the Middle Ages : the historical consciousness of a Christian humanist / by István Bejczy. – Leiden ; Boston ; Köln : Brill, 2001
  (Brill's studies in intellectual history ; Vol. 106)
  ISBN 90–04–12218–4

ISSN   0920-8607
ISBN   90 04 12218 4

PRINTED IN THE NETHERLANDS

For Erika Rummel

Mala tempora, laboriosa tempora, hoc dicunt homines. Bene vivamus, et bona sunt tempora. Nos sumus tempora: quales sumus, talia sunt tempora.

Augustine, *Sermo* 80.8

CONTENTS

ACKNOWLEDGEMENTS

The Netherlands Organisation for Scientific Research (NWO) generously subsidised my research from the outset, appointing me research fellow at the Catholic University of Nijmegen and enabling me to visit several centres of research abroad: the Pontifical Institute for Mediaeval Studies and the Centre for Reformation and Renaissance Studies in the University of Toronto, Canada (1994, 1995, 1996, 1999); the Catholic University of Louvain (Leuven), Belgium (1997); the Centre d'Etudes Supérieures de la Renaissance at Tours, France (1998). I wish to thank the Catholic University of Nijmegen for institutional support, and all the scholars attached to the above-named institutions who helped me in my work. I am particularly grateful to Hilmar Pabel and Peter Raedts for their detailed comments on a manuscript version of this book; to Kate van Liere, Karen Lindsey, and Michael Milway for their corrections of my English; and to Erika Rummel, to whom I owe my greatest debts in Erasmian studies.

Quotations of Erasmus in English translation are taken from *Collected Works of Erasmus* (University of Toronto Press, 1974–) whenever available. All other translations are my own.

INTRODUCTION

Few appraisals of history have so forcibly and durably imposed them-selves as the contempt of Renaissance humanists for the millennium which preceded them. Not only have we accepted their concept of the Middle Ages, but their judgement of the period is, in common parlance at least, still influential: despite the apologetic zeal of gen-erations of medievalists, and despite the many upswings of medieval nostalgia since the days of Romanticism, in most European languages "medieval" can be used as a synonym of "backward" or "barbarian".

By studying the Renaissance view of the Middle Ages, medieval-ists may come to understand the earliest conceptualisation of their own period of interest. Also, and perhaps more important, such study offers Renaissance scholars a chance to grasp the identity of the Renaissance movement.[1] As the Renaissance centred around the idea that civilisation had to be restored to its ancient splendour after cen-turies of medieval decline, the Renaissance conception of the Middle Ages is fundamental to a proper understanding of the Renaissance itself, however unfair the humanist attitude to medieval culture may have been.[2]

The aim of this book is to examine Erasmus' attitude toward the medieval past and to relate it to his historical consciousness in gen-eral, that is, to his view of the world in its temporal dimension and

---

[1] For the view of the Renaissance as a movement (rather than a period), i.e. as a conscious association of human beings around a programme (the restoration of civilisation after its medieval decline) see Ernst H. Gombrich, *In Search of Cultural History* (Oxford 1969); idem, "The Renaissance—Period or Movement?", A.G. Dickens et al., *Background to the English Renaissance: Introductory Lectures* (London 1974), 9–30.

[2] Cf. Wallace K. Ferguson, *The Renaissance in Historical Thought: Five Centuries of Interpretation* (Cambridge MA 1948), 18: "the Middle Ages are an essential prereq-uisite to the Renaissance in the conceptual as well as the chronological sense". Actually Ferguson's monumental survey of Renaissance conceptualisations since early humanism can be read as a history of the perception of the difference between the Middle Ages and the Renaissance. See also Charles G. Nauert, *Humanism and the Culture of Renaissance Europe* (Cambridge 1995), 21: the "sense of being deeply engaged in the restoration of true civilisation after many centuries of barbarian darkness" is "the defining characteristic of Renaissance humanism, and anyone attempting to understand humanism must take it into account".

of his own place in it. As Erasmus was, according to his contemporaries as well as to modern commentators, the most important and the most influential figure of the Northern Renaissance, his attitude toward the Middle Ages is surely deserving of scholarly attention. Indeed, the desirability of a study on Erasmus' view of the Middle Ages has been pointed out before.[3]

The case of Erasmus is particularly rewarding. More than any other Renaissance figure, the humanist from the Low Countries was committed to the goal of building an alternative to medieval civilisation. Using the past as an instrument to correct the present, he organised his immense knowledge of the intellectual and religious traditions of Western Christendom into interpretative schemes, drawing a crucial distinction between "ancient" and "recent" elements. As a rule, the ancient elements were essential to him, whereas he tended to discard most "recent" (that is, medieval) phenomena as superfluous or harmful.[4] His ideas on the intellectual and religious renewal of Christian civilisation thus lay embedded in his conception of history. As several scholars have noticed, Erasmus' most important historical thought actually pertains to his ideas on the reform of Latin Christendom rather than to his formal treatment of the past.[5] Accordingly, this study will focus on the interaction between Erasmus' perception of the medieval past and his project of creating a better future.

In studying Erasmus' historical consciousness, we must bear in mind that Christian history was what mattered most to him. Indeed to Erasmus all history was, in a sense, Christian history. With good reason his conception of history has been characterised as Christocentric. In Erasmus' view, all history sacred and profane was the work of God—"nothing happens either in human or in heavenly affairs unless with divine consent", as he wrote in one of his Psalm

---

[3] See Franz Bierlaire, "Pour une étude du temps chez Erasme", *Le temps et la durée dans la littérature du Moyen Age et à la Renaissance*, ed. Y. Bellenger (Paris 1986), 117–23:118–9.

[4] John W. O'Malley, "Introduction", CWE 66 ix–li:xvi–xvii.

[5] Cf. Ferguson, *The Renaissance in Historical Thought*, 40: "[Erasmus'] most influential historical thought ... was that implicit in his whole program for the reform of religion and good letters"; Myron P. Gilmore, "Fides et Eruditio: Erasmus and the Study of History", *Humanists and Jurists: Six Studies in the Renaissance* (Cambridge MA 1963), 87–114:111: although "history as a formal subject was allotted but a small place" in Erasmus' educational programme, "the whole scheme nevertheless depended on Erasmus' conquest of the historical world of antiquity and early Christianity".

commentaries[6]—and inclined toward the spiritual maturity of mankind.[7] Naturally, the Incarnation constituted the pivotal moment in this process, but not its completion. For Erasmus, the caesura between Mosaic law (the flesh) and the reign of the New Testament (the spirit) lived on in every human being personally as well as in Christian history in its entirety.[8] But not every epoch had witnessed progress. In fact, Christian history had long been proceeding in the wrong direction. In the Middle Ages, especially in the last few centuries, faith had grown cold, and humanity had become distracted by care for mere outward things. Erasmus saw it as his task, at least in his mature years, to redirect the process and to lay the foundations for a liberation of the soul.

As the above statements imply, Erasmus' views on sacred and pro- fane history do not receive a separate treatment in this study. We cannot agree with the idea advanced by some scholars that Erasmus drew a fundamental distinction between the two.[9] He did recognise

---

[6] *Enarratio psalmi XXXIII* ASD V-3 98:108–9. Curiously, Fiorella De Michelis Pintacuda, "Erasmo e le origini della storiografia moderna", *La storia della filosofia come sapere critico: studi offerti a Mario Dal Pra* (Milan 1984), 659–683:682 infers from these words that "in questo modo è garantita alla storia sacra una posizione tutta particolare e indubbiamente superiore rispetto alla storia profana".

[7] See esp. Jean-Pierre Massaut, "Humanisme et spiritualité chez Erasme", *Dictionnaire de spiritualité* 17 vols. (Paris 1937–95) VII 1006–28:1008: "Pour chaque individu, comme dans l'histoire humaine, la culture profane, même païenne, est justifiée par sa fonction propédeutique et auxiliaire en vue de la "théologie" . . . Cette sorte de *translatio studii* . . . est possible parce que le Christ est le centre de l'histoire et la fin de toute la création . . . L'histoire culturelle s'intègre ainsi dans l'histoire du salut, selon une perspective christologique et eschatologique". Cf. Marjorie O' Rourke Boyle, *Christening Pagan Mysteries: Erasmus in Pursuit of Wisdom* (Toronto 1981), 10ff. See also below #. [Ch 1]

[8] Cf. *Commentarius in psalmum II* CWE 63 96/ASD V-2 118:665–72: "In the course of its history, the world passed through a sort of universal childhood, so to speak, and its tutor then was Moses' law. Each of us, too, goes through a sort of child- hood in Christ, and the church has certain rituals of its own which cater for the weakness of youth until, growing up in the faith and charity of the gospel, we acquire sufficient strength. God tolerates the life of the flesh for a while, if it is gradually dissolved into the spirit, but he does not tolerate it for ever".

[9] See P.G. Bietenholz, *History and Biography in Erasmus of Rotterdam* (Geneva 1966), 38; Jacques Chomarat, "More, Erasme et les historiens latins", *Moreana* 22.86 (1985), 71–107:100–01; idem, "La philosophie de l'histoire d'Erasme d'après ses réflexions sur l'histoire romaine", *Miscellanea Moreana* [= *Moreana* 26.100 (1989)], 159–67. Chomarat's first study repeats Bietenholz's opinion that sacred and profane history, for Erasmus, operate on different planes. His second study is more nuanced: Erasmus would perceive history "sur trois plans, ou dans trois domaines" (159; the difference between these two formulae is, of course, considerable), pertaining to politics, religion, and literature. Religious history, however, offered important parallels with literary

different facets within historical reality (political, cultural, religious, etc.) and valued those on different scales, as most historians do nowadays, but this is not to say that he saw these facets as different "planes" which interfered with each other only incidentally. To isolate Erasmus' view of sacred history is to ignore the essential correlation existing, in his understanding, between the developments in the field of literature and learning on the one hand and the moral and spiritual growth of humanity on the other. Insofar as Erasmus' perception of history allows for the notion of separate development, a dichotomy between *Geistesgeschichte* (intellectual, cultural, and religious history in a broad sense) and political history would seem to be of greater relevance, although for him even these two fields were connected (since politics may favour or harm cultural and religious life, intellectuals may influence political rule, etc.). In Erasmus' conception, however, sacred and cultural history were inextricably intertwined.

In accordance with his general concept of history, Erasmus consistently argued that the neglect of good (that is, ancient) letters had caused the downfall not only of secular culture but also of true Christian piety and virtue. Consequently, the restoration, dissemination, and study of ancient literature (Greek and Latin classics, the New Testament, the church fathers) would result in an elevation of cultural and intellectual as well as moral and spiritual standards.[10] Yet these very assumptions, which one may consider constitutive of the reform programme of Christian humanism, appear to be challenged by Erasmus' specific observations on the course of history up to his own day. Our study will permit us to explore the challenge. Did Erasmus' view of the past allow him to suppose that learning produced moral effects?[11] Did literary and religious culture, in his

---

history (164–5), whereas political history was hardly relevant to it. To support the latter statement, Chomarat alleges that with Erasmus one does not even find the traditional argument that the domination of Rome over the world facilitated the spread of the gospel (160). Chomarat is mistaken: Erasmus used the argument at least twice, cf. *Antibarbari* CWE 23 59–60/ASD I-1 82:28–83:5, *Ecclesiastes* ASD V-4 180:919–22.

[10] In this study the terms "moral" and "spiritual" will be used rather loosely. Both terms refer to Erasmus' conception of *pietas*, which can hardly be rendered in English, cf. O'Malley, "Introduction", CWE 66 xi–xii.

[11] Albert Rabil, "Desiderius Erasmus", *Renaissance Humanism: Foundations, Forms, and Legacy* II *Humanism Beyond Italy* (Philadelphia 1988), 216–64:222 rightly identifies the concept "that learning will make one a better person" as "the key to Erasmus's program of scholarship and reform".

perception, really decline together and later, during his lifetime, revive together?[12] Although the relation between the intellectual and the moral dimensions of Erasmus' programme of reform has been critically examined before,[13] the present study is the first to show a fault line between the basic assumptions of Erasmus' Christian humanism and his view of the actual development of humanity through the ages.

Thesis

The study of Erasmus' historical consciousness poses several methodological problems. First of all, Erasmus was no historian (and certainly no medievalist), nor was he a philosopher of history. The medieval past does not occupy a dominant place in any of his writings. As a Renaissance humanist, Erasmus tried rather to reach back across the medieval period to the literary and religious culture of the first centuries, to make it inform his own day. Moreover, he hardly ever subjected his historical thought to sustained reflection. We cannot therefore proceed by analysing in detail a limited number of key writings which clearly express Erasmus' ideas on history. We must try to gather his view of the Middle Ages, and of history in general, from incidental remarks throughout his work. Naturally not all of his particular and mostly unreflective statements agree perfectly with each other, so that in some cases we must subsume Erasmus' ideas in conflicting parallel schemes. Further, some of his ideas underwent modifications in the course of his life, especially in the Reformation era, when he became more explicit on the relative merits of medieval civilisation. On the whole, however, Erasmus' views were fairly consistent. The real conflict is not among his various statements on history themselves, but between these statements on the one hand and the fundamental claims of Christian humanism on the other.

problem 1

A second problem concerns terminology. Erasmus never gave the medieval period a name of its own, and his sparse substantial statements on the course of Western history are for the most part so

problem 2

---

[12] As is stated by Ferguson, *The Renaissance in Historical Thought*, 46.

[13] See most notably Anthony Grafton and Lisa Jardine, *From Humanism to the Humanities: Education and the Liberal Arts in Fifteenth- and Sixteenth-Century Europe* (London 1986), 138–49 which concentrates, however, on Erasmus' writings on grammar and rhetoric. In Erasmus' view, these subjects were not sufficient to produce good Christians, as Grafton and Jardine seem to assume, but had a propaedeutic function. Yet Grafton and Jardine are right to point to the problematic character of Erasmus' assumption that accurate reading of good texts would result in moral improvement.

diffuse that it is difficult to extract from them a distinct notion of the Middle Ages at all. However, he usually employs the term *recentior* to refer to medieval times, especially if opposed to *vetustior, antiquus*, etc. The term extends, of course, to Erasmus' own lifetime, but then Erasmus did not think that the Middle Ages had come to an end. As a rule, Erasmus' suggestion of a contrast between different epochs helps to solve problems of interpretation. Whenever he sets off modern developments against ancient situations, one may assume that he is pointing to medieval events. A more elaborate discussion of Erasmus' terminology can be found in Chapter Two.

The present study is divided into six chapters. The first three examine Erasmus' conception of the past and concentrate on passages in his work which reveal his view of the direction, the nature, and the sense of the historical development of the Christian world. Chapter One opens with an investigation of some of Erasmus' general statements on history and then proceeds with a discussion of successive historical epochs, taking Erasmus' own periodisation as a point of reference. Pagan classical antiquity, which Erasmus considered most relevant to Christian civilisation, will be briefly treated, but our main interest lies with Christian history proper. The "apostolic" and "patristic" periods, together composing Christian antiquity, are reviewed in the first chapter. Our primary concern is the extent to which these ancient periods of history could serve, in Erasmus' view, as a model for contemporary society.

The second and third chapters are devoted to what Erasmus called the "modern" history of Christendom and what we call the Middle Ages. The "monastic" period (roughly the sixth to twelfth centuries) is the subject of Chapter Two. Chapter Three deals with the ensuing "scholastic" period, which in Erasmus' opinion still dominated his age and therefore receives a comparatively extensive treatment in his writings. Our discussion focuses on the analysis of cultural and spiritual decline. When and how did Christian civilisation, according to Erasmus, fall away from ancient ideals? What caused this lapse? Were the developments in learning and piety contingent upon each other?

The next three chapters explore the relationship between Erasmus' view of the past and his ideas on the reform of Christian civilisation. Chapter Four examines to what extent, in Erasmus' assessment, contemporary society had left the medieval past behind and how much work still needed to be done. Special attention is paid to his evaluation of his own role in the process and to his expectations for the future. Again, the relationship between culture and piety is central to our argument: did Erasmus' perception of his own age confirm his idea that learning and religion would revive hand in hand?

Erasmus' claim that his project of reform aimed at nothing new but envisaged the restoration of pre-medieval culture is measured in Chapter Five against his New Testament edition. As the chapter tries to demonstrate, Erasmus was, knowingly and willingly, an innovator of biblical prose. Moreover, some of the arguments he put forward in defence of his edition seem to suggest that religion could do very well without the aid of letters and thus defy the essence of Christian humanism.

Chapter Six asks to what extent Erasmus saw medieval civilisation, for all its alleged inferiority, as worthy of respect. His confrontation with two movements which, in his perception, tried to dispense with the medieval past altogether—Ciceronianism and Lutheranism—turned him into a defender of tradition in the domains of both literary and religious culture. The chapter argues, however, that Erasmus' attachment to tradition is consistent with the outlook on history which he had developed in his early years. The Reformation did not change Erasmus into a conservative, but accentuated an existing attitude. He never favoured a revolution which would destroy the medieval experience.

What readers should not expect to find in any chapter is a systematic study of Erasmus' reception of medieval authors. No doubt he owed more to them than he would have liked to admit. But our concern is with Erasmus' historical consciousness, not his formal indebtedness to the Middle Ages. The study of the influence of medieval ideas on Erasmus' thought, or of his originality in comparison to medieval intellectual life, falls outside the scope of this book.

CHAPTER ONE

THE IDEA OF HISTORY

In 1517, at the height of his fame and influence, Erasmus wrote a letter to his friend Guillaume Budé, the leader of humanism in France, in which he pretended to reveal the source of his inspiration. Whereas Budé drew strength from reading the classics and Italian humanists, for Erasmus the situation was different:

> And then, if I summon up my courage to write something, it is other men's amazing impudence that drives me to it who, though they cannot write and have read nothing, have the effrontery to teach what they do not know. You get the urge to write from Pliny and Ermolao and Poliziano; in me the passion is aroused by Passavanti and Hugo and their like, the compilers of summaries; for though more than tongue-tied compared with your great scholars, in this unmusical company even a lark like me dares to give tongue.[1]

Although Erasmus' confession is obviously cast to be witty, there can be little doubt that he consciously worked to create an alternative to the intellectual and religious civilisation of the Middle Ages. He conceived of his scholarly activities not only as contributions to the restoration of true and ancient culture, but also as a struggle against medieval barbarism.

Our earliest testimonies regarding Erasmus' life and thought show that, in his twenties, the future prince of humanism was bent on expelling the Middle Ages from the world, especially from his own country. Probably his aversion to his predominantly medieval school education in part explains his radical stance, even though under the rectorate of Alexander Hegius (c. 1433–98) his school at Deventer had adopted a curriculum which was progressive for its day, including lessons in Greek.

---

[1] CWE Ep. 531:162–9/Allen 148–53. The references are to the preacher Jacopo Passavanti (1302–57) and, probably, to either the philosopher-theologian Hugh of St. Victor († 1141) or the exegete Hugh of St. Cher (c. 1190–1263). Cf. CWE Ep. 1581:97–8/Allen 88–9: "But, for some reason which I cannot explain, whenever I take up these modern writers, I begin to feel my own inadequacy less".

The earliest work of Erasmus may have been his paraphrase of the *Elegantiae linguae latinae* of Lorenzo Valla (1407–57), the champion of classical Latin in Renaissance Italy and the young Erasmus' personal idol. Erasmus composed his paraphrase about 1488 and never intended it for publication. The work nevertheless appeared in print in 1529, without his consent and with substantial changes in both order and content. But what we may duly ascribe to Erasmus are the recurrent references to the "barbarians" who spoil the Latin language, references for which there is often no parallel in Valla's text. True, Valla had blamed the decay of classical Latin on the Goths and the Gauls, but Erasmus continually accuses barbarous modern grammarians (*neoterici*) of distorting the language of ancient Rome even when Valla does not. Moreover, Erasmus frequently attacks the barbarians in model phrases of his own making, devised to illustrate the proper use of Latin. We find nothing of this kind in Valla, who instead had offered phrases from classical authors as examples. Erasmus' own phrases express the idea that the literary culture of antiquity had all but perished during the uncivilised ages which were still holding sway.[2] Twice he voices the hope that barbarism could soon be crushed and literature saved.[3]

Several other writings from the same period confirm that the young Erasmus considered himself stationed at an outpost in a world-wide combat initiated by Italy against medieval barbarism. His short tragicomedy *Conflictus Thaliae et Barbariei*, written about 1489, stages a fight between the muse Thalia and Barbary, a monstrous character who has as her stronghold the school of Zwolle in the Low Countries, with its medieval curriculum. Barbary, who believed that she had subdued Thalia long ago, sees that the latter has come to life again. Still, Barbary affirms that it is she who rules the world. Thalia does not deny this, but thinks that her own brave companions are by far the more distinguished. She ridicules Barbary and her followers (the medieval grammarians) and finally bests her opponent in a poetic contest.[4]

---

[2] Cf. *Paraphrasis in Elegantias Vallae* ASD I-4 244:5; 286:208–9, 214; 304:664–5, 310:829. For a more detailed discussion see my "Overcoming the Middle Ages: Historical Reasoning in Erasmus' Antibarbarian Writings", *Erasmus of Rotterdam Society Yearbook* 16 (1996), 34–53:35–6. The present and next sections are dependent on this article.

[3] ASD I-4 304:654, 330:386–7.

[4] LB I 889–94; see also *Carmina* 128 CWE 85 350–3/ASD I-7 436–7 (the poetic

Barbary is also under attack in various letters and poems dating from 1489, addressed mostly to Cornelis Gerard (Cornelius Aurelius, c. 1460–1531).[5] To "repel the barbarians' assaults" is, in Erasmus' view, the common cause of both men.[6] Many of these letters and poems contain arguments against medieval barbarism which correspond closely to passages in *Antibarbari*, the first version of which Erasmus was completing at the time. Again Erasmus' main ally in the struggle is Valla and his main opponents are the medieval grammarians as well as their contemporary followers. Although their barbarism "now prevails almost from pole to pole",[7] Erasmus sees the cause of good (read "ancient") literature advanced not merely in Italy but even in Germany by a few outstanding men, who, if they persevere, will be able to defeat barbarism completely in the near future.

Erasmus' statements on the struggle against barbarism are embedded in his view of the past. True civilisation is identified with (Roman) antiquity, and barbarism with the ages which followed antiquity and which are still dominating the present day. In a letter of 1489 to Cornelis, Erasmus summarises his view of Western history as follows:

> But, my dear Cornelis, the change in the fortunes of literature seems to me to be just that which has occurred in the other functions of craftsmen—those, I mean, that are called mechanical. For the poems of nearly all the bards bear witness that in the earliest ages there flourished craftsmen of vast renown. As to later times, if you examine reliefs or paintings or sculptures or buildings or indeed works of art of any sort more than two or three hundred years old, you will, I think, be astonished and laugh at the artist's extreme crudity; but in our age, again, the diligence of craftsmen has once more achieved every effect of art. In just the same way it is generally agreed that in ancient times, while the pursuit of the arts was flourishing, that of eloquence flourished with particular distinction, but afterwards, in the obstinate growth of barbarism, so completely disappeared that not a trace of it remained to be seen. This was when the most uneducated of mankind, who had never learned, began to teach that of which

---

contest), CWE 86 711–6/ASD I-7 432–6 (commentary, also concerning the disputed authorship of the work). It should be noted that the school of Zwolle was a municipal institution, not an establishment founded by the Brethren of Common Life, as is stated at CWE 86 711/ASD I-7 432.

[5] Cf. Epp. 22, 23, 26, 29–32; *Carmina* 93 (with 135), 98 CWE 85 182–97, 226–9, 364–7/ASD I-7 268–82, 306–9, 447–9.

[6] CWE Ep. 22:24/Allen 23.

[7] CWE Ep. 32:55/Allen 50.

they were ignorant . . . This was the period when men turned their
backs on the precepts of the Ancients and had recourse to newfangled rules, framed by ineptitude: modes of signifying, long-winded
explications, and countless fancies added to absurd rules of grammar.
When, with infinite toil, they had got all this by heart they had reached
such a peak of literary skill and eloquence that they were incapable
of delivering a single discourse in good Latin. In fact, as far as I can
see, if this uncivilized race of human beings had carried to its end the
process it began, it would have turned our art into I know not what
kind of new jargon; but at that point both our good Lorenzo Valla,
and Filelfo with admirable scholarly application rescued it from death
when it had all but expired. Valla's books, known under the title of
Elegantiae, will inform you how zealously he fought to refute the foolish notions of the barbarians and to bring back into use the regular
practices of authors of prose and verse, long since buried and forgotten.[8]

Here Erasmus accepts a view of history which is compatible with a
tripartite division of the past into a positively valued antiquity, neg-
atively valued Middle Ages, and a Renaissance present which restores
the positive achievements of the ancients. Significantly, he considers
history from a secular point of view only, leaving religion out of the
picture. As a Christian, and a professed religious, he must have
believed that Western history had made progress since classical antiquity by adopting the Christian faith. But as far as secular culture
was concerned, history, according to Erasmus, had changed for the
worse since antiquity, intellectually as well as artistically; classical
style had succumbed to Gothicism (as it is called today) in the arts
and to scholasticism in the liberal disciplines. Only a few men in
the present age had begun to move beyond the pernicious influence
of the barbarous centuries and to restore civilisation to its ancient
glory.

For our purposes, Erasmus' preoccupation with the expulsion of
what he saw as medieval barbarism offers ample compensation for
his undeniable lack of interest in medieval history proper. In fact,
his formal historical interest was limited to biblical and ancient history. In his opinion, only biblical history was entirely trustworthy,[9]

---

[8] CWE Ep. 23:90–111/Allen 86–106. Erasmus' observation concerning an artis-
tic Renaissance is astounding: in the Low Countries Gothic art remained predom-
inant until the 1520s. Ferguson, *The Renaissance in Historical Thought*, 43–4 suggests
that Erasmus borrowed his remarks from Valla's preface to the *Elegantiae*.

[9] Cf. *Divinationes ad notata Bedae* LB IX 472B, *Annotationes in Novum Testamentum*
CWE 56 20/Reeve 339 on Rom. 1:4 "Ex resurrectione mortuorum Iesu Christi";

even though it lent itself, within certain limits, to various interpretations and conjectural assumptions.[10] Ancient history constituted a traditional ingredient of the humanist curriculum,[11] even though most humanists did not treat it as a separate subject but as a part of literary or moral instruction.[12] Erasmus was no exception to the rule. Recognising that (ancient) history comprised a distinguished literary genre[13] and that it had an exemplary value, especially for Christian rulers,[14] he included it in his educational programmes more often than not, all the while expressing important reservations about its use.[15] And although he edited or prefaced several works of ancient history,[16] he did not think those works absolutely reliable, since many

see also *Ciceronianus* CWE 28 393/ASD I-2 645:4–8: the fabulous tales of ancient historians like Herodotus, Diodorus, and even Livy (who is too inconsistent to be trustworthy) are largely inferior to biblical history.

[10] Cf. *Responsio ad annotationes Lei* LB IX 152B (justifying his conjecturing by pointing to Bonaventure as a precedent), *Supputatio* LB IX 594B–C (idem by pointing to Gerson); for the limits in question cf. *Ecclesiastes* ASD V-5 146:850–148:858 (reproving Bonaventure's conjectures as frivolous), Allen Ep. 2951:19–20 (admitting to have made mistakes himself by putting too much trust in Jerome, Bede, and more recent authors).

[11] The classic study of the humanist curriculum—comprising grammar, rhetoric, history, poetry, and moral philosophy—is Paul Oskar Kristeller, "Humanism and Scholasticism in the Italian Renaissance", *Renaissance Thought: The Classic, Scholastic, and Humanist Strains* (New York 1961), 92–119.

[12] Cf. Erich Meuthen, "Humanismus und Geschichtsunterricht", *Humanismus und Historiographie*, ed. August Buck (Weinheim 1991), 5–50.

[13] Cf. CWE Epp. 312:55–8/Allen 50–2, 586:57–60/50–3, 919:64–6/60–2. Even fictitious elements could offer valuable reading, cf. Allen Ep. 2431:206–9.

[14] Cf. *Copia* CWE 24 591/ASD I-6 216:504: history is "the teacher of life"; *Adagia* CWE 31 5, 16/ASD II-1 48:76–7, 63:351–2 (prolegomena): several adages are borrowed from history, and many historians used adages to support the truth of their narratives. See also below pp. 14–16. J. IJsewijn and C. Matheeussen, "Erasme et l'historiographie", *The Late Middle Ages and the Dawn of Humanism outside Italy*, ed. G. Verbeke and J. IJsewijn (Louvain-The Hague 1972), 31–43 point out that although Erasmus' talents and interests kept him from writing history, he certainly did not have a negative opinion of historiography, as is alleged by Bietenholz, *History and Biography*—except for medieval historiography.

[15] Included: *De ratione studii* CWE 24 675/ASD I-2 124:1–3, *Ratio* Holborn 185/LB V 79E; absent: *De recta pronuntiatione* CWE 26 387/ASD I-4 30:556–31:570. The study of history was helped by geography (CWE Ep. 760:14–5/Allen 13), chronology (Allen Ep. 2435:91–101), cosmography and mathematics (*Ecclesiastes* ASD V-4 258:255–6), and visual aids like the portraits of popes and emperors (*Colloquia* CWE 39 206/ASD I-3 264:1065–7). For Erasmus' use of ancient history see also Walther Ludwig, "Erasmus und Schöfferlin—vom Nutzen der Historie bei den Humanisten", *n. 12 above* *Humanismus und Historiographie*, 61–88 esp. 61–7; Silvano Cavazza, "Erasmo e l'uso della storia", *Renaissance Studies in Honor of Craig Hugh Smyth*, ed. A. Morrogh et al. 2 vols. (Florence 1985) I 53–63. For Erasmus' reservations see below pp. 15–16.

[16] In 1517 he edited Q. Curtius Rufus, *Historia Magni Alexandri*; in 1518 Suetonius,

historians had mixed fictitious elements into their accounts, for instance by putting speeches into the mouths of their characters.[17] Indeed, Erasmus argued that because of the many falsehoods in ancient biographies of great men Augustine "preferred to be his own historian" and composed his *Confessiones.*[18]

Medieval historiography, on the other hand, seems to have left Erasmus largely indifferent, although his recommendation that princes acquaint themselves with the past of their country[19] and that Christian scholars study the history of their church and religion[20] would seem to include some attention for the Middle Ages as well. The only product of medieval historiography which he genuinely admired is the *Gesta Danorum* by Saxo Grammaticus (c. 1150–c. 1220).[21] For the rest we find only vague references[22] and a handful of condemnations

---

Vita caesarum, and some works of Flavius Josephus. Suetonius' work was included in Johann Froben's edition of *Historiae augustae scriptores* which Erasmus at least partially revised; for an assessment of his share in the project see J.S. Hirstein, "Erasme, l'Histoire Auguste et l'histoire", *Actes du colloque international Erasme,* ed. Jacques Chomarat et al. (Geneva 1990), 71–95 esp. 74–86. Moreover, Erasmus prefaced the Livy editions of Nikolaus Karbach (1519) and of Simon Grynaeus (1531), see Epp. 919, 2435.

[17] Cf. *Copia* CWE 24 649–50/ASD I-6 272:890–5, *Vita Hieronymi* CWE 61 19–22/Ferguson 134–6 (e.g. Herodotus, Xenophon), *Spongia* ASD IX-1 137:368–72 (the stories of Alexander the Great), Allen Ep. 2431:206–9; see also above n. 9. As a rule, Christian historians had no right to do this, although one could find notable exceptions like the story of the Maccabees, the lives of the martyrs, and (Pseudo-)Ambrose's life of Agnes (mentioned at *Copia;* cf. also *Ecclesiastes* ASD V-5 146:820–43). For veracity as a requirement of historiography see also CWE Epp. 45:51ff./Allen 45ff., 645:7–9/4–7.

[18] Scholia on *Retractiones* and *Confessiones* in Augustine, *Opera* 10 vols. (Basel 1528–9) I 44 (= PL 47 198B): "maluit ipse sui historiographus esse".

[19] *Institutio principis christiani* CWE 27 253/ASD IV-1 182:529–31.

[20] *Ciceronianus* CWE 28 387, 400/ASD I-2 640:21–3, 650:21–2; cf. *Ecclesiastes* ASD V-4 258:254–5: preachers should have some knowledge of history. Jerome is praised for his knowledge of history at *Edition of Jerome* CWE 61 69/Jerome *Lucubrationes* II fol. 2 (praefatio).

[21] Cf. the short eulogy at *Ciceronianus* CWE 28 424/ASD I-2 679:14–680:6 which was reprinted under the title "Des. Erasmi Roterodami de Saxone censura" on the front page of Saxo Grammaticus, *Danorum historiae libri XVI* (Basel 1534). The edition is mentioned in Ferdinand Vander Haeghen, *Bibliotheca Erasmiana. Répertoire des oeuvres d'Erasme* (Ghent 1893) [III] 52, but Erasmus was not involved in it.

[22] Cf. *Adagia* I iii 1 CWE 31 229/ASD II-1 306:68–71: ancient and modern chronicles teach that nearly all monarchs caused disasters by their stupidity; Reeve 473 on 1 Cor. 7:39 "Liberata est a lege": "si qua fides historiis", the Sorbonne condemned Pope Alexander III who permitted divorce; CWE Ep. 1196:280–1/Allen 258–60: "the histories of Christianity record the disgraceful acts of Christians, not even sparing their names"; Allen Ep. 2177:11–5: why do princes not learn from history that their discord encourages the pope to extend his power over them? Cf.

in passing.[23] The only medieval historian whom Erasmus used with some regularity is Peter Comestor (c. 1100–1187), who had written on biblical, not on medieval, history. And yet the Middle Ages were almost constantly on Erasmus' mind. Not even in writings exclusively dedicated to the heritage of antiquity could he refrain from expressing misgivings about the deplorable products of medieval civilisation. The Romans, Erasmus related in *Apophthegmata* (1531), banished Greek philosophers, who taught the young nothing useful; what would they have done with the scholastics? Alcibiades caused a scene at school because his master was unwilling to teach Homer; what if he had been forced to study the medieval grammarians?[24] In his *Parabolae* (1515) Erasmus repeated after Pliny the Elder that the panther had a sweet smell to other wild animals, but not to human beings. He went on adding on his own account: "Scotus is like that, evil-smelling to enlightened minds, but to those stupid numbskulls more fragrant than any spice".[25]

The omnipresence of the Middle Ages in Erasmus' writings does not imply that he had a well-founded view of the medieval past. His statements consisted mostly of humanist commonplaces. Scrutinising the medieval period historically was of little importance to him. "It is not really important to decide how someone fell into a well; the main thing is how to get him out", as he wrote in *Antibarbari*.[26] None

---

also *De bello turcico* ASD V-3 38–50 for a historical survey of the spread of Turkish power during "the last 700 years" (40:230). Probably it is the fact that the Turks were not mentioned in ancient history which made Erasmus qualify their origins as obscure (38:192, 50:349–50). An obvious disregard for medieval historiography is implied by the remark at CWE Ep. 45:4–5/Allen 1–2 (epilogue to Robert Gaguin, *De origine et gestis Francorum*) that the achievements of the French kings "heretofore lay well-nigh buried in darkness for lack of a fitting historian".

[23] At *In Nucem Ovidii commentarius* CWE 29 138/ASD I-1 153:36–154:9 Erasmus ridicules the tale from Holland chronicles on the countess of Henneberg (13th c.) who produced 365 babies in a single birth (for a legendary statement from Holland chronicles which apparently Erasmus did not reject cf. *Paraphrasis in Elegantias Vallae* ASD I-4 288:243–4: the Hollanders take their origin from the Trojans). Moreover, he ridiculed preachers taking foolish anecdotes from the *Speculum historiale* (c. 1250) of Vincent of Beauvais (*Moria* CWE 27 134/ASD IV-3 166:641–5) and from the mid-14th c. *Gesta Romanorum* (ibid., likewise *Ecclesiastes* ASD V-4 310:546–51). Cf. also *Responsio ad annotationes Lei* LB IX 262B–C: the author (Werner Rolevinck) of the *Fasciculus temporum* (1474) is of little value, except to Erasmus' medieval-minded critics.

[24] LB IV 143D, 247D.

[25] CWE 23 273/ASD I-5 318:570–1.

[26] CWE 23 42/ASD I-1 68:6–8.

the less, we have to expound his view of the past in some detail
before we can examine the relationship between his concept of history and his programme of reform. We shall therefore discuss some
notable passages from Erasmus' work commenting on the course of
secular as well as religious history, with special attention to the Middle
Ages. Our starting point will be *Antibarbari*, a work which more than
once has been called a manifesto of Erasmus' Christian humanism.[27]

Discussing History in Antibarbari

The original version of *Antibarbari*, written about 1489, comprised a
refutation, in monologue form, of the barbarians' objections to classical learning. That text is now lost. What have come down to us
are a manuscript version, dated circa 1500,[28] and a version which
appeared in print in 1520 and was reprinted nine more times in
Erasmus' day. In both versions *Antibarbari* is fashioned as a conversation between Erasmus and four humanist companions at Halsteren
near Bergen op Zoom in Northern Brabant, in 1494 or 1495. The
beginning of the conversation is dominated by a genuinely historical question:

> Finally . . . we fell to discussing that prime topic of complaint in our
> times, long-standing indeed but absolutely justified: we tried to dis-
> cover, and not without sharp wonder, what the disaster was that had
> swept away the rich, flourishing, joyful fruits of the finest culture, and
> why a tragic and terrible deluge had shamefully overwhelmed all the
> literature of the ancients which used to be so pure. How did it hap-
> pen that there is such an enormous distance between ourselves and
> the writers of antiquity; that men who are now at the summit of learn-
> ing, a few only excepted, hardly seem worthy to enter the literary
> arena against women and children, mere beginners, of the ancient
> world; and that the present generals of our army would not deserve
> enrolment among their common soldiers, nor would those who now
> steer the ship of learning find a place in the hold?[29]

---

[27] Margaret Mann Phillips, "Introductory Note", CWE 23 8; Brendan Bradshaw,
"The Christian Humanism of Erasmus", *Journal of Theological Studies* ns 33 (1982),
411–47:430–1, 447. Rabil, "Desiderius Erasmus", 222 speaks of Erasmus' "credo".
[28] Silvano Cavazza, "La cronologia degli 'Antibarbari' e le origini del pensiero
religioso di Erasmo", *Rinascimento* II 15 (1975), 141–79 argues for 1500/01 instead
of 1494/5, the date found in older literature (also in ASD I-1 and CWE 23). James
D. Tracy agrees with him in "Against the Barbarians: The Young Erasmus and
His Humanist Contemporaries", *Sixteenth Century Journal* 11.1 (1980), 3–22:3n.2.
[29] CWE 23 23–4/ASD I-1 45:15–27.

The "prime topic" of Erasmus' day which the five men make their own ("long-standing indeed", for it can be traced back in the history of humanism to Petrarch)[30] concerns the emergence of the Middle Ages, the *immensum interuallum* between antiquity and the humanists themselves. What calamity put medieval darkness in the place of ancient literature and civilisation, and why?

In answering these questions, Erasmus' friends turn out to be historians of different kinds. The physician Joost van Schoonhoven ascribes the decay of learning to the influence of the stars; Willem Colgheenes, burgomaster of Bergen op Zoom, believes that the rise of Christianity has put an end to ancient culture; the poet Willem Hermans attributes the degeneration of knowledge and eloquence to the senescence of the world. *Persona* Erasmus neither makes a choice in favour of one of the views exposed by his friends nor offers one of his own. But Jacob Batt, the protagonist of the dialogue, rejects the judgements of all three men, accusing them of making circumstances responsible for the faults of human beings and criticising the burgomaster in particular because of his tolerance of ignorant schoolmasters in Bergen op Zoom. If only these schoolmasters were replaced by competent ones, argues Batt, literary culture would revive soon enough.

In spite of Batt's fierce rejection of the burgomaster's view, both of these men agree on the actual development of Western history since antiquity. The burgomaster's account of the past, vastly expanded in the 1520 edition of *Antibarbari*,[31] is confirmed rather than contradicted by Batt in the course of the dialogue, and actually reflects Erasmus' opinion. What we have here is Erasmus' view of the history of Western Christendom in a nutshell.

In the manuscript version, the burgomaster's account comprises only a few lines. Having stated that the decline of letters should be related above all to Christian religion, the burgomaster surveys the reasons why early Christians remained ignorant of classical learning and even despised it. Inspired by a devotion more ardent than wise,

---

[30] See Theodor E. Mommsen, "Petrarch's Conception of the 'Dark Ages'", *Speculum* 17 (1942), 226–42; M.L. McLaughlin, "Humanist Concepts of Renaissance and Middle Ages in the Tre- and Quattrocento", *Renaissance Studies* 2 (1988), 131–42.

[31] In ASD I-1 the manuscript account comprises 15 lines (46:7–47:7), the 1520 account 49 lines (46:21–47:37), whereas the accounts of the other two men are only slightly extended.

they disdained anything which the world held in honour and therefore shunned secular learning. In addition, they wanted to have nothing in common with the pagan enemy. Partly they cloaked their
indolence in the name of religion. Some, perhaps the large majority, hated learning because they had learnt nothing themselves; others were satisfied with their own simplicity. Because of disrespect and
neglect of learning, literary culture eventually died out.

Like Erasmus in his letter to Cornelis Gerard as quoted above,
the burgomaster suggests that medieval decay followed classical antiquity almost immediately, thus bracketing together pagan history
and true culture on the one hand, and Christian history and barbarism on the other. But in the 1520 version of *Antibarbari* his argument has become more refined. The reasons that the first Christians
turned their backs on classical learning are more or less identical,
but he adds an account of what happened after the initial stages of
Christendom. Certain despots closed the schools to the Christians,
thinking that the faith would fade away without intellectual support.
The Christians, however, devoted themselves all the more eagerly to
learning, in order to defeat the pagans with their own weapons. As
a result, the faith triumphed over paganism. Then violently zealous
men appeared, wanting to do away with pagan literature as well.
Possibly they thought that religion was incompatible with the critical attitude inherent in learning; moreover, they knew that the ignorant are more tractable than the educated. The best books were
destroyed or perished through neglect. Princes and bishops avoided
erudition and relegated the care of literature to the monks, who initially managed their business not too badly. But later on, as the
monks turned to luxurious living, languages and ancient culture were
neglected and "there grew up a confused sort of teaching, a kind of
uneducated erudition, which corrupted not only humane studies but,
in distressing ways, theology itself".[32]

The account of the burgomaster accords very well with Batt's view
of Christian history, at least on a factual level. In the course of the
antibarbarian dialogue Batt adopts the same division of Christian
history as the burgomaster, distinguishing an apostolic, a patristic, a
monastic, and a scholastic period. He grants that Christianity took
its beginning from untutored founders, observing that in the early

---

[32] CWE 23 25–6/ASD I-1 47:35–7.

church there were many martyrs but few doctors.[33] He concedes that
Christians have been lazy in accepting classical literature, that they
have cloaked their ignorance with religion, and that they have suppressed learning because the ignorant are more compliant.[34] He
agrees that in the patristic period Christians were able to destroy
both paganism and heresy, thanks to the union of faith and erudition.[35] He also agrees that the monks did relatively well in keeping
up letters during the early and high Middle Ages, expressing a moderate esteem for two monastic authors from the period, the Venerable
Bede (673–735) and especially Bernard of Clairvaux (1090–1153).[36]
What the burgomaster discerns as the later period, marked by piti-
ful moral and intellectual decay which affected theology itself, we
have to understand as the later Middle Ages; the "confused sort of
teaching" dominating the period refers to scholasticism. Again Batt
agrees. He observes a gradual degeneration of theology after the
church fathers and authors like Bede. "For several centuries scholars were fewer, and of an inferior stamp, although they were never
altogether lacking", Batt asserts, pointing to Thomas Aquinas (1225–
1274) and John Duns Scotus (c. 1266–1308) as writers who were
still willing to use classical sources. "There is little need to mention
more recent writers, or those still living", Batt continues. He notes,
however, that classical learning is not completely absent even among
them, "although their erudition is much inferior".[37] He frequently
condemns scholasticism (his attacks are even extended in the 1520
version) and alleges that when he forces himself to read modern theologians, "nausea overcomes me as I go on, I am so disgusted by
the barbarous style and confusion of thought".[38]

In sum, both antibarbarian interlocutors express the same opinion on the cultural history of Christendom. The criterion of their
assessment is the willingness of Christians to incorporate classical

---

[33] Ibid. 113, 83/130:11–2, 104:2.
[34] Lazy: ibid. 61/84:9; cloaked ignorance: 33, 43, 48/57:10, 68:15–6, 74:17–8;
suppressed learning: 80/101:19–24.
[35] Ibid. 83/104:5–8.
[36] Ibid. 105, 109, 118–20/125:2–7, 129:2–5, 134:32–136:13. Erasmus' appraisal
of those two authors was not exceptional in his time, not even among humanists.
Flavio Biondo likewise respected them, see Ferguson, *The Renaissance in Historical
Thought*, 23. Bede was appreciated by men like Philipp Melanchthon (ibid. 45) and
Thomas More; Bernard was admired by Luther. See also below pp. 47–50, 52–54.
[37] CWE 23 112/ASD I-1 129:13–6.
[38] Ibid. 74/96:18–9.

learning. This willingness was absent in the first centuries, but reached its peak in the next period, dominated by the church fathers. After them the monks tried to save learning as well as they could, but they had most of their contemporaries against them. The decline of learning became more acute, probably in the course of the twelfth century, because of a simultaneous degeneration of moral and intellectual standards, and has been deteriorating ever since, although classical learning never completely vanished. The task of the present generation, then, is to restore the union of learning and religion.

It is this view of history which underlies Erasmus' programme of intellectual, moral, and religious reform that we commonly associate with Christian humanism. Although many humanists of his day endorsed similar views, Erasmus' perception that learning and religion had grown apart and had thus caused the downfall of Christian civilisation bears his personal stamp. Rather than separate intellectual and religious decline as independent phenomena, Erasmus assumed a causal connection between the two. His suggestion is that the neglect of letters had provoked the corruption of the Christian spirit—and that, consequently, the restoration of letters would lead to a renewal of piety.

Erasmus' view of history thus functioned to legitimate his calls for reform. We have reason therefore to study more closely the relatively few passages in his work which reiterate or substantiate (and sometimes modify or contradict) his view of the past as expressed in *Antibarbari*. We will proceed along the line drawn by Erasmus himself, distinguishing various successive epochs marked by their degree of integration of learning and Christianity. With regard to ancient history, to be treated in the remainder of this chapter, we will be especially concerned with the question of to what extent it represented Erasmus' cultural ideal. As for medieval history, the subject of the next two chapters, our main interest is Erasmus' conceptualisation of the origin and the development of cultural decline.

Ancient History: Classical Rome

Antibarbari repeats the view expressed earlier in Erasmus' letter to Cornelis Gerard which has been quoted at length above: all culture, whether intellectual or material, springs from classical antiquity. With the obvious exception of their religion, Christians have inherited everything from the pagans: the Latin language, literature, eloquence, all arts and crafts, science, and agriculture (Erasmus ignores here the inventions of the Middle Ages; in other works, he wrongly ascribes some of them to antiquity, for instance letters of credit and—a stock misinterpretation by humanists—the Carolingian minuscule).[39] Christians have never added anything to the inventions of the ancients which was not crude; instead, they have been preserving the earlier discoveries badly, damaging many of them and throwing everything into confusion.[40]

When referring to antiquity, Erasmus meant above all ancient Rome, although he admitted that the Greeks were the true founders of culture.[41] Pre-classical Rome was for him an archaic society which did not offer any cultural standard.[42] His real point of reference was the golden age of Cicero and Augustus, when Rome had fully integrated the achievements of Greek civilisation and ruled the world in relative stability. It is against this golden age that he measured the cultural development of Western Christendom and found many symptoms of decay, especially in literary culture. Erasmus may have thought that the Greek East had undergone a similar process of decline, but his historical scope was limited largely to the Latin West.

Erasmus' glorification of antiquity was carried to extremes, and sometimes even verged on the comic. Practically everything seemed to have been better in the days of old. As in the case of other humanists, his preference for classical Latin led him to affect unfamiliarity with medieval terms or with Gothic script and even drove him to adopt anachronisms (for instance, when calling a burgomaster *tribunus plebis* or *consul* in order to avoid the medieval but more appropriate term *magister civium*).[43] Moreover, according to Erasmus,

---

[39] Letters of credit: *Adagia* IV ix 60 ASD II-8 208:659–71. Minuscule: *De recta pronuntiatione* CWE 26 390–1, 393/ASD I-4 34:655–63, 35:718–9. Cf. *Adagia* II i 1 CWE 33 12/LB II 404A: "I do not deny that the moderns can make some discoveries which have escaped [the ancients]", but only by adding details to existing bodies of knowledge. For exceptions see below pp. 51, 155–6.

[40] CWE 23 56–7, 61–2/ASD I-1 79:17–80:25, 84:23–9.

[41] Ibid. 60/83:7–9, cf. *Moria* CWE 27 117/ASD IV-3 128:68, *Ecclesiastes* ASD V-4 262:354–7.

[42] Cf. *Ciceronianus* CWE 28 366, 404, 409/ASD I-2 624:3–4, 653:36–9, 657:20–1; *De recta pronuntiatione* CWE 26 393, 446, 471/ASD I-4 36:723–44, 81:240–82:249, 99:884–7; *Apologia adversus Stunicam* LB IX 398E; CWE Ep. 47:58–60/Allen 53–5; Allen Ep. 3032:381–2.

[43] Terms: *De conscribendis epistolis* CWE 25 55/ASD I-2 286:7–19 (here also "tribunum plebis"; in *Antibarbari* the burgomaster of Bergen op Zoom is called "consul"); Gothic script: CWE Ep. 396:187–9/Allen 172–4.

the ancients valued friendship more than Christians did, took more
care of public hygiene, disdained the game of dice which was now
popular among Christian princes, did not care much about lawyers
who now ruled the roost, had better music, held literature and good
libraries in higher esteem (the learned even lived longer in antiquity
than in Erasmus' day), still appreciated true learning instead of mere
academic titles, and were more reluctant to corrupt literary texts.[44]
By way of irony he staged in his colloquy *Senatulus* (1529) a group
of women who complained that even the position of the female sex
had been better in antiquity and who asked for a restoration, thus
creating a feminist variant of the Renaissance.[45]

Of course we have to bear in mind that contrasting a perfect
antiquity to a deplorable present constituted in many of these instances
a rhetorical device. Erasmus' main intention was not to expound
ancient history but to appeal to his contemporaries for intellectual
and moral improvement. Shaming his contemporaries by comparing
their bad habits to a supposedly better past was a useful strategy.
But this strategy could be successful only if Erasmus' statements on
the past did not seem implausible. One wonders whether his readers could have taken seriously what he praised most in the ancients:
their alleged pacifism. Erasmus asserted in several writings that instead
of making war, the rulers of antiquity invested their money and
energy in building works for the public good. Their courts were centres of literary culture, and they took pains to excel in knowledge.[46]
If by chance a war broke out, they fought more humanely than we
do, as Erasmus notes in his lengthy and repeatedly expanded commentary on the adage *Dulce bellum inexpertis* (1515). Turning over the
pages of pagan history, one finds countless examples of Roman war-

[44] Friendship: CWE Ep. 187:22–9/Allen 21–8. Hygiene: *Encomium medicinae* CWE
29 46–7/ASD I-4 182:328–41. Dice: scholia on Ps.-Cato, *Disticha moralia* in *Opuscula
aliquot Erasmo Roterodamo castigatore et interpraete* (Louvain 1515), fol. Aiiii v at "Aleas
fuge": "Alea infamis erat apud gentiles. Nunc principum christianorum lusus est".
Lawyers: *Apologia contra Latomi dialogum* CWE 71 48/LB IX 86B. Music: *Adagia* I ii
63 CWE 31 202–6/ASD II-1 276–82; Allen Ep. 1756:93–112. Literature and
libraries: CWE Epp. 30:5–6/Allen 4–6, 47:16–7/13–5, Ep. 396. Learned grew
older: CWE Ep. 1347:230–4/Allen 213–7. Appreciation of learning: CWE Ep.
145:130–3/Allen 114–6, Allen Ep. 2750:95–102. Corruption of texts: Allen Ep.
2774:108–10.
[45] *Colloquia* CWE 40 906–7/ASD I-3 630:20–35.
[46] *Colloquia* CWE 39 504/ASD I-3 407:152–3; CWE Epp. 919:39–45/Allen 36–41,
964:122–4/112–4; Allen Ep. 2200:17–21.

riors who did everything to come to terms with the enemy, and who tried to avoid bloodshed as much as possible. Provinces they had subdued in war they turned into prosperous and civilised regions, so that it became an advantage to be conquered.[47] Of course the main reason for Erasmus to give such accounts of the past was to restrain the warlike princes of his own day and to turn them to the study of literature. But if those princes had had an Erasmian education, they would have been the first to recognise that Erasmus was not telling the truth. Reading a single page of ancient history would have been sufficient to inform them that the Romans had been anything but pacifists; and it was especially for Christian rulers that Erasmus thought ancient history instructive "as a mirror for the amendment of their own lives and behaviour".[48]

In order to demonstrate the usefulness of ancient history for Christian rulers, Erasmus stressed that some pagan emperors had ruled in a Christian spirit. Others had been tyrants, but offered a valuable negative example in their private ambition, cruelty, and hasty innovations. Moreover, the fact that their deeds were recorded by historians was effective as a stimulus for good princes, and as a warning for bad ones.[49] Yet history had to be taken in small doses. Reading too much about ancient tyrants like Alexander the Great or Julius Caesar could infuse a young prince with the most destructive ideas, in particular because ancient historians sometimes praised their heroes for actions a Christian prince should avoid. Christians had to pick up suitable examples from ancient history like jewels from a dung-heap.[50] One could ask why Erasmus hardly ever invoked Christian rulers from the past as examples for behaviour in the present. In

---

[47] *Adagia* IV i 1 ASD II-7 30:543–32:600, cf. Margaret Mann Phillips, *The "Adages" of Erasmus: A Study with Translations* (Cambridge 1964), 333–5. See also *Querela pacis* CWE 27 308/ASD IV-2 82:491–5. For similar statements on the Greeks see *Colloquia* CWE 40 938/ASD I-3 644:49–50, 646:93–5; *Apophthegmata* LB IV 100B–C, 104F–105A.

[48] CWE Ep. 586:73–4/Allen 65–6; for the seeming incongruity between Erasmus' educational goals and his use of ancient history cf. Chomarat, "More, Erasme et les historiens latins", 97–9.

[49] CWE Ep. 586:25–8, 37–45, 74–80/Allen 20–4, 31–40, 66–71; *Institutio principis christiani* CWE 27 252/ASD IV-1 181:478–182:498.

[50] *Adagia* I iii 1 CWE 31 234/ASD II-1 312:237–313:242, *Institutio principis christiani* CWE 27 251/ASD IV-1 180:452–64. Cf. *Parabolae* CWE 23 272/ASD I-5 316:557–61: like mythology, gentile history is pleasant in small doses, but ceases to please at closer inspection.

such educational works for Christian princes as *Institutio principis chris-tiani* (1516) and *Apophthegmata* he referred almost exclusively to pagan rulers from antiquity;[51] moreover, he made only ancient history avail-able to them in humanist editions—even including a life of Alexander the Great, whom Erasmus qualified in his preface as a shocking example for a good prince and a scourge who fortunately died young.[52] Erasmus had a cogent argument when he could point out that even heathen rulers sometimes behaved better than their Christian successors,[53] but why would he have preferred to divulge the blame-worthy career of Alexander rather than the exemplary life of some Christian prince? The preface of *Apophthegmata*, dedicated to the future Duke William of Cleves, offers an explanation. History is full of lessons for the Christian prince, but nobody could remember all of them. Therefore Erasmus made a selection from ancient Greek and Latin historians. Although the moderns had sometimes made valu-able statements as well, the authority of the ancients was much greater (nevertheless the work concludes with a small section con-cerning Alfonso X the Wise, King of Castile 1252–84).[54] Thus it would seem that Erasmus' low opinion of medieval civilisation, includ-ing historiography, made him ignore the period even if he could have drawn more expedient examples from it than from antiquity.

Erasmus, then, knew that many ancient rulers had not been peace-ful lovers of literature but rather warlike lovers of power. He also knew that Roman society in particular had taken delight in specta-cles of cruelty such as triumphal processions (more splendid as more victims had been claimed and more material damage had been done, so Erasmus believed), gladiatorial games, and bull-fights.[55] Erasmus' persistent assertion of Roman pacifism may have been partly rooted in his conviction that a flowering of literary culture stimulated peace-

---

[51] *Institutio principis christiani* mentions Alexander and Caesar most often, along with other pagans and Old Testament kings like David and Solomon; also Christ is frequently invoked (but obviously his kingdom is not of this world). *Apophthegmata* concentrates on various Greek and Roman rulers, but contains one item on emperor Sigismund (1410–37; LB IV 366F–367A) and a brief section on the Castilian king Alfonso the Wise (1252–84; ibid. 377E–379A).

[52] CWE Ep. 704:31–8/Allen 27–35.

[53] Cf. e.g. *Apophthegmata* LB IV 100B–C, 143D–E, 146A–B, 203A, 240D, 284E, 369E.

[54] Allen Ep. 2431:24–8, 165–9. For Alfonso see above n. 51.

[55] Triumphal processions: Allen Ep. 2090:17–22; gladiators: *Adagia* IV vii 26 ASD II-8 86:260–1; bull-fights: *Adagia* IV iv 29 ASD II-7 198:312–5, Allen Ep. 3032:417–9.

ful behaviour. For Erasmus, letters had a civilising effect, even in a moral sense. The humanities were, quite literally, humanising; without them, human beings were but beasts, prey to savage instincts.[56] Although ancient history showed that a bright literary culture actually often coincided with war and tyranny, Erasmus may have preferred to uphold the notion that in antiquity, as a consequence of the flowering of literature, morality had blossomed as well.

In spite of Erasmus' tremendous, if partly inaccurate, admiration of Roman antiquity, he had little sympathy for the Italian dream of restoring the Roman empire. According to Erasmus, medieval and contemporary emperors hardly had anything in common with their Roman predecessors except their title, "the shadow of a mighty name".[57] Thus Erasmus avoided putting his own sovereign, who became Emperor Charles V in 1519, on equal terms with the ancient Roman rulers. After Charles' election, Erasmus expressed the hope that the emperor would match the glories of his (Habsburg) ancestors.[58] A few years later he called him "of all the emperors whom the world has known in the last eight hundred years the greatest . . . and the best"[59] (that is to say, since Charlemagne, not since Augustus, even if Charlemagne could also be portrayed as a good prince who cared for literary culture).[60] Many Italians no doubt agreed that the contemporary empire had little in common with the ancient institution, but Erasmus may have thought that the world was actually better off without Roman emperors. As he asserted in the preface of his edition of Suetonius (1518), the empire had originated as something criminal, violating the authority of the senate, the laws, and the liberty of the people; it had enslaved the world and had been itself the slave of a brute army.[61] To a certain extent the medieval *translatio imperii* had been a step forward:

---

[56] Cf. *Antibarbari* CWE 23 84/ASD I-1 104:27–8, *Adagia* IV v 1 ASD II-7 242:243; CWE Epp. 1554:46–7/Allen 43–4: "men who are ignorant of letters (which are not called the humanities for nothing) scarcely deserve the name of men", 1572:31–3/ 29–31; Allen Epp. 1767:3–6, 2432:18–9, 2584:15–6. Without the humanities civilisation would sink into barbarism and tyranny, cf. *Adagia* II i 1 CWE 33 12/LB II 404A–B; CWE Epp. 1582:88–91/Allen 79–82, 1584:12–25/11–22, 1591:60–3/52–6, 1645:17–20/13–5; Allen Ep. 2636:7–9. See also below p. 121 ("taming the mind").
[57] CWE Ep. 586:137–9/Allen 126–7, cf. 1009:25–6/16–7, Allen Ep. 1855:132–6.
[58] CWE Ep. 1009:22–4/Allen 13–5.
[59] CWE Ep. 1333:81–3/Allen 72–5.
[60] Cf. Allen Ep. 2435:38–42.
[61] CWE Ep. 586:180–4, 193–6/Allen 161–5, 174–8.

> But the majesty of the Roman empire gradually faded in the brilliant
> light of the Gospel . . . Finally it was swept away by the flood of bar-
> barian invasions, and after many centuries restored by the Roman
> pontiffs more in name than in reality. For what else could they do?
> At least it was right to transfer the right of election from a military
> mob to certain specific princes, who could be relied upon to give the
> world, with a full and proper sense of responsibility and no interfer-
> ence from hopes of reward, the prince whom they knew most likely
> to be a blessing to mankind.[62]

Rather than attempt to revive the ancient empire or its splendour,
one should strive for peace and unity under Christ, the one ruler of
all humankind. For Rome never dominated the whole world: some
parts never recognised its rule; other parts were still unknown.[63]
Moreover, true Romans were not those who longed for its ancient
glory, but those who considered themselves citizens of the Rome
Paul had created. This community had actually made progress since
antiquity and even since the day of Jerome: ancient and Christian
Rome were related as death is to life, superstition to faith, despo-
tism to salvation, corruption to eternity.[64] Thus, although ancient
Rome was for Erasmus a model of secular culture and sometimes
of civilised life in general, he never considered it a blueprint for his
own day.

Ancient Christian History: The Apostolic Period

In *Antibarbari* the protagonist of the dialogue, Jacob Batt, unfolds a
Christocentric conception of history.[65] According to the principle of
divine economy, all events from the beginning of the world were
predisposed to the coming of Christ. The *aureum saeculum* in which
Christ was born is superior to any other era which came before or

---

[62] Ibid. 214–22/193–200.
[63] Ibid. 207–14, 231ff./185–93, 209ff.; Allen Ep. 2126:17–20. Especially the latter passage may involve implicit criticism of the policy of Charles V. According to
Hirstein, "Erasme, l'Histoire Auguste et l'histoire", 90–4 Erasmus saw in the biographies included in the *Historia Augusta* implicit warnings against the dream of universal rule.
[64] CWE Ep. 710:54–113/Allen 49–106 (preface to *Paraphrasis* on Romans), cf.
Ciceronianus CWE 28 431–2/ASD I-2 694:1–16, *Moria* CWE 27 117/ASD IV-3
128:66–7.
[65] Cf Boyle, *Christening Pagan Mysteries*, 10ff.; Bejczy, "Overcoming the Middle
Ages", 42–4.

followed after. This does not make pre-Christian history meaning-less, however: it is rather Christ who renders it meaningful, by using it for the *saeculum Christianum*. Batt forwards two traditional argu-ments to substantiate this view: the domination of Rome over the world facilitated the spread of the faith, and the prevailing medley of cults and superstitions made the victory of Christian religion all the more glorious. But his real interest lies with literary culture. According to Batt, Christ himself established the discovery and flowering of the arts before his birth, so that "the best religion should be adorned and supported by the finest studies".[66] The harvest of pagan learning was a gift of Christ to the preceding centuries, but more so to his own age. The trouble of discovering the arts was taken away from the Christians. They had merely to apply what had already been invented, so that they could concentrate on the diffusion of Christianity.

Erasmus did not always value the period preceding the birth of Christ so favourably. Using a traditional metaphor, he sometimes stated that Christ was born to bring light in an age of darkness. In *Commentarius in hymnos Prudentii* (1524) he explained that the moment of Christ's birth was chosen on purpose, not because of the flowering of learning but because of the low point reached by moral life. "Everywhere charity had grown cold; the world lay beneath the dark-ness of ignorance and the shadow of sins", desecrated as it was by foolish philosophers, blinded Pharisees, cannibalism, and the worship of statues, animals, and lifeless things.[67] At the time of Christ's com-ing the Jews and the gentiles had reached "the summit of wicked-ness", and Rome and Athens especially were seats of corruption.[68] Christ came to rescue the world from its depravity, not to crown any positive development. Rather than being born in a golden age, he restored it in an age of iron.[69]

Regardless of whether the initial period of Christian history suffered a great deal from pagan vileness, it could only serve, in Erasmus' estimation, as a limited model for the present, since the first Christians

---

[66] CWE 23 60/ASD I-1 83:16–7.

[67] *In hymnos Prudentii* CWE 29 175/LB V 1339B–C, cf. *In psalmum IV concio* CWE 63 183–5/ASD V-2 200:208–201:248.

[68] Jews and gentiles: *Hyperaspistes II* LB X 1354C; Rome and Athens: *De vidua christiana* CWE 66 198/LB V 732B.

[69] *In hymnos Prudentii* CWE 29 186/LB V 1344C.

had shunned a literary education. Erasmus did not consider the simplicity of Christ and the apostles an example for his own age insofar as it meant a lack of culture, in particular of refined speech. As
he stated in *Antibarbari*: "the Christian religion [took] its beginning
from untutored founders . . . This was appropriate to those times,
but what about our own? These times demand another kind of life,
other ways of living". One must imitate the spirit of the apostles but
the scholarship of the church fathers.[70]

Of course apostolic simplicity was a commendable example insofar as it implied abstinence from strife and worldly concerns, and,
above all, a commitment to the moral and spiritual precepts of the
gospel, for which Erasmus employed the term *philosophia Christi*. It
has been observed that, for Erasmus, Christ was first and foremost
a transhistorical teacher of this philosophy, not a historical exponent
of it.[71] Still, Erasmus believed that even the moral pronouncements
of Christ and the apostles did not always need to be interpreted to
the letter but should be understood in their historical context or, as
he put it, in accordance with the times (*pro ratione temporum*). In *Ratio
verae theologiae* (1519), his manual for theological study, Erasmus emphasised that in reading the Bible "we should not only take into account
what is said, but also by whom it is said, to whom, by what words,
at what moment, on what occasion, what is preceding, what is following", adding many examples of regulations instituted by Christ
and Paul "for the use of those times" which afterwards had rightly
been changed or had fallen into oblivion. Sometimes, Erasmus
explained, they admonished the believers to moderate their behaviour in order not to offend the Jews and the heathens, something
which had become pointless in the present, for who would abstain
from pork out of consideration for the Jews? In other instances they
made statements which strike sixteenth-century believers as all too
harsh, for example concerning the beatitude of those who castrate
themselves for the realm of God (Matt. 19:12).[72] This latter statement, noted Erasmus in *Encomium matrimonii* (published in 1518, when

---

[70] CWE 23 113/ASD I-1 130:4–5, 11–5; for the apostles' lack of education cf.
ibid. 24, 112–3/46:24–6, 129:29–30; at 103/122:13–123:1 Erasmus tries hard not
to depict their speech as too rustic.

[71] Cf. John O'Malley, "Grammar and Rhetoric in the *pietas* of Erasmus", *Journal
of Medieval and Renaissance Studies* 18 (1988), 81–98:94ff.; idem, "Introduction", CWE
66 xxii–xxiii, xxvii.

[72] Holborn 196, 200–1/LB V 85E, 87C–88B.

he was composing his *Ratio*), chiefly applied to the epoch of Christ, when preachers were obliged to detach themselves from the world as much as possible. In the present century, however, it is among the married that one finds the best examples of a holy life.[73] Imposing the faith by strict rules had been suitable for the early church, as Erasmus explained elsewhere; the present, in which piety was endangered by superstition, called for a relaxation of rules and ceremonies.[74] If times change, doctrines and ecclesiastical practices should change with them, Erasmus remarked to his critic Noël Bédier.[75] Rituals in particular should be adjusted as circumstances require. Paul himself, after the death of Christ, introduced many regulations in view of his times.[76] And although everything Paul said was in some way or another applicable to the present as well, as Erasmus wrote in his *Paraphrasis* on Romans (1517), "a great many of these things were more specifically appropriate to that age, in which the church, composed of Jews and gentiles and subject to heathen rulers, was gradually taking shape, but still not fully formed".[77] Thus not only the Old Testament[78] but also the New Testament must, to some extent, be read as a historical document, as not all of its pronouncements applied with identical significance to every age.

Erasmus subsumed his ideas on the historical understanding of the New Testament under the rhetorical principle of *accomodatio*. Orators and preachers had to adapt their messages to changing circumstances in order to prevent opposition, as did God. For faith had not been revealed in apostolic times all at once, but gradually and prudently. Step by step humanity was taught, under Christ's guidance, to detach itself from the flesh and to submit itself to the spirit.[79] This process

---

[73] ASD I-5 402:211–8, cf. 404:239–42.

[74] Cf. Reeve 473 on 1 Cor. 7:39 "Liberata est a lege", *Declarationes ad censuras Lutetiae* LB IX 829A.

[75] *Divinationes ad notata Bedae* LB IX 488C; cf. also CWE Ep. 1581:640–50, 820–2/Allen 577–86, 736–7 (written to Bédier as well); Allen Ep. 1744:16–26.

[76] *Epistola ad fratres Inferioris Germaniae* ASD IX-1 338:255–7.

[77] CWE 42 12/LB VII 777–8 (argumentum).

[78] Cf. *Institutio principis christiani* CWE 27 252/ASD IV-1 182:499–503: there is a vast difference between what was permitted for Jews in accordance with the standards of the time and what is laid down for Christians; hence, the prince should not imitate straightaway what he finds in the Old Testament.

[79] See Jacques Chomarat, *Grammaire et rhétorique chez Erasme* 2 vols. (Paris 1981), 655–8, 1107–12, giving many examples from the *Paraphrases* and *Ecclesiastes* respectively. Cf. also Hilmar Pabel, *Conversing with God: Prayer in Erasmus' Pastoral Writings* (Toronto 1997), 13–5.

still awaited its completion. Not that Christ had left Revelation
unfinished, but certain aspects of it were not fully grasped until post-
apostolic periods. In fact, every century since the first had received
gifts from the Spirit which contributed to salvation.[80] The continuation of history, then, was not necessary for the completion of Christ's
teaching to humanity, but for its understanding, its diffusion, and,
above all, its implementation in life.

An important example of a practice from apostolic times which
had lost at least part of its validity for the present was the toleration of heretics. In contrast to what many modern commentators
like to believe, Erasmus did not oppose in principle the punishment
of heretics, although he did disapprove of the heresy-hunters' zeal,
which he regarded as a symptom of the spirit of contention that had
ruined Christian civilisation. Granted, Christ had called for toleration in the parable of the tares, as Erasmus indicated in his *Paraphrasis*
on Matthew (1522). Until the day of harvest (the Last Judgement),
the tares (heretics and false apostles) were not to be pulled out but
should stay in the midst of the wheat (the true believers).[81] Like some
of Erasmus' contemporaries, quite a few modern scholars have understood this exegesis as indicative of Erasmus' opinion of his own age.
But reporting on Christ's opinion is different from stating one's own,
as Erasmus himself repeatedly explained. Christ recommended toleration in his own day when speaking to the apostles who possessed

---

[80] Cf. CWE Ep. 1581:618–24/Allen 557–61: "If through the gift of the Spirit
certain insights, which had escaped for centuries many of the great luminaries of
the church, have been revealed to men of relatively recent date, that is, if Gerson
and Ockham saw what Chrysostom and Basil and Ambrose and Augustine and
Jerome did not see, is there anything to prevent this same Spirit from revealing to
someone of our time a truth which no one has noticed before?" This passage, taken
from a letter to Erasmus' critic Noël Bédier, is obviously coloured by polemical
rhetoric. Erasmus may not really believe that Gerson or Ockham saw truths which
the fathers did not see, but assumes that Bédier believes so and uses this idea in
order to claim freedom of thought for himself. Cf. the apparently serious statement
at *Apologia adversus Sutorem* LB IX 759B–C: "Sic coelestis Spiritus distribuit dotes
suas, ut nulli aetati defuerint praesidia, quae requirebantur ad salutem . . . Quaedam
vel ignoravit, vel in dubiis habuit prisca Ecclesia, quae post per Concilia sunt
explanata. Recentioribus etiam Theologis aliquid revelatum est, quod fugerat veteres. Scotus alicubi est Thoma oculatior. Et his nonnulla contulit Gerson. Nec
adhuc interclusa est Spiritus liberalitas"; see also *Apologia contra Latomi dialogum* CWE 71
52/LB IX 88B: "We now have quite a few articles of the faith which were unknown
to our forbears: so what is to prevent advances being made on the knowledge of
the early critics of biblical scholarship as well?" See also below pp. 131, 179.

[81] LB VII 79C–81B, paraphrasing Matt. 13:24–30, 36–43.

only a spiritual sword; the attitude to be adopted by modern princes wielding real swords was a different matter.[82] One is entitled to believe, however, that Erasmus' insistence upon the tolerant attitude prevailing in early Christian history has some connection with his plea for moderation in the present. During the first eight centuries excommunication had been the ultimate punishment, he pointed out to his readers,[83] and in the eleventh century Berengar of Tours († 1088) had still been able to deny the real presence of Christ in the Eucharist without incurring violent reprisals.[84]

The fact that early Christians had to tolerate evil in the church at all is another reason that Erasmus could not consider the initial period of Christian history an ideal age. To be sure, he asked in his *Precatio pro pace ecclesiae* (1532) for a restoration of the peace and the unity of the church which Christ himself had given it at the moment of its foundation.[85] We also find numerous passages in his work contrasting the pure and simple church of the apostolic period with the degeneration of later times. But Erasmus knew, and often said in so many words, that Christ had enemies like Herod, Caiphas, Annas, Pilate, and the Pharisees, and would always have them.[86] The sufferings of the just constituted a historical constant: from its birth, the church had been menaced by Jews, by cruel princes ordering exiles, crucifixions, and murders, and most important by false believers in its own midst.[87] Significantly, Erasmus' accentuation of the perpetual threat of internal enemies in the church grew more intense during the Reformation. On the one hand, he took the Lutherans to be such enemies, trying to convince himself that the church would overcome this particular challenge as well. On the other hand, he warned

---

[82] Cf. *Supputatio* LB IX 582A, *Declarationes ad censuras Lutetiae* LB IX 905D–F; *Apologia adversus monachos hispanos* LB IX 1056D, 1059D–E; *Epistola contra pseudevangelicos* ASD IX-1 288:126–31. See also my "Tolerantia: A Medieval Concept", *Journal of the History of Ideas* 58 (1997), 365–84:377–8.

[83] *Apologia adversus monachos hispanos* LB IX 1056C–D, cf. CWE Ep. 1033:251–67/Allen 229–43.

[84] *De bello turcico* ASD V-3 59:538–60:539, *Apologia adversus monachos hispanos* LB IX 1057D.

[85] CWE 69 115/LB IV 655C, 656A–B/LB V 1218A, B–C.

[86] Cf. *Commentarius in psalmum II* CWE 63 99/ASD V-2 120:740–2, *Interpretatio in psalmum LXXXV* ASD V-3 402:983–403:988, *Paraphrasis in Joannem* CWE 46 227/LB VII 649–50 (Erasmus . . . pio lectori).

[87] Cf. *Interpretatio in psalmum LXXXV* ASD V-3 402:974–82, Reeve 210 on Luke 22:36 "Sed nunc qui habet sacculum", *Supputatio* LB IX 524B.

Lutherans to have patience with what they considered inimical, that is, with traditional forms of Catholicism. The fact that in all phases of its history the church had endured many evils should restrain Lutherans from casting out everything at once.[88]

The conclusion that, on close inspection, the initial period of Christian history had in fact little relevance to contemporary society would not be a fair reflection of Erasmus' thought. The period had, after all, provided the gospel teaching, which for all its succinctness constituted an enormous treasure and, under the flag of *philosophia Christi*, inspired an immense reform programme for Erasmus' day which clung, as he saw it, to degenerated forms of learning and morality. But this is not to say that for him the first centuries of the church constituted the pinnacle of history. Although Christ allocated the highest good—the gospel—to his own era, Erasmus did not consider this era to be an epoch of universal felicity. The general impression in his writings is that Christ, rather than creating or restoring an age of gold, gave his followers the possibility of building a golden age themselves by accumulating the intellectual and spiritual gifts he had progressively disclosed to humanity. Through their neglect of intellectual gifts, the first Christians had not fully realised this possibility. Being in personal contact with Christ and the apostles themselves, they could perhaps afford such neglect.[89] For later generations, however, a literary education was indispensable in order to understand and implement the Word properly.

Ancient Christian History: The Patristic Period

At first sight the patristic period would seem to constitute, from an Erasmian point of view, a most propitious phase of history. The fathers eventually combined the gospel teaching of the initial days of Christianity with the intellectual heritage of classical antiquity (literary rather than philosophical, to be sure, for "in those days Aristotle was not yet accepted as an authority in the theological schools, and the philosophy current in our universities nowadays was not yet

---

[88] Cf. *Epistola contra pseudevangelicos* ASD IX-1 303:594–304:618, *Detectio* ASD IX-1 260:665–8. See also below pp. 176–8.
[89] Cf. *Antibarbari* CWE 23 102–3/ASD I-1 121:25–122:13: the lack of formal education of the apostles was amply compensated for by the presence of Christ.

invented").[90] Elevating the intellectual standard of Christendom and the moral standard of learning, the fathers seem to synthesise perfectly the fruits of earlier periods of history. In addition, numerous passages from Erasmus' work suggest that religious life in the patristic age struck him as still fairly uncorrupted. Priests were fewer, but much more pious than in Erasmus' day and held in higher esteem.[91] Bishops (including the Roman pontiff) saw themselves as the spiritual leaders of their communities and did not wield much more power than ordinary priests.[92] Monks were men who lived a holy life without specific rules or ceremonies.[93] Being nearer to the time of the apostles and still breathing the pure spirit of Christ undefiled by worldly goods, the "holy men of old" could produce writings very much at variance with "the pattern of these times".[94] The superiority of ancient Christian literature was so evident to Erasmus and his humanist contemporaries that he could even feign acquaintance with the quality of lost writings. "I can scarcely refrain from tears as I read the lists of ancient authors and see what wealth we have lost", he wrote in his edition of a letter from Eucherius of Lyon, a minor patristic author. "My grief increases when I compare the quality of our losses with what we now commonly read".[95] Is the patristic age, then, Erasmus' true age of gold?

---

[90] CWE Ep. 456:153–5/Allen 139–42. See also below pp. 38–40.

[91] Cf. *Parabolae* CWE 23 226/ASD I-5 242:333–5, *Vita Origenis* LB VIII 427E, *Epistola de esu carnium* ASD IX-1 26:214–28:231, *Apologia invectivis Lei* Ferguson 302, Allen Ep. 2284:147–61; see also CWE Ep. 447:714–5/Allen 645: "In the old days men were seldom admitted to the priesthood before the age of thirty"; scholia on *Regula Augustini* in Augustine, *Opera* I 591 [= PL 47 237D]: ". . . in clericos eius temporis, quorum tum erat maior et libertas et dignitas".

[92] Cf. scholia on *Ad Euagrium, De gradu presbyteri et diaconi* in Jerome, *Lucubrationes* III fol. 150v (antidotus): "[Hieronymus] aequare videtur omnes episcopos inter se, perinde quasi omnes ex aequo apostolis successerint . . . non putat episcopum quouis sacerdoto praestantiorem esse, nisi quod ius habet ordinandi". See also *Julius exclusus* CWE 27 176, 183, 192/Ferguson 82–3, 99–100, 116–7.

[93] Cf. *De contemptu mundi* CWE 66 173/ASD V-1 82:167–83:179, *Vita Hieronymi* CWE 61 29/Ferguson 145–6, scholia on *Ad Rusticum monachum, Vivendi forma* in Jerome, *Lucubrationes* I fol. 20r (antidotus): "Nam illis temporibus monachi nihil aliud erant, quam uita seueriori mundi contemptum profitentes, nihilominus episcopo suo parebant sicut caeteri, et clericorum munere fungebantur, sicut et caeteri"; see also below pp. 55–57.

[94] *Edition of Jerome* CWE 61 153/scholia on *Ad Nepotianum, De vita clericorum* in Jerome, *Lucubrationes* I fol. 6v (aliud [antidotum]). As examples, Erasmus mentions the Greeks, Jerome, Ambrose, and, surprisingly, Bernard of Clairvaux.

[95] CWE Ep. 676:32–5/Allen 30–3.

The answer is no. Despite his admiration for the learning and
eloquence of the Latin fathers, Erasmus felt compelled to admit that
in their times the decay of literary culture had already set in. Up
to the century of Jerome, theology in the Latin world had been
"practically incapable of effective speech";[96] when finally theology
sought the aid of eloquence, Latin itself had degenerated from its
pristine purity, a decline which affected the writings of fathers like
Jerome, Augustine, and Ambrose. In addition, the fathers had been
obliged to compromise the quality of the language because they had
been writing for the ignorant.[97] Erasmus does not appear to have
made similar remarks in relation to the Greek fathers, who in any
case were preferable, in his opinion, to the Latins.[98] But his primary
concern was with the civilisation of the Latin West. In his view
the Latin fathers were born too late in history to profit fully from
the flowering of classical Latin during the very first centuries of the
Christian era.

Still more significant is Erasmus' estimation that in the patristic
age, among Latins and Greeks alike, religious life had been anything
but pure and peaceful. Discord, private ambition, and rivalries in
matters of faith prevailed in Rome and even more so in the East,
as he pointed out in his Jerome edition.[99] With regard to the age

---

[96] *Vita Hieronymi* CWE 61 27/Ferguson 143 (Erasmus is rendering here Jerome's
own impression).

[97] *Annotationes in Novum Testamentum* CWE 56 286/Reeve 401 on Rom. 10:16
"Domine quis credidit auditui nostro". Cf. *De conscribendis epistolis* CWE 25 54/ASD
I-2 284:18–9: even fathers like Jerome, Augustine, and Gregory the Great "bowed
to the custom of their times", using strange formulas of salutation in their letters;
Apologia adversus Stunicam LB IX 395A–B: neither Tertullian nor Ambrose offer stand-
ards of good Latin; *Responsio ad collationes gerontodidascali* LB IX 1005E: Ambrose,
Cyprian, Augustine, and Jerome made many concessions to the taste of their times,
when Roman eloquence was already on the decline; scholia on *De moribus ecclesiae
catholicae* and *De moribus manichaeorum* in Augustine, *Opera* I 519 [= PL 47 234D]:
Augustine "stilum dimisit ad imperitorum intelligentiam". Cf. also *Apologia in Novum
Testamentum* Holborn 172/LB VI **3: not only Thomas' (exegetical) mistakes, but
also those of Augustine could perhaps be blamed on their times; CWE Ep.
1304:63–71/Allen 54–62 (preface to the edition of the Psalm commentary of Arnobius
Minor, fl. c. 450, but ascribed by Erasmus to Arnobius Afer, d.c. 330): Arnobius'
flaws "are so obvious that scarcely a Holcot or a Bricot could have made grosser
blunders", but "should be ascribed not to the man but to the age in which he
lived". Erasmus' remarks qualify the current opinion, voiced e.g. by Bietenholz,
History and Biography, 36, that the fathers "of all Christians inherited the full benefit
of the classical civilization", including language.

[98] Cf. *Ecclesiastes* ASD V-5 200:981–2; CWE Ep. 844:153–4, 235/Allen 139–40,
216–7.

[99] CWE Ep. 1451:56–70/Allen 50–63.

of Lactantius (c. 240–c. 320) Erasmus lamented: "O misery, even in those days Christian piety had so much cooled off that the gospel was ill reputed among the heathens, because of the impious and impure life of many men"; the ruling classes in particular were Christians in name only, if at all.[100] Likewise, he observed in his biography of Chrysostom (c. 347–407) that this Greek father had to face many problems after his ordination to the priesthood. The city of Constantinople was given over to luxury, while heterodox sects had infected the people; the imperial court—a mixture of orthodox, heretic, pagan, and Jewish elements—suffered from utter corruption, and the clergy had lapsed into a worldly life while dragging the common believers with them.[101] In the Latin West, Chrysostom's contemporary Jerome (345–420) bore witness to "how far the church of Rome fell away even in the old days from its zeal for the purity of the Gospel".[102] Several observations of Erasmus in his edition of the Latin father expand on this idea. In Jerome's lifetime the wealth of the church was increasing while charity was decreasing. The majority of those who professed Christ were Christians in name rather than practise. Clerics and bishops were preoccupied with honours, wealth, and worldly concerns, and the priestly devotion characteristic of "earlier times" was degenerating into tyranny and arrogance.[103] Indeed, "this whole age in which Jerome lived was an incredible hotbed of heretical discord and confusion, such that in those days it needed some special gifts even to be a Christian"; the original faith was found on paper rather than in the heart, there existed almost as many creeds as there were believers, private ambition and rivalries caused much disaster, and the papal see was almost overthrown.[104] Augustine, writing in the same century as Jerome, likewise noted that ritualism had buried the faith.[105] Thus the idea that

---

[100] Scholia on Lactantius *De opificio Dei* in *Vidua christiana* . . . (Basel 1529), 218 at ch. 1 "Male audiant": "O miseriam, etiam illa aetate sic refrixerat Christianorum pietas, ut euangelium apud ethnicos male audiret, ob impiam et impuram multorum uitam"; ibid. at ch. 1 "Nam licet": "Rarum erat illo seculo Christianam pietatem inuenire in proceribus, aulicis et magistratibus, Magnum erat illos, nomine Christianos esse".

[101] *Vita Chrysostomi* LB III 1334A–B.

[102] CWE Ep. 1202:16–21/Allen 14–9 (cited 16–7/14–5), cf. *Apologia ad blasphemias Stunicae* LB IX 358A, *Responsio ad epistolam Pii* LB IX 1108C; CWE Epp. 1173:192–3/Allen 172–3, 1469:31–5/26–31.

[103] *Vita Hieronymi* CWE 61 28–9, 38/Ferguson 145, 158.

[104] CWE Ep. 1451:31–63/Allen 26–57.

[105] *Epistola de esu carnium* ASD IX-1 24:138–41. Cf. ibid. 20:49–55, *In epistolam de*

Christ had enemies in every age applied also to the patristic period, as Erasmus pointed out on several occasions. The fourth and fifth centuries especially boiled over with heresies (first of all Arianism),[106] not only among the common people but also among bishops and within the imperial court. In addition, there were still many pagans in the empire, and barbarian invasions threatened Christian civilisation from outside.[107] It was, again, during the age of the Reformation that Erasmus increasingly emphasised the negative aspects of the patristic age, thus encouraging himself with the idea that the church had been able to withstand periods of serious discord earlier in its history. But his Jerome edition, which amply illustrates his gloomy view of the period, was first published in 1516, when Erasmus still joyfully welcomed an imminent age of peace and true culture.[108]

The eruption of heresies in the fourth and fifth centuries once drove Erasmus to divide the patristic period into a *prisca vetustas* ('old antiquity'), including fathers like Irenaeus, Origen, and Tertullian who lived in or directly after the days of the apostles (so Erasmus claimed; actually none of them was born before the second century), and a *media vetustas* ('middle antiquity'), including Basil, Chrysostom, Augustine, Ambrose, and Jerome. The latter period was characterised by the definition of dogmas, a measure of control to which the church was impelled by the impudence of heretics, whereas during the *prisca vetustas* dogmas were not yet fixed and doubt was still permitted.[109] We will see in the next chapter that the definition of dogma in reaction to heresy represented for Erasmus the first step in the

---

dilectu ciborum scholia ibid. 68:83–6: in the early church the people abstained voluntarily from meat, but later (in the 4th c.?) charity cooled down so that bishops and finally the pope had to make rules for fasting.

[106] Cf. *Vita Origenis* LB VIII 428E: "[Arius] orbem universum horrendo schismate perturbavit".

[107] Cf. *Epistola ad fratres Inferioris Germaniae* ASD IX-1 423:117–425:134; Allen Epp. 1790:87ff.; 2366:39–52; 2383:42–8; 2643:26–33, 95–108; 2651:41–2.

[108] For this latter aspect see below pp. 113–7. To be sure, Erasmus' negative assessments of the patristic period became more dominant in later versions of the Jerome edition; his Ep. 1451 was first published in the second edition (1524).

[109] *Ecclesiastes* ASD V-5 200:981–98; cf. below p. 142 n. 62. Cf. also his scholia on Irenaeus, *Opus . . . in quinque libros digestum, in quibus mire retegit et confutat haereseon . . . opiniones* (Basel 1526), 206 "Argumentum in quartum librum": "Tanta erat sanctissimis de rebus diuinis loquendi reuerentia, priusquam ecclesia super huiusmodi mysteriis pronunciaret explanatius. Opinor et ob eam causam priscos doctores de multis parcius ac tectius fuisse loquutos, ne si sanctum proiecissent canibus, Ethnicis ac Iudaeis praeberent ansam blasphemiae".

process of religious decline: it was thus that the faith became the object of disputation. The *media vetustas*, then, more or less announces the Middle Ages. It would hardly seem accidental that the period coincides with the age of Christian imperial rule, when orthodoxy became a state concern and thus the object of legislation and political conflict.

It seems evident that the patristic age was not Erasmus' ideal period of history, unless perhaps we consider only the *prisca vetustas*, the second and third centuries; this period, however, was dominated by the Greek fathers, whereas the Latin West had hardly more to offer than Tertullian, who for Erasmus was a champion neither of orthodoxy nor of eloquence.[110] In Erasmus' estimation, the church fathers set individual examples of learning and holiness, which surpassed rather than epitomised their century.[111] Similarly, early monasticism, far from mirroring the religious climate of the age, harboured the scant remnants of true piety. "In every generation, however blessed, the best things have always appealed to the minority", as Erasmus knew.[112] Only the fathers, not the patristic period as a whole, embodied the combination of *eruditio* and *pietas*. In addition, not every father stood as a model for the present in every respect, and none had been perfect. They all had been human beings liable to err, as Erasmus made evident, notably in his edition of the New Testament, which corrected many of their exegetical mistakes. More important, they showed serious moral shortcomings. They fought not only against the heretics but sometimes even with each other, although Erasmus now and then tried to mask their differences,[113] doubtless in order to avoid depicting the fathers as the predecessors of the

---

[110] Cf. *Ciceronianus* CWE 28 413, 443/ASD I-2 660:10–1, 705:26–8; CWE Epp. 1000:58–65, 165–70/Allen 56–64, 160–5; 1232; 1304:217–9, 304–7/196–8, 278–80 (in Tertullian, Origen, and almost all the early fathers there are "elements of manifest error or of dubious doctrine"); 1334:326–9/307–11.

[111] Cf. Bietenholz, *History and Biography*, 35–7: although the fathers set a "true historical precedent" for Christian humanism, Erasmus did not idealise the patristic age as a whole.

[112] CWE Ep. 1171:82–5/Allen 78–81 (adding immediately: "But was there ever a generation that gave more scope to ignorance, affrontery, shamelessness, stupidity, and abusive language?").

[113] Cf. Allen Ep. 2284:59–60: the fathers seem to have written "interim obscurius, interim varie, ne dicam diuerse" on the Eucharist; on closer inspection, however, they appear to be in harmony. For references to serious discord among the fathers see e.g. *Enarratio psalmi XXXVIII* ASD V-3 242:704ff., *Responsio ad annotationes Lei* LB IX 244D, Allen Ep. 1841:61–75.

quibbling scholastics. Still, he conceded that many of them had stooped to ignominious dispute, dragging their opponents through the mire and even distorting Scripture in order to slay their adversaries.[114] Human affairs are like that, as Erasmus observed in one particular instance: once the spirit of contention has been introduced, victory, not concord, is what counts most.[115] Finally, many fathers had expressed heterodox ideas, in particular during the early period. Erasmus did not make a fuss about this: he was perfectly capable of admiring authors without sharing all of their ideas, stressing that no author, ancient or modern, could escape the charge of heresy from overly zealous readers. But he did not deny their doctrinal shortcomings.[116] Once he implied an excuse for the errors of the fathers from his sense of history: in the preface to his (partial) translation of Origen's commentary on Matthew (1527) he insisted that one must understand the Greek father in the light of opinions and customs prevailing in Origen's century instead of measuring his pronouncements by modern standards. The latter approach would be no less absurd than treating the scholastics as if they had lived in patristic times, or dealing with Thomas Aquinas as if he had given his Aristotelian and Averroist definitions of dogma in the present, which would make them plainly indigestible.[117]

One father in particular may be considered, from an Erasmian perspective, a figure of transition to medieval decline. In Augustine (354–430) Erasmus could already foresee the Middle Ages, not only because the bishop of Hippo did not know Greek, but because more than other patristic authors he was given to logical disputation and defining the faith.[118] According to Erasmus, he was not the most

---

[114] Cf. *Ratio* Holborn 287–91/LB V 129A–130F; *Responsio ad annotationes Lei* LB IX 270E, 275C–D.

[115] Reeve 667 on 1 Tim. 1:17 "Soli deo": "Verum ita sit in rebus humanis, ubi semel studiorum pugna incaluit, non hoc agit quisque quod ad concordiam facit, sed quod ad victoriam". Erasmus is commenting here on the Greek fathers' adding "sapienti" to the Bible verse in question ("soli sapienti Deo") to counter the Arians.

[116] For references to dubious doctrine in patristic authors see notably *Enarratio psalmi XXXVIII* ASD V-3 192:795–197:978; see also e.g. *In psalmum XXII enarratio triplex* ASD V-2 346:583–7, *Apologia pro declamatione matrimonii* CWE 71 95/LB IX 110E–F, *Apologia adversus Sutorem* LB IX 772C, *Responsio de divortio* CWE 83 168/LB IX 961A, CWE Ep. 1033:49–51/Allen 43–5, Allen Epp. 1687:80–4. See also above n. 110.

[117] Allen Ep. 1844:20–34.

[118] Cf. Allen Ep. 2037:171–3: Augustine was considered an invincible dialectician

popular father among the scholastics without reason. Apart from the fact that he might be easier to understand, his pronouncements were more definite than those of contemporaries like Jerome and Ambrose, who had been more reluctant to lay down the law.[119] Small wonder that some preferred to ascribe dogmas of recent date to Augustine, "because he was of great help to the theological schools with his definitions".[120] Erasmus even called him "the fountainhead and father of all scholastic theology";[121] indeed, scholastic theology was born from Augustine's brain as Minerva from Jupiter's head.[122] Thomas Aquinas in particular had often followed Augustine and had therefore deviated less from the ancients than other scholastics—but Augustine, for his part, had been audacious enough to deviate from all other Greek and Latin fathers.[123] At one point Erasmus went so far as to mention Augustine in the same breath with Thomas and Scotus as authors from a recent generation.[124] Is it a coincidence that Augustine is Erasmus' primary example of the few fathers "from later times, when the fervour of the gospel was weakening", who in certain circumstances approved of war?[125]

One is tempted to think that, in Erasmus' view, religion and learning never merged in their purest and highest forms during ancient history, not even in the patristic age. When the faith was still pure, there were few Christians of supreme erudition, especially in the Latin West. When finally the Latin Christians turned to classical learning, the corruption of the faith had already set in with the degeneration of Latinity. Some individual fathers had reached a splendid synthesis of religion and learning, but there were always weak

---

in his day because he had read Aristotle's *Categoria*. Cf. also CWE Ep. 1334:165–7/Allen 156–8 on his joy of doctrine.

[119] CWE Ep. 844:175–82/Allen 159–65.

[120] *Ecclesiastes* ASD V-5 200:998.

[121] *Apologia adversus monachos hispanos* LB IX 1058D.

[122] *Hyperaspistes II* LB X 1495D.

[123] Allen Ep. 1844:26–8.

[124] Scholia on Sophronius, *Vitae scriptorum ecclesiasticorum* in Epiphanius, *De prophetarum vita* . . . (Basel 1529), 165 at ch. "Papias" at "Iudaicam aedidisse δουτέρωσιν": "Iudaei δουτερώσεις uocant, posteriorum interpretationes, cuius generis apud nos sunt Augustinus, Thomas et Scotus".

[125] *Adagia* IV i 1 ASD II-7 34:676–9, cf. Phillips, *The "Adages" of Erasmus*, 339; *Institutio principis christiani* CWE 27 283–4/ASD IV-1 215:512–22, cf. Reeve 212 on Luke 22:36 "Sed nunc qui habet sacculum". See also Rudolf Padberg, "Erasmus contra Augustinum. Das Problem des bellum justum in der erasmischen Friedensethik", *Colloque érasmien de Liège*, ed. Jean-Pierre Massaut (Paris 1987), 279–96.

points in their work. Generally speaking, the spiritual and intellectual climate was becoming unfavourable. The need to repel the
heretics did much to worsen the situation: eloquence was gradually
replaced by logical disputation, charity by dogma, investigation by
definition, doubt by arrogance. Augustine already embodied some of
those defects, which would become omnipresent in the course of the
next millennium.

CHAPTER TWO

MEDIEVAL HISTORY: THE MONASTIC PERIOD

Although no period of ancient history could count as an ideal in Erasmus' eyes, his admiration for the achievements of classical and Christian antiquity remained intense. In the fields of literature, thought, morality, and religion (which for Erasmus were all that really mattered) the ancients, in his view, had been allotted the highest possible gifts, even though they had never combined those gifts into a perfect synthesis involving all humankind.

Erasmus' exalted picture of the accomplishments of antiquity permitted him to lament in his writings the loss of culture since the days of old, and to contrast a highly favourable *olim* to a poor and degenerated *nunc*. It is with such a lamentation that the historical discussion in *Antibarbari* begins. In fact, the contrast between a glorified past and a distressing present is by far the most frequent allusion to history in Erasmus' work. As a consequence, the tripartite division of history into antiquity, Middle Ages, and Renaissance is less prominent in his writings than the older, bipartite division of the past generations into *antiqui* and *moderni*[1]—or, as Erasmus more often put it, into *veteres, vetusti,* or *prisci* on the one hand, and *recentes, recentiores,* or *neoterici* on the other.

With Erasmus the latter set of terms sometimes refer to all those who followed the church fathers, and sometimes more specifically to the scholastics. The church fathers, however, were definitely *veteres* in Erasmus' opinion. His distinction between *veteres* and *recentiores* has nothing to do with a division of history into a pre-Christian and a Christian epoch. Although in some instances Erasmus resorted to a more traditional view of history—for example, when talking of the infancy, the progress, and the adulthood of the church (and occasionally of its old age as well, alluding to the *mundus senescens* metaphor), ignoring intermediate periods of decay[2]—his works normally reveal

---

[1] For the development of the bipartite and tripartite schemes in Italian humanist thought see McLaughlin, "Humanist Concepts of Renaissance and Middle Ages".

[2] Cf. *Julius exclusus* CWE 27 196/Ferguson 122, *Epistola contra pseudevangelicos* ASD

a historical sense typical of the Renaissance, based on the opposition between antiquity, which set the standard of both secular and
religious culture, and a later period which added nothing valuable
to the heritage of the ancients but distorted everything. The first
centuries of Christian history (the apostolic and patristic periods) were
for Erasmus part of antiquity; modern history (the monastic and
scholastic periods) only began after the patristic age.

Preferring a bipartite to a tripartite division of history, Erasmus
never clearly demarcated a "medieval" period. What he regarded as
the beginning of modern times we may consider the start of medieval
history, but naturally Erasmus did not think that modern times had
come to an end in his own era (although he certainly thought that
his age had put an end to the universal reign of "modern" barbarism,
as we will see in Chapter Four). He never employed the concepts
medium aevum or *media aetas*, which in any case did not become current in Northern Europe until the seventeenth century,[3] nor the
adjectives derived from them. He was, however, among the first
Northern humanists to use some related terms. In his *Apologia de "In
principio erat sermo"* (1520) he referred to the monastic authors of the
early Middle Ages as *mediae vetustatis scriptores*.[4] *Media vetustas* seems to
echo the phrase *media antiquitas* introduced in 1519 by Erasmus' friend
and correspondent Beatus Rhenanus. However, Beatus' phrase has
a different meaning: it concerns the period between the Roman conquest of Germany and the barbarian migrations. Only afterwards,
from 1525 on, did Beatus extend the phrase to encompass later periods. A real parallel is offered by another correspondent of Erasmus,
Joachim Vadianus, who frequently designated the early Middle Ages
(from about the fifth to the twelfth centuries) as *media aetas*, a period
which was followed by the *infima aetas* of scholasticism. However,
Vadianus' earliest use of the expression dates from 1522.[5]

IX-1 304:623–4; adding old age: *Responsio ad epistolam Pii* LB IX 1109A, CWE Ep.
1400:405–8/Allen 390–2, Allen Ep. 1844:30–1. At *Ciceronianus* CWE 28 400/ASD
I-2 650:22 Erasmus uses the formula "the origins, progress, and decline of the
Christian world", which may correspond to his division of Christian history into
the apostolic, patristic, and modern (monastic and scholastic) periods. For the *mundus
senescens* metaphor cf. *Antibarbari* CWE 23 26/ASD I-1 47:37–48:13, *Apologia in Novum
Testamentum* Holborn 167/LB VI **2v, CWE Ep. 1347:233/Allen 216.

[3] See Uwe Neddermeyer, *Das Mittelalter in der deutschen Historiographie vom 15. bis
zum 18. Jahrhundert. Geschichtsgliederung und Epochenverständnis in der frühen Neuzeit* (Cologne
1988), 101–232.

[4] *Apologia de "In principio erat sermo"* LB IX 118C; for a fuller quotation see below
p. 45.

[5] On Beatus and Vadianus see Neddermeyer, *Das Mittelalter in der deutschen*

In two other instances Erasmus seems to have conceived some sort of historical period corresponding to what we would call the Middle Ages. In 1525 he wrote to his critic Noël Bédier: "If I cannot trust the accepted authorities of the past or of the present or of the period between the two (*medioximi*), what rule shall I follow to correct what I have written?"[6] The "period between the two" might refer to the Middle Ages as a whole, although it would also seem possible that Erasmus was alluding only to the early Middle Ages, the monastic period. In another letter, written one year later, Erasmus pointed out that in his biblical studies he had corrected many mistakes of Augustine and Ambrose, "lest I should mention other authors of *recentior antiquitas* like Thomas, Lyra, Hugh of St Cher etcetera".[7] The term *recentior antiquitas* obviously includes the scholastics, but it is not entirely clear what part of the further past is covered by it.

Erasmus did, however, use some other designations, of a negative character. The term *intervallum*, introduced in *Antibarbari*, recurs in one of his letters.[8] Twice he indirectly compared the medieval period to winter.[9] But his favourite metaphors were "exile" or "captivity" and, above all, "slumber". Several times he compared the renascence of literature in his own day to a return to citizenship after a period of forced absence (*postliminium*).[10] Still more frequently he stated that the world had been profoundly asleep, resting on scholastic doctrine and superstition, until it was aroused from its lethargy by Erasmus himself or, with much more violence, by Martin Luther.[11] Erasmus

---

Historiographie, 105–124. Neddermeyer ignores Erasmus' phrase "media vetustas" as well as both Erasmian expressions discussed in the next paragraph. He does, however, point to the following passage from the preface (1515) to Erasmus' edition of Jerome: "mediis illius commentariis passim admiscerunt suas naenias", suggesting that the reference is to "medieval" commentaries on Jerome (ibid. 105). But "mediis illius commentariis" simply means "in the middle of his [Jerome's] commentaries". The translation at CWE Ep. 396:168–9: "they have mixed in their own rubbish into his expositions", is adequate.

[6] CWE Ep. 1581:701–3/Allen 631–3.

[7] Allen Ep. 1687:83–4.

[8] *Antibarbari* CWE 23 23/ASD I-1 45:7; Allen Ep. 1805:55.

[9] *Antibarbari* CWE 23 61/ASD I-1 84:1–2; CWE Ep. 542:9–16/Allen 6–12.

[10] *Adagia* IV v 1 ASD II-7 240:180–2, 242:244–7; Allen Epp. 1805:54–8, 1876:14–5, 1885:28–9, 2379:427–8.

[11] In Ep. 64 Erasmus for the first time connects sleep with medieval tradition (Scotist theology). Cf. also *Colloquia* ASD I-3 38:213–39:217, 83:205–10, CWE 39 121/ASD I-3 187:2034–188:2040; *Detectio* ASD IX-1 236:63–4; CWE Epp. 531:589–92/Allen 531–3, 1341A:34/Allen I 2:23; Allen Ep. 2588:7–9. For his image of the world arousing from its sleep partly or mainly by his effort see CWE Epp. 943:11–4/Allen 9–12, 966:13–4/10–1, 1581:784–97/704–16; Allen Epp. 1700:39–40;

may well have thought that the slumber of the Middle Ages had lasted for a thousand years. In one of his letters he called the decay of religious life "a disease which has by now grown chronic over a thousand years",[12] and to his adversary Jacobus Latomus he wrote that "over a thousand years [the church] has taken up a definite stand on many issues which used to be argued from various points of view as matters of dispute".[13] Accordingly, he repeatedly pointed out to his Protestant critics that they would be unable to undo at once the wrongs which had been accumulating during a whole millennium.[14]

The Emergence of the Middle Ages

Erasmus' works do not clearly show when he thought the period of cultural decline had set in. Two events which in his day were already conventionally regarded as starting-points were the reign of Constantine the Great and the fall of the Roman empire. In contrast to most Italian humanists, Erasmus seems not to have considered the latter event a landmark in history. As we have seen, he attached much more importance to the dominion of Christ than of Rome. He deplored the loss of Roman culture, but not of Roman rule, even though the limits of the ancient empire seem to have defined what he considered the civilised world.[15] Once he stated that the dissolution of Roman rule by the Goths and other barbarians was actually a sign of historical progress willed by God: at first the empire had

---

1805:96–102, 209–13; 1891:185–95; for Luther or the Lutherans as those who woke up the earth see *Epistola ad fratres Inferioris Germaniae* ASD IX-1 336:175–6; CWE Ep. 1313:23–37/Allen 21–35; Allen Ep. 1672:24–6, 30–2; 1804:118–20. Rudolph Agricola already depicted the Middle Ages as a period of sleep, cf. Herbert Weisinger, "The Renaissance Theory of the Reaction Against the Middle Ages as a Cause of the Renaissance", *Speculum* 20 (1945), 461–7:462. The metaphor is related to the much more common image of literature being (almost) dead and/or buried, used by Erasmus e.g. at CWE Ep. 23:103–11/Allen 98–106.

[12] CWE Ep. 1341A:1170–1/Allen I 30:27.

[13] *Apologia contra Latomi dialogum* CWE 71 52/LB IX 88B.

[14] *Epistola contra pseudevangelicos* ASD IX-1 300:466–8; *Epistola ad fratres Inferioris Germaniae* ASD IX-1 338:240–1, 362:748ff.; see below pp. 171–2, 174, 176. Cf. also Maarten van Dorp's observation at CWE Ep. 347:64–5, 102–6/Allen 57–8, 93–7 that Erasmus rejected as "modern" a theological tradition of 1000 years.

[15] As is shown by his references to nations never subjugated to Roman rule as remote and naturally savage people, cf. my "Erasmus Becomes a Netherlander", *Sixteenth Century Journal* 28 (1997), 387–99:393 with n. 40.

helped the diffusion of Christianity, but after that it had to be removed in order to eliminate the last remnants of paganism.[16]

To Erasmus, the reign of Constantine the Great was of more importance to Christian history. Constantine's acceptance of Christianity in 313 could be interpreted as a victory of the faith after centuries of persecution, but also as the beginning of a reprehensible mixture of religion and worldly affairs. Erasmus seems occasionally to have taken the second view. In his[17] *Julius exclusus*, written in 1513 or 1514, he staged a discussion between the deceased pope Julius II, claiming a right to enter heaven, and the apostle Peter, who demands of Julius an account of his deeds. Appalled by Julius' lust for worldly power, Peter asks who the first to defile the church with such ambition was; Julius answers that it was Constantine, who transferred the majesty of the empire to the pope. True enough, Julius admits that the *Donatio Constantini* is probably a forgery,[18] but the interference in religious matters by Christian emperors was for Erasmus certainly a symptom of the decline of the church. As he asserted in his edition of Jerome, the decline of the church started when "gradually wealth came to her, and the favour of princes now Christian also came to her";[19] likewise, he admitted in the preface to his edition of Hilary (1523): "the intervention of imperial authority . . . did not improve much the purity of faith".[20] His opinion is particularly clear from his *Ratio verae theologiae* (1519). In this work Erasmus divided sacred history into five epochs. First came the age of Old Testament law. Next followed the age of John the Baptist, when the law was moderated in a spirit foreshadowing Christ. The third period belonged to Christ himself, who taught the true precepts of religion. In the fourth period Christianity, now spread over the world, was protected

[16] *Ecclesiastes* ASD V-4 180:919–22.

[17] Erasmus' authorship of *Julius exclusus* is more often accepted than not, but has recently been called into question again by Jozef IJsewijn, "I rapporti tra Erasmo, l'umanesimo italiano, Roma e Giulio II", *Erasmo, Venezia e la cultura padana nel '500*, ed. Achille Olivieri (Rovigo 1995), 117–29 esp. 123–5.

[18] *Julius exclusus* CWE 27 192/Ferguson 116–7. Cf. also CWE Ep. 1451:64–6/Allen 58–60: "under the emperor Constantius [Rome] maintained a dubious hold upon that rock on which rests the Catholic church". Nicholas of Cusa and Lorenzo Valla had exposed the *Donatio* as a falsification.

[19] *Edition of Jerome* CWE 61 153/scholia on *Ad Nepotianum, De vita clericorum* in Jerome, *Lucubrationes* I fol. 6v (aliud [antidotum]).

[20] CWE Ep. 1334:397–9/Allen 372–4.

by the emperors. New laws which seemed at odds with the commandments of Christ were introduced. In the final period the church
fell away from the Christian spirit altogether. Thus the degeneration
of the church had its roots in the fourth period, which started, as
we must assume, with Constantine.[21]

It is not the emperors, however, who were primarily to blame for
the regrettable course Christian history had taken. Erasmus' writings
contain several passages on the origins and the subsequent stages of
the degeneration of Christendom which point to a different cause.
In the preface (dated 1515) to his Jerome edition, he raised the question of what had caused the mutilation and the loss of so many
ancient texts. When princely rule had degenerated into tyranny,
Erasmus argued, and bishops had begun to love their power more
than their duty to teach, the business of instruction was abandoned
to the religious. Sound learning began to be neglected, the knowledge of Greek and Hebrew vanished along with history and geography, while Latin survived in a corrupt form. Ancient learning was
only found in compilations, mingled with the notes of the monks;
the genuine texts of the fathers fell out of use or, more likely, were
deliberately suppressed to save the monks from the charge of pla-
giarism or ignorance, while scholastic theologians and exegetes ruled
supreme.[22]

This exposition accords fairly well with the views set forth in
Antibarbari and discussed in the previous chapter. But in the same
year he wrote the preface of his Jerome edition, Erasmus composed
his commentary on the adage *Dulce bellum inexpertis*, which offers a
different perspective. In the commentary Erasmus explained that the
corruption of civilisation had crept in little by little. Erudition and
eloquence, first neglected and opposed by Christians, were approved
as means for confuting the heretics. Then, under the pretext of combating heretics, a taste for controversy manifested itself. Finally,
Aristotle was accepted as an integral part of theology, which was
like mixing water and fire. From him we learned that worldly goods
and private ownership were indispensable to human happiness. Roman

---

[21] Holborn 199–201/LB V 87A–88C; see also Cornelis Augustijn, *Erasmus: His
Life, Works, an Influence* (Toronto 1991), 85; Chomarat, "La philosophie de l'histoire
d'Erasme", 164. For Petrarch the Middle Ages indeed set in with Constantine, see
Ferguson, *The Renaissance in Historical Thought*, 8.
[22] CWE Ep. 396:80–105/Allen 70–94.

law, too, had exercised a bad influence on the gospel teaching: it
allowed the use of force, striving for one's own rights, bargaining,
usury, and warfare. In sum, Christ's teaching had been contaminated by all sorts of learning from the pagan world; his precepts
were ignored or twisted in accordance with alien doctrine. Honour,
wealth, and power came in after this, and finally there evolved incessant warfare.[23] According to Erasmus' commentary, it is not the rejection of classical civilisation which has brought us down, as he had
asserted in *Antibarbari*, but the improper use of it, which started at
some moment in or after the patristic age and became endemic
under scholasticism. Apparently the justification of secular concerns by
pagan learning eventually led Christians to care for nothing but this
world, and to kill each other so as to satisfy their base aspirations.

In several other instances Erasmus viewed the excessive interest
in pagan learning, in particular philosophy, as being responsible for
the degeneration of Christianity. In the preface (dated 1520, the year
of the *Antibarbari* edition) of his *Paraphrase on Ephesians* he wrote: "In
olden days the Christian philosophy was a matter of faith, not of
disputation; men's simple piety was satisfied with the oracles of Holy
Scripture, and charity, a natural growth, had no need of complicated rules, believing all things and never coming to a stop". Later,
theology became the business of learned men (the fathers), who were
mainly schooled in rhetoric. "Gradually philosophy came to be applied
more and more, Platonic first and then Aristotelian", and ethical
and metaphysical questions began to be asked. "At first this seemed
almost fundamental; but it developed by stages until many men,
neglecting the study of the ancient tongues and of polite literature
and even of Holy Writ, grew old over questions meticulous, need-
less, and unreasonably minute". Theology began to be a form of
skill and a showpiece, spoiled by ambition, avarice, flattery, strife,
and superstition. Thus it happened that Christ was almost overlaid
by human disputations, and that the rules of Holy Scripture were
bent to fit our appetites. At that point the humanists "tried to recall
the world to the simpler studies of an earlier day", insisting on a
knowledge of the tongues and liberal studies, "for it was neglect of
them, it seemed, that brought us down to where we are".[24]

---

[23] *Adagia* IV i 1 ASD II-7 28:492–30:542, cf. Phillips, *The "Adages" of Erasmus*,
330–3.
[24] CWE Ep. 1062:23–49/Allen 19–44.

Thus the dependence of Christian learning on the support of philosophy "was the first step of the church on the downward path",
as Erasmus put it in the preface to his edition of Hilary. Although
faith was originally more "a way of life" than "a profession of articles", the stubbornness of the heretics necessitated its definition. As
a result, faith became trapped within the written word. The number of articles increased along with the spirit of contention, while
charity grew cold. Wealth, power, and imperial interventions made
things worse. Spoilt by sophistic controversy and the eruption of
thousands of articles, religion "became a matter of intimidation and
threats".[25]

Obviously Erasmus' view of the past in these passages is coloured
by the controversy between humanist rhetoric and scholastic philosophy.[26] The decay of Christianity did not begin, according to Erasmus,
when Christians lost their intellectual innocence and became acquainted
with pagan learning (this was actually a big leap forward), but when
within the realm of pagan learning Christians came to prefer philosophy to literature. The emergence of heresies impelled them to
resort to logical reasoning in order to refute the falsehoods of Christ's
enemies. For some reason—Erasmus does not tell us why exactly—
they acquired a taste for strife in the process and carried the application of philosophy beyond its due limits. Argumentation, and hence
the condemnation of heterodox opinion, became an end in itself, as
was still the case, in Erasmus' opinion, for contemporary scholasticism. Aristotle, the hero of the scholastics, had exercised a particularly pernicious influence. Erasmus' summons to return to "the simpler
studies of an earlier day" was thus first of all an appeal to push
back the influence of philosophy and consequently of scholasticism;
it is not really a longing for apostolic simplicity, for it involves a
profound study of classical languages and literature.

It seems evident that the intellectual degeneration of the church,
with its negative implications in the field of morality, weighed more
in Erasmus' conception of the decline of the West than did the
defilement of the church with secular goods and concerns. Obviously,
he did condemn the latter development as well, contrasting the force
of the primitive church, bereft of all worldly advantages, to its weak-

---

[25] CWE Ep. 1334:386–401/Allen 362–76.
[26] On this controversy see the discussion below p. 72ff.

ness in later times when it had gained many material but lost many spiritual goods.[27] In itself, however, the enrichment of the church was not necessarily a bad development. "In the old days [the Church] had no literature and no eloquence, and she lacked wealth and power; now she has both, but it does not follow that Christ has deserted his spouse".[28] It was the misuse of wealth and power which had harmed the church, just as it was the misuse of pagan learning which had perverted Christian civilisation. But Erasmus' primary criterion for judging Christian history remained the way Christians had dealt with the classical heritage. His implicit division of Christian history into an apostolic, a patristic, a monastic, and a scholastic age was based on this criterion and remained valid for him throughout his life.

The Monastic Period

We have seen that the degeneration of Christian culture consisted for Erasmus in two developments which germinated in the patristic age: the waning of religious vigour accompanied by the increase of strife and worldly concerns on the one hand, the decay of Latin literary culture on the other. As a Christian humanist, Erasmus claimed that a revival of literary culture would lead to a restoration of religion and morality. Accordingly, he often ascribed the degeneration of religion and morals in the past to a neglect of literature. Nevertheless he did not deny that the *philosophia Christi* had been at its purest in the initial age, when Christians had abstained from learning altogether. Conversely, the fathers had embraced literature with enthusiasm, setting individual examples of Christian culture but not being able to avert the corruption of religion in their century. Thus ancient history offered hardly any support for Erasmus' crucial assumption that a literary education would lead to moral improvement. One might rather conclude from his own picture of the ancient past that literature and religion had developed independently from each other. But Erasmus did not draw this conclusion. He preferred to believe that he could contribute to a better world by making people study

---

[27] Cf. e.g. *Julius exclusus* passim; *Edition of Jerome* CWE 61 153/scholia on *Ad Nepotianum, De vita clericorum* in Jerome, *Lucubrationes* I fol. 6v (aliud [antidotum]).
[28] CWE Ep. 843:256–8/Allen 228–30.

key literary and religious texts, upholding the idea that a neglect of
such study had been responsible for the decay of civilisation during
the last thousand years.

Erasmus' more specific utterances on what was the recent past to
him (and what to us is medieval history) do not give an exact idea
of how the degeneration of culture came about and who was responsible for it. We do not know the identities of the violently zealous
men blamed in *Antibarbari* for the deliberate destruction of pagan
culture at the dawn of the Middle Ages. We do not see how or why
kings and bishops, according to the same work, lost their interest in
literature and left its care to the religious. What Erasmus does substantiate in his work, however, is his opinion that the religious tried
to save literary culture to the best of their abilities before the devastating period of scholasticism set in.

In Erasmus' view, the decline of literary culture, which had already
begun in the time of the fathers, steadily continued during the monastic period. In the patristic age, literary and intellectual culture were
best preserved in Rome,[29] just as the faith was,[30] but in the course
of the sixth and seventh centuries the decay of letters became general. The first person in history called *recentior* by Erasmus appears
to be Boethius (480–524), whom he once included among the ancients
as well (today Boethius is sometimes still referred to as "the last
Roman").[31] Erasmus spared Boethius from severe criticism, but charged

---

[29] Cf. *Vita Hieronymi* CWE 61 25/Ferguson 140–1, CWE Ep. 1304:140–3/Allen
125–7 (in the days of Gregory the Great Latin in Rome was "still comparatively
unspoiled"). But see above p. 26 on falling literary standards in and before Gregory's
day; cf. also scholia on *De moribus ecclesiae catholicae* and *De moribus manichaeorum* in
Augustine, *Opera* I 519 [= PL 47 234D–235A]: "et textores et textrices id temporis [in Augustine's day] intelligebant latinam orationem simplicibus verbis ac sensi-
bus contextam, qualis est divi Gregorii"; *Ciceronianus* CWE 28 413/ASD I-2 660:26:
Gregory's Latin was quite unciceronian, "but that is what he was taught at school".
[30] Cf. *Explanatio symboli* CWE 70 253–4/ASD V-1 220:416–9, *Edition of Jerome*
CWE 61 198/scholia on *Ad Damasum* in Jerome, *Lucubrationes* III fol. 60v at "Super
illam petram".
[31] Boethius as a *recentior*: *Adagia* II v 93 CWE 33 283/LB II 579C ("his recentior", i.e. in comparison to Apuleius, Lucian, Dion, and Athenaeus); reckoned with
the ancients: CWE Ep. 269:19/Allen 16. Cf. *Ciceronianus* CWE 28 411/ASD I-2
659:6–13: Boethius constitutes, with Ausonius, a category of "half-Christian" authors
between the ancient Romans and the church fathers. At *Edition of Jerome* CWE 61
72/Jerome, *Lucubrationes* II fol. 2v (praefatio) Erasmus calls Boethius a distinguished
philosopher. Edward A. Synan, "Boethius, Valla, and Gibbon", *The Modern Schoolman*
69 (1992), 475–91 discusses Boethius' reputation as "the last Roman" and "the first
scholastic"; the first epithet may go back to Valla, who grudgingly called Boethius
"eruditorum ultimus".

the latter's younger contemporary Cassiodorus (c. 490–580) with a lack of literary discipline.[32] The sixth-century poet Venantius Fortunatus does not seem to have met with his approval either,[33] and with Isidore of Sevilla (c. 570–636) the decline of literature, in Erasmus' eyes, had become as good as complete. Although Erasmus once called him "not . . . completely unlearned",[34] he often scoffed at Isidore as well as at medieval scholars like Peter Lombard and Nicholas of Lyra who had been careless enough to follow him ("the blind leading the blind"). Isidore would not have been able to express his thoughts in good Latin even once, and his etymologies were often especially absurd.[35] Isidore, then, may be considered the first fully "modern" writer in Erasmus' eyes. He is also the earliest author whose name was sometimes scornfully put in the plural by Erasmus, in phrases like "what have I to do with those Isidores".[36] Pluralising the names of medieval authors was a device typical of Erasmus; he never maligned the names of the church fathers in the same way.

Apparently Erasmus did not think Isidore's utter incompetence a unique phenomenon in its age. In *De conscribendis epistolis* (published in 1522 but composed by 1499) he identified the seventh-century Parisian monk Marcolphus as the initiator of the abominable misuse of the *vos* form of address in courteous discourse instead of the plain *tu* from classical Latin (thus also, Erasmus could denounce a

---

[32] Allen Ep. 2315:163–4.

[33] Cf. Allen Ep. 2178:13–8.

[34] Cf. *Apologia ad Fabrum* CWE 83 67/ASD IX-3 150:1625–7: "Granted that this preface [of the Epistle to the Hebrews] is not the work of Jerome, whether it is by Bede or Isidore or someone else it is certainly not the work of any completely unlearned person".

[35] On Isidore's Latin: CWE Ep. 260:56–8/Allen 50–2, cf. *Copia* CWE 24 399/ASD I-6 112:60–1. On his scholarship cf. e.g. *Ratio* Holborn 186/LB V 80D; Reeve 173 on Luke 3:23 "Qui fuit Heli", 178 on Luke 6:1 "In sabbato secundoprimo" (even a Jew would give a better explanation than Isidore); CWE Ep. 26:99–101/Allen 88–90 (Isidore included among "the ringleaders of barbarism"). Isidore followed by Lombard: Reeve 7 on Matt. 1:19 "Nollet eam traducere" (unless the scribe is to blame), *Edition of Jerome* CWE 61 148/scholia on *Ad Nepotianum, De vita clericorum* in Jerome, *Lucubrationes* I fol. 5v at "Si acolytus, si psaltes" ("the blind leading the blind"), CWE Ep. 750:43–5/Allen 34–7. Followed by Lyra: Reeve 74 on Matt. 17:24 "Non solvit didrachma", cf. 142 on Mark 14:3 "Nardi spicati". However, at *In psalmum IV concio* CWE 63 238/ASD V-2 245:674–9 with n. Erasmus himself follows Isidore, *Etymologiae* 9.4.31, wrongly stating that "baron" is derived from the Greek βάρος ("weight", "respect").

[36] Cf. CWE Ep. 260:56–8/Allen 50–2 (the plural form is lost in translation), *Supputatio* LB IX 575D.

tradition of almost a thousand years as an objectionable modern departure from ancient standards). Erasmus' dogged struggle against this habit, regrettably not yet extinct despite "the gradual coming of age of sound learning", indicates that he believed he was dealing with an important step in the process of linguistic corruption.[37] By the seventh century, then, learning suffered from universal decline.

Nevertheless, Erasmus recognised in his later writings that until the twelfth century many monastic authors had made laudable efforts to save learning from utter ruin. Repeatedly he expressed his respect for early medieval scholars who had been willing to continue the tradition of Christian learning as best as they could. Incapable of great achievements themselves, they had summarised the existing knowledge from antiquity. The writings of the (Latin) fathers, often too subtle for the learned and too tedious for the common people, had been condensed by those monks in brief tracts which were easy to understand. Their work had been useful to the church and was all the more valuable when one took into account the uncultivated times and regions in which the authors had been living. The brevity and the clarity of their work contrasted favourably with the scholastic subtleties of more recent theologians as well as with some frivolous literary products of Erasmus' own age. As examples of deserving monks from the early Middle Ages Erasmus often mentioned Bede, Claudius or Claudian of Turin († c. 827), Remigius of Auxerre (after 841–c. 908), and Anselm (either Anselm of Canterbury, c. 1034–1109, or Anselm of Laon, † 1117);[38] incidentally, he also mentioned Haimo of Halberstadt († 853), Guitmund of Aversa († c. 1095), and Alger of Liège († 1131/2).[39] In the Greek world they had had their counter-

---

[37] CWE 25 45–50/ASD I-6 266:9–276:14 (citation at 45/266:14).

[38] Both Anselms were already confounded in the Middle Ages, cf. Beryl Smalley, *The Study of the Bible in the Middle Ages* (Oxford 1952), 68. Erasmus' references to "Anselm" are too faint to decide which Anselm he meant.

[39] See Allen Epp. 1790:20–8 (Bede, Claudius, Remigius), 2284 (Guitmund, Alger), 2771:5–21 (Bede, Claudius, Haimo, Anselm); cf. *Ciceronianus* CWE 28 414/ASD I-2 660:33–661:2 (bracketing together Isidore, Bede, Claudius, Remigius, Anselm—and, surprisingly, also the Greek author Hesychius—as representatives of a "sick" eloquence). Cf. also *Declarationes ad censuras Lutetiae* LB IX 880D ("Haymones, Anselmos, Rupertos, & Hugones"); Reeve 150 on Luke 1:2 "Qui ab initio ipsi viderunt", *Apologia adversus monachos hispanos* LB IX 1048E (Bede, Remigius, and Anselm mentioned as early medieval examples in a list of Christian authorities). At *Apologia contra Latomi dialogum* CWE 71 78/LB IX 102F Erasmus brackets Haimo of Halberstadt together with the scholastic theologians. "Altisiodoraeus" and William of Paris, mentioned

part in the Bulgarian bishop Theophylact († c. 1108).[40] Once Erasmus qualified these generations of learned monks ("Anselm, Remigius, and their like") as *mediae vetustatis scriptores*, "whose authority could neither seem to be obsolete because of their excessive antiquity, nor to be slight because of their novelty".[41] The post-patristic, pre-scholastic Christian scholars, then, are those Erasmus considered almost literally "medieval".

Erasmus' qualified respect for the monastic authors of the early and high Middle Ages is also clear from his reception of their works. Twice he deigned to bring out early medieval texts personally: in 1530 he published Alger of Liège's tract on the Eucharist (originally composed to refute Berengar of Tours), followed three years later by an edition of what he took to be the Psalm commentaries of Haimo of Halberstadt (in reality the work of an anonymous author of the late eleventh or early twelfth century).[42] In his preface to the first publication, Erasmus praised Alger along with Guitmund of Aversa (whose tract on the Eucharist had appeared in print shortly before) for their philosophical competence which never degenerated into ostentation, for their knowledge of the Bible and patristic writings, and even for a certain eloquence, adding that nobody could, of course, expect sharp-witted and powerful rhetoric from them. But at least their arguments had been solid, as usually appeared to be

---

in the same passage, are wrongly identified in CWE 71 78, 158n.49 as Isidore and William of St. Thierry (1080/85–1148/9) respectively. The first reference is either to the theologian William of Auvergne († 1249) or to Remigius of Auxerre ("Antissidorensis"); the second to William of Auvergne, to the inquisitor William of Paris († before 1314) who was confessor of King Philip IV the Fair of France, or to the 15th-c. Dominican William of Paris who wrote a commentary on the New Testament. William of Paris is also mentioned at *Colloquia* CWE 40 634–5/ASD I-3 480:375ff. without being identified by the editors.

[40] Cf. CWE Ep. 916:451–4/Allen 402–5, Allen Ep. 1790:20–8. In *Annotationes in Novum Testamentum* Erasmus makes ample use of Theophylact and almost puts him on a par with the fathers, although he often calls him *recentior* (or *abbreviator Chrysostomi*). At *Responsio ad annotationes Lei* LB IX 147A he calls him "non adeo recens, neque malus"; sometimes he reckons him with the *veteres*, cf. e.g. *Detectio* ASD IX-1 248: 369–70.

[41] *Apologia de "In principio erat sermo"* LB IX 118C, cf. 117E.

[42] See Paul Gerhard Schmidt, "Erasmus und die mittellateinische Literatur", *Erasmus und Europa*, ed. August Buck (Wiesbaden 1988), 129–37 esp. 135–6: the author might be Anselm of Laon, but the issue is open to debate. Schmidt corrects the attribution of the work to Haimo himself by Marjorie O'Rourke Boyle, "For Peasants, Psalms: Erasmus' *editio princeps* of Haymo (1533)", *Mediaeval Studies* 44 (1982), 444–69 who also states wrongly that (Pseudo-) Haimo's commentary was the only medieval text edited by Erasmus (445).

the case with the generations preceding the quibbling scholastics. Erasmus professed himself to have profited from their writings, having been convinced once more of Christ's real presence in the Eucharist (a doctrine challenged in Erasmus' time by some Protestant movements).[43] As for the edition of (Pseudo-) Haimo, Erasmus praised the author's brevity, his simplicity, and his perspicuity, and again expressed his admiration for the diligence of the early medieval intelligentsia. Haimo's plain style should not deter anybody from reading his work; one should rather take his piety to heart. Erasmus admitted that he added this remark because he himself was once appalled by writings which lacked rhetorical ornament, as many people were in his day; however, he had overcome his youthful whim.[44]

With the exception of Bede, Erasmus did not make an extensive use of the early medieval authors, but when he did refer to their works, he often expressed a moderate respect for them. In fact, Isidore is the only author from the period he subjected frequently to severe and sarcastic criticism. To the others he showed more benevolence, without closing his eyes to such defects as an imperfect style, strange literary habits, and especially a deficient (though not in every case completely absent) knowledge of Greek.[45] In the annotations on the New Testament we find the majority of Erasmus' references to the authorities of the monastic age.[46] Anselm and Remigius are quoted a few times;[47] Bede is even mentioned in more than a hundred instances.[48] In addition, Erasmus referred repeatedly

---

[43] Allen Ep. 2284:34–53, 174–8; cf. Allen Ep. 2375:11–3.

[44] Allen Ep. 2771:5–14, 104–10. See also *Annotationes in Novum Testamentum* CWE 56 436/Reeve 436 on Rom. 16:25 "Missa fuit a Corintho": Erasmus' sarcastic remarks on Haimo from 1516 were excised in the 1522 edition.

[45] Cf. e.g. *Ratio* Holborn 282 (not in LB): Rabanus forced theological subjects to suit literary patterns. Imperfect knowledge of Greek: cf. Reeve 310 on Acts 17:18 "Epicurei et Stoici" (Rabanus probably consulted a faulty dictionary—but at least he consulted one); *Apologia contra Latomi dialogum* CWE 71 49, 50/LB IX 86E, 87A (mentioning Remigius). See also below n. 60.

[46] Our survey expands on the brief discussion in Erika Rummel, *Erasmus' Annotations on the New Testament: From Philologist to Theologian* (Toronto 1986), 69–70.

[47] Anselm: Reeve 150 on Luke 1:2 "Qui ab initio ipsi viderunt" (first mentioned in *1522*); 219 on John 1:1 "Erat verbum" (*1522*). Remigius: Reeve 74 on Matt. 17:18 "Et increpavit eum" (*1535*), 150 on Luke 1:2 "Qui ab initio ipsi viderunt" (*1522*), 219 on John 1:1 "Erat verbum" (*1522*), 485 on 1 Cor. 9:13 "Qui altario deserviunt" (*1516*), 647–8 on 1 Thess. 1:8 "Diffamatus est" (*1516*), 714 on Heb. 3:3 "Habet domus" (*1516*).

[48] For a complete list of references see my "Bede in the Renaissance: The Case of More and Erasmus", *Erasmus of Rotterdam Society Yearbook* 18 (1998), 89–103:100–03.

to the biblical historian Peter Comestor as well as to Rabanus or Hrabanus Maurus (c. 780–856), the one non-patristic exegete Erasmus followed in his paraphrase of the parable of the tares; the Carolingian scholar Alcuin (c. 730–804) is quoted once.[49] The majority of the references in question were added in later editions, from 1522 on. Moreover, the later references tend to be more favourable than the earlier ones: Erasmus agreed with his early medieval predecessors more often than not,[50] and when he disagreed, he sometimes tried to find explanations for the errors in question: for instance by blaming them on the copier of the text rather than on the author.[51] All this points to a growing concern and sympathy with early medieval scholarship after 1520.

There can be little doubt that among the aforementioned writers Bede was Erasmus' favourite, even if Bede's merits were only relative. Erasmus did not rank Bede with the church fathers, as did Thomas More, although a few passages from Erasmus' work could perhaps suggest otherwise.[52] The English monk remained for him primarily an early medieval author who had been summarising ancient knowledge rather than making original contributions,[53] a man "not

---

[49] Rabanus: Reeve 19 on Matt. 3:4 "Esca autem" (first mentioned in *1535*), 281 on Acts 2:23 "Praescientia dei traditum" (*1527*), 291 on Acts 7:6 "Annis quadrin-gentis" (*1527*), 294 on Acts 8:39 "Spiritus domini rapuit Philippum" (*1527*), 307 on Acts 16:1 "Filius mulieris viduae fidelis" (*1522*), 310 on Acts 17:18 "Epicurei et Stoici" (*1527*), 327 on Acts 24:21 "Nisi de hac solummodo voce" (*1522*), 329 on Acts 26:10 "Detuli sententiam" (*1522*), 331 on Acts 27:14 "Ventus typhonicus" (*1522*). Erasmus' source seems to have been the *Glossa ordinaria*. At *Declarationes ad censuras Lutetiae* LB IX 906B he claims to have consulted Rabanus for his paraphrase, calling him ibid. 858C "vir nec indoctus, nec illaudatus", but at Reeve 310 on Acts 17:18 "Epicurei et Stoici" he introduces him with the words "quisquis is fuit". Comestor: Reeve 79 on Matt. 19:12 "Qui facti sunt" (*1519*), 146 on Marc 15:25 "Erat autem hora tertia" (*1519*), 161 on Luke 2:5 "Uxore praegnante" (*1519*), 164 on Luke 2:14 "Hominibus bonae voluntatis" (*1527*), 166 on Luke 2:35 "Et tuam ipsius animam" (*1527*), 170 on Luke 3:1 "Tetrarcha autem" (*1535*), 178 on Luke 6:1 "In sabbato secundoprimo" (*1519*), 321 on Acts 22:9 "Et qui mecum erant . . ." (*1527*). Alcuin: Reeve 251 on John 10:24 "Animam nostram tollis" (*1535*, quoted from the *Catena aurea*).

[50] See e.g. the references to Remigius quoted above n. 47: the three references dating from 1516 all reiterate criticisms of Remigius in Valla's annotations on the New Testament; the other three references, added in 1522 and 1535, express agreement with Remigius' opinion.

[51] See e.g. above n. 35 (Lombard), below n. 63 (Bede).

[52] Cf. *De taedio Jesu* CWE 70 52/LB V 1283D, *Apologia ad blasphemias Stunicae* LB IX 365D; see also below n. 59. For a detailed study of More's and Erasmus' reception of Bede see my "Bede in the Renaissance".

[53] Cf. *Colloquia* CWE 40 661/ASD I-3 661:312–3, *Apologia adversus rhapsodias Pii* LB IX 1190C.

completely unlearned",[54] "not to be despised",[55] "who lacked neither learning nor industry by the standards of his time".[56] Prior to 1516 Erasmus did not take much interest in Bede's work. But for both editorial projects which Erasmus completed in 1516, the New Testament and the works of Jerome, Bede served as a source of some importance. Erasmus acknowledged this in both cases. In the Jerome edition he called him a truly learned man whose writings had helped him to solve some problems of interpretation.[57] As for the New Testament, Bede's influence was still modest in the first and second editions (1516, 1519), but this changed in the third edition of 1522, when Erasmus started to make ample use of Bede's work[58] and even went so far in his preface as to include Bede as the only post-patristic figure among the "fully and universally approved" authors against whose work he had checked his emendations.[59] Meanwhile Erasmus did not always agree with Bede in his annotations, but often took a different stand, indicating where Bede had gone astray and occasionally belittling his scholarly merits.[60]

---

[54] *Apologia ad Fabrum* CWE 83 67/ASD IX-3 150:1627. Cf. *Antibarbari* CWE 23 105/ASD I-1 125:4–5: Bede's style is "even-toned and dull, but learned, considering his century"; the positive half of this qualification was first added in the 1520 version.

[55] Reeve 745 on 1 Pet. 1:2 "Secundum praescientiam".

[56] CWE Ep. 1112:37–38/Allen 30–1.

[57] *Edition of Jerome* CWE 61 93/Jerome *Lucubrationes* II fol. 190v (praefatio), cf. CWE Ep. 361:6–10/Allen 5–10; Erasmus acknowledges his debt to Bede (esp. to his works on calculation, cf. *Adagia* II iv 91 CWE 33 234/LB II 550A) in his scholia on *Adversus Iovinianum* in Jerome, *Lucubrationes* III fol. 25v at "Nam ipsa digitorum coniunctio", 31r–v (appendix scholiorum); for other mentions of Bede see scholia on *Adversus Montanum* ibid. fol. 58v at "Super quem fundauit", on *Ad Demetriadem virginem, De virginitate* ibid. II fol. 4v (censura).

[58] That is, in the annotations on books of the New Testament upon which Bede had commented: Mark, Luke, Acts, and the Catholic Epistles; Bede is also sometimes mentioned in the rest of the annotations. In addition, Erasmus consulted Bede for his paraphrases on the New Testament, see CWE Ep. 1112:37ff./Allen 30ff. and the relevant notes in CWE 44, 49, 50 and ASD VII-6. Since the paraphrases were put into the mouth of the apostles, Erasmus naturally could not mention Bede in his texts.

[59] CWE Ep. 373:34–43/Allen 31–8 (all five editions include this preface; the reference to Bede was first added in the third edition of 1522).

[60] Pointing e.g. to his deficient knowledge of Greek, cf. Reeve 760 on 2 Pet. 2:4 "Sed rudentibus", 762 on 2 Pet. 3:1 "In quibus"; Allen Ep. 1680:134–5. Cf. however *Responsio ad annotationes Lei* LB IX 276D = *Apologia ad Stunicam* ASD IX-2 254:469–70 = Reeve 768 on 1 John 1:5–7 "Tres sunt...": "Nec huic tamen viro defuit... linguarum peritia"; see also Reeve 740 on James 2:13 "Superexaltat autem misericordia iu." for praise of Bede's consulting Greek sources. For other mentions of Bede's modest abilities cf. *Ratio* Holborn 288–9/LB V 129E–130A, *Capita argumentorum* LB VI ***2, CWE Ep. 1112:48/Allen 40–1.

One reason for Erasmus' increasing use of Bede in the 1520s may have been the publication, in 1521, of a handsome edition of Bede's Bible commentaries.[61] Before then, Erasmus knew Bede only from two exegetical compilations (the *Glossa ordinaria* and the *Catena aurea*) and one or two manuscripts.[62] But many of the quotations from Bede first added in his 1522 edition of the New Testament were still drawn from the *Glossa*; in addition, his use of Bede not only extended, but also became more circumspect, as it did with other early medieval authors.[63] Some of his quotations served polemical ends. If he could demonstrate that Bede stood on his side, he had a stronger case against the Protestants, who were not insensitive to Bede's authority,[64] and even more so against Catholic critics who charged him with unorthodox views. Apart from three Bede quotations against Luther,[65] then, we can find a few dozens of quotations in Erasmus' defences against his Catholic accusers. Erasmus inserted some of these quotations in later editions of his annotations on the New Testament. Some other references to Bede, which first appeared in his New Testament edition, could be seen as anticipations of future criticism by Catholic opponents.[66] But this would only hold true for the instances in which Erasmus agreed with Bede. In the majority of

---

[61] *Secundus operum Venerabilis Bedae presbyteri tomus, in quo subsequentes continentur eiusdem commentarii* (Paris: J. Bade and J. Petit 1521). No first volume was ever published. Erasmus confirmed that he used this edition at Reeve 276 on Acts 1:14 "Cum fratribus eius", 769 on 1 John 5:7–8 "Tres sunt . . ." A copy of it was in his library, see Fritz Husner, "Die Bibliothek des Erasmus", *Gedenkschrift zum 400. Todestage des Erasmus von Rotterdam* (Basel 1936), 228–59:240 no. 160.

[62] At Reeve 747 on 1 Pet. 2:2 "Rationabiles sine dolo lac" and 768–9 on 1 John 5:7–8 "Tres sunt . . ." Erasmus states that he had used a manuscript from the Franciscan convent in Antwerp. For his Jerome edition he used a manuscript lent to him by Ludwig Baer, see his scholia on *Adversus Iovinianum* in Jerome, *Lucubrationes* III fol. 31r (appendix scholiorum). See also CWE 44 263–4nn.28–9; Henk Jan de Jonge, "Erasmus und die *Glossa Ordinaria* zum Neuen Testament", *Nederlands Archief voor Kerkgeschiedenis* 56 (1975), 51–77:57, 59.

[63] E.g. by ascribing failures not to Bede himself but to later copiers of his work, cf. Reeve 142 on Mark 14:3 "Nardi spicati", 208 on Luke 21:38 "Et omnis populus manicabat", 277 on Acts 1:23 "Qui cognominatus est Iustus", 740 on James 2:13 "Superexaltat autem misericordia iu.", 750 on 1 Pet. 2:18 "Sed etiam discolis", 756 on 1 Pet. 5:13 "In Babylone collecta".

[64] See my "Bede in the Renaissance", 93–4.

[65] *Hyperaspistes II* LB X 1374E, *Detectio* ASD IX-1 252:473ff., *Purgatio adversus epistolam Lutheri* ASD IX-1 455:362ff.

[66] Cf. *Capita argumentorum* LB VI ***1: "Beda, Rabanus, Thomas, Lyrensis & Carrensis, aliique his obscuriores . . . videntur rem utilem praestare. Et nobis obstrepitur, qui tot argumentis ac summorum virorum auctoritate veram lectionem restituimus?"

cases we should not suppose that Erasmus quoted Bede for strate-
gic reasons, but because Bede's commentary was interesting enough
for him to mention, even if he did not always agree with it.[67]

To be sure, Erasmus did not respect every early medieval author
of the Latin West, and neither did he always give due honour to
those he did appreciate. An example of a monastic writer whom he
did not greatly value is the founder of the Carthusian order, Bruno
(c. 1030–1101). Erasmus thought that Bruno's Psalm commentaries
were of poor literary quality, recommending them for their piety
rather than their erudition.[68] With the *Glossa ordinaria*, composed in
the early twelfth century under the supervision of Anselm of Laon,
he showed even less patience, despite his extensive use of the work
in *Annotationes in Novum Testamentum* as a sourcebook of early medieval
exegetical commentaries.[69] An example of an appreciated but neglected
author is Walter of Châtillon, whose *Alexandreis* (c. 1180) Erasmus
quoted without acknowledgement in his *Adagia*, apologising that the
name of the author did not come to his mind at the moment. This
moment lasted for thirty-six years: from the first edition of 1500 to
the last one of 1536, Erasmus retained his excuse.[70] Finally, there
were some authors from the early Middle Ages of whom he simply
did not know. John Scotus Eriugena (mid-ninth century), for instance,
was the most original philosopher of the period and an outstanding
Greek scholar at that, but Erasmus does not make any reference to
his work.[71]

---

[67] The same thing is true for Erasmus' use of the *Glossa ordinaria*, see De Jonge,
"Erasmus und die *Glossa Ordinaria*", esp. 71.

[68] Cf. Allen Epp. 2143:27–31, 2315:164–5. Bruno is sometimes called Bruno of
Carinthia, although he was born in Cologne.

[69] Erasmus frequently condemned the *Glossa* as a disorderly patchwork, cf. *Apologia
ad Stunicam* ASD IX-2 144:664–6, *Apologia ad Caranzam* LB IX 409E, CWE Ep.
1112:39–41/Allen 31–4; instead of strengthening the faith, the *Glossa* would cast
doubt on it, cf. *Apologia ad Stunicam* ASD IX-2 258:523–5 = Reeve 769 on 1 John
1:5–7 "Tres sunt qui testimonium dant in coelo". For a detailed study of Erasmus'
use of the *Glossa* in his *Annotationes* see De Jonge, "Erasmus und die *Glossa Ordinaria*".

[70] *Adagia* I v 4 CWE 31 389/ASD II-1 482:187–9, cf. Schmidt, "Erasmus und
die mittellateinische Literatur", 132–3 who concludes: "Sein Verhalten mag mit
dazu beigetragen haben, daß vielfach der Eindruck eines Vakuums zwischen Antike
und Renaissance entstanden ist".

[71] He knew, however, Eriugena's homily on the prologue of the gospel of John
(PL 122 283–96) which was commonly ascribed to Origen. Erasmus rejected Origen's
authorship at Reeve 222 on John 1:3 "Et sine ipso factum est nihil" but included
the text in his Latin edition of Origen, *Opera* 2 vols. (Basel 1536) II 291–8, indicating in his introduction (LB VIII 435F) that some of the homilies in question
were spurious. He clearly had no idea that the text was Eriugena's.

In spite of his modest esteem of the early and high Middle Ages, Erasmus did not recognise either a Carolingian or a twelfth-century Renaissance (which should not come as a surprise, for both concepts are inventions of modern medievalists).[72] Once he praised Charlemagne as a monarch who equipped the monasteries of his realm with libraries to stimulate literary culture,[73] but he seems to have regarded the emperor's attitude as a relic of antiquity rather than as an attempt at restoring civilisation. Likewise Erasmus considered the Carolingian minuscule an ancient letter; some other Carolingian inventions which he knew to be at least post-classical, like the use of interspaces, he actually welcomed as improvements.[74] For the rest, the literary culture of the Carolingian age seems hardly to have existed for Erasmus.[75] He largely, if not entirely, disregarded worthy scholars like Alcuin and Walafrid Strabo (808/9–849).

The twelfth century, in Erasmus' view, ushered in the breakdown of Christian civilisation because of the emergence of scholasticism, as we will see in the next chapter. Yet the century produced two intellectuals for whom he expressed not only respect but admiration. The first one is Thomas Becket (1118–1170), the famous archbishop

---

[72] See however Ferguson, *The Renaissance in Historical Thought*, 45: according to Philipp Melanchthon, a literary revival had been realised in Carolingian times thanks mainly to Alcuin; the rise of scholasticism had put an end to it. Like many other German scholars, Melanchthon greatly valued Charlemagne as the first "German" emperor and tended to think favourably of the Carolingian age, see Dieter Mertens, "Mittelalterbilder in der frühen Neuzeit", *Die Deutschen und ihr Mittelalter. Themen und Funktionen moderner Geschichtsbilder vom Mittelalter* ed. Gerd Althoff (Darmstadt 1992), 29–54:42–3; Neddermeyer, *Das Mittelalter in der deutschen Historioraphie*, 21–4, 202–5.

[73] Allen Ep. 2435:38–42. This unique Erasmian reference to Charlemagne is inexact: according to Erasmus, Charlemagne founded the monastery of Lorsch 700 years earlier, but 700 years before 1531 (the year of Erasmus' letter), in 831, Charlemagne was dead. In reality the monastery was founded in 762/3 by a noble family who transferred it to Charlemagne in 772; after that, intellectual life at Lorsch started indeed to flower. The mention of Charlemagne at CWE Ep. 1000:51 is a mistranslation: the reference is to Charles the Bold. Erasmus possessed a book called *Vita et gesta Caroli Magni*, see Husner, "Die Bibliothek des Erasmus", 238 no. 31.

[74] For the minuscule cf. above p. 13; interspaces: *De recta pronuntiatione* CWE 26 396/ASD I-4 38:799–812.

[75] Except, of course, for the exegetes quoted above; see also Daniel J. Sheerin, "A Carolingian Cure Recovered: Erasmus' Citation of Hucbald of St. Amand's *Ecloga de caluis*", *Bibliothèque d'Humanisme et Renaissance* 42 (1980), 167–71 for the identification of "the poem in praise of baldness" mentioned at *De recta pronuntiatione* CWE 26 407/ASD I-4 48:143–5 as a work of Hucbald of St. Amand (c. 840–930). Jean-Claude Margolin, "Erasme et Charlemagne", *Moreana* 27.101–2 (1990), 125–32:127 with 132n.13 draws attention to Allen Ep. 2473:17–21 where Erasmus states that Roland died of thirst in Spain. According to Margolin, Erasmus' source may have been Rabelais' *Pantagruel*, but certainly not the *Chanson de Roland*.

of Canterbury who because of his assassination by four servants of
the king of England was venerated as a martyr. According to Erasmus,
Becket acted as a true bishop should: putting learning above everything, he protected the arts, and, keen on the liberty of the church,
he excommunicated those who occupied her property, which was
the cause of his death.[76]

The second one is Bernard of Clairvaux. Bernard appears already
in Erasmus' earliest writings as an author of some distinction.[77]
Erasmus considered Bernard's commentary on the Canticle an especially impressive achievement.[78] Moreover, Erasmus frequently appealed
to Bernard's view on divine grace (mostly in connection with Augustine)
in his dispute with Luther on free will.[79] There are even a few passages in Erasmus' work where he seems to credit Bernard with the
same authority as the church fathers.[80] But it would not be correct

---

[76] Learning: *Commentarius in psalmum II* CWE 63 141/ASD V-2 153:804–154:815,
Reeve 649 on 1 Thess. 2:7 "Sed facti sumus parvuli". Excommunication: *Lingua*
CWE 29 343/ASD IV-1A 111:795–803 (but see CWE Ep. 1400:255–74/Allen
243–64: Becket asserted the liberty of the church in a case of small importance;
his death gave the priests so much authority and wealth in England that this has
made them unpopular). See also *Julius exclusus* CWE 27 190/Ferguson 113. The
devotion to Becket in England struck Erasmus as exaggerated, cf. *Colloquia* CWE
39 199, CWE 40 641–9/ASD I-3 257:791ff., 486:589ff.; *Modus orandi Deum* CWE
70 198/ASD V-1 154:150–7. Cf. also *De bello turcico* ASD V-3 72:865–70: as a
result of Becket's martyrdom, only the archbishop of Canterbury is allowed to mint
coins in England.

[77] Cf. CWE Ep. 39:165–7/Allen 150–2 (1494?); *De contemptu mundi* CWE 66 167,
170/ASD V-1 76:993–4, 79:74 (c. 1488/9); *Antibarbari* CWE 23 105, 118ff./ASD
I-1 125:2–3, 134:32ff. (c. 1500). For a detailed study of Erasmus' reception of
Bernard see my "Erasme explore le moyen âge: sa lecture de Bernard de Clairvaux
et de Jean Gerson", *Revue d'Histoire Ecclésiastique* 93 (1998), 460–76 which corrects
the assessment of Gerhard Winkler, "Die Bernhardrezeption bei Erasmus von Rotterdam", *Bernhard von Clairvaux. Rezeption und Wirkung im Mittelalter und in der Neuzeit*, ed.
Kaspar Elm (Wiesbaden 1994), 261–70.

[78] CWE Ep. 1334:139–46/Allen 129–37, cf. *Apologia adversus Sutorem* LB IX 745F.

[79] References to Bernard: *Hyperaspistes I* CWE 76 151, 231, 272, 281/LB X
1272C, 1306C, 1324D, 1328B; *Hyperaspistes II* LB X 1338A, 1338E–1339A, 1343E,
1356D, 1360F, 1430B, 1522A–E (comparing Bernard's and Augustine's views).
Augustine and Bernard were Luther's own most appreciated authorities. On the
importance of Bernard for Luther see Theo Bell, *Divus Bernhardus. Bernhard von
Clairvaux in Martin Luthers Schriften* (Mainz 1993; originally Dutch, 1989). Erasmus
insisted that Luther's work showed more parallels with the writings of Bernard than
with his own, cf. *Acta contra Lutherum* CWE 71 102/Ferguson 320, *Apologia ad prodromon Stunicae* LB IX 379E; CWE Epp. 1033:93–4/Allen 82–4, 1236:174–8/156–60,
1418:37–8/35–7.

[80] Cf. above p. 25 n. 94; *Supputatio* LB IX 523D, 547A–B; *Purgatio adversus epistolam Lutheri* ASD IX-1 480:45–6.

to say that he considered Bernard a patristic figure. First, Erasmus seriously criticised Bernard on occasion, especially for his frivolous way of dealing with scriptural texts[81] and for his militarism.[82] Second, and more important, he normally treated the abbot of Clairvaux as an exponent of medieval instead of patristic learning. In *Antibarbari* he mentioned Bernard along with Bede as deserving authors of the monastic age, calling the abbot of Clairvaux "one of a more recent generation and both learned and eloquent as well as having a reputation for sanctity", "highly instructed not only in philosophic writings but in the poets too, at any rate the secular ones", whose style was "choice, not unpolished, but with an ecclesiastical ring".[83] In later writings, too, Erasmus ranked Bernard with other medieval scholars rather than the fathers,[84] indicating, however, that among all medieval authors Bernard was the one he liked best. In *Ciceronianus*, Bernard's candidacy for the title of Ciceronian is turned down after all church fathers have been rejected as well. Bernard, however, is presented not only as a good person, but as "a man of inherent refinement with a natural charm of style". This judgement strikes one almost as a eulogy in comparison to the words spent on the other authors from the early Middle Ages (including Bede), whom he describes as "just choppers and mutilators" who spoil what they take from others and hardly speak at all when setting forth their own views. In them, eloquence was sick; later, under scholasticism,

---

[81] Cf. *Ratio* Holborn 287/LB V 129A: "Sunt, qui ludant verbis scripturae divinae, ac veluti fit in centonibus poetarum, ad alienum sensum ceu per iocum abutuntur. Quod aliquoties facit divus Bernardus, venuste magis quam graviter, meo quidem judicio. Sic enim imbiberat vir ille praeclarus sacras litteras, ut nusquam non occursarent". The Cistercian monk Georg Schirn begged Erasmus to revise his judgment (Ep. 1142); it recurred, however, in all later editions of *Ratio* (but at *Ecclesiastes* ASD V-4 268:466–9, 274:605 Erasmus recommends Bernard as a model for preachers precisely because of his wit). In *Annotationes in Novum Testamentum* Erasmus cites Bernard three times, disagreeing with him in every case (though using respectful vocabulary): Reeve 147 on Mark 16:14 "Qui viderant eum resurrexisse", 155 on Luke 1:28 "Gratia plena", 335/CWE 56 5 on Rom. 1:1 "Vocatus apostolus". At *Apologia adversus monachos hispanos* LB IX 1084F–1085A Erasmus repeats his view on Bernard's pious but faulty interpretation of Luke 1:28; at *Enarratio psalmi XXXVIII* ASD V-3 184:490–512 he rejects Bernard's interpretation of Luke 1:38.

[82] Cf. *Adagia* IV i 1 ASD II-7 35:686–9, *Institutio principis christiani* CWE 27 284/ASD IV-1 215:513–5; *De bello turcico* ASD V-3 66:735–6, cf. 68:769–72; *Responsio ad annotationes Lei* LB IX 251C, Allen Ep. 2285:118–20.

[83] CWE 23 118, 120, 105/ASD I-1 134:32–3, 136:5–6, 125:3.

[84] Cf. *Enarratio psalmi XXXVIII* ASD V-3 196:948–51, *Apologia adversus Sutorem* LB IX 772C.

eloquence died out altogether.[85] Hence it is clear that Bernard did
better, according to *Ciceronianus*, than any medieval author before or
after him.

A confirmation of this view is offered by Erasmus' defence against
the Sorbonne theologians, who in 1531 had condemned numerous
passages from his writings. One of their *censurae* concerned Erasmus' remark in the preface of his *Paraphrase on John* (1523) that "in
no centuries have men been lacking to pay the gospel the honour
that is its due; but all the same in these last four hundred years its
energy in most hearts had grown cold".[86] The Paris theologians, criticising Erasmus for his derogatory view of medieval civilisation, set
against it, in chronological order, the names of a dozen scholars
from the twelfth century onward, from Bernard to Thomas Waldensis
(c. 1372–1431), as examples of particularly holy and learned men.
Erasmus responded:

> I shall not scrutinise the list of names which they are objecting. I do
> believe that all of them were good men, but to be a good man is
> something different from breathing the vigour of the gospel. Among
> those mentioned, Bernard seems indeed to be burning with passion,
> but how cold does he become when compared with someone like
> Cyprian or Jerome![87]

These words leave little doubt about Erasmus' appreciation of Bernard.
Compared to the fathers, Bernard was of small value. Only when
contrasted to other authors from the Middle Ages did he command
respect and admiration.

Thus far we have concentrated on the literary and intellectual
aspects of early and high medieval civilisation as observed through
Erasmus' eyes. We have seen that, according to the humanist from
the Low Countries, learning suffered greatly in the monastic period
without succumbing completely, thanks to the efforts of good men
of modest abilities. If we turn to the moral and religious aspects of
civilisation in the period, it would seem that, according to Erasmus,
decline was less serious than in the field of learning. Had he dated
the beginning of ecclesiastical corruption at the early seventh cen-

---

[85] CWE 28 414/ASD I-2 660:29–661:13.
[86] CWE Ep. 1333:345–8/Allen 322–5.
[87] *Declarationes ad censuras Lutetiae* LB IX 911B–C; the Sorbonne *censura* at 910F–
911A. Cf. *Divinationes ad notata Bedae* LB IX 481B–E, *Supputatio* LB IX 624B–E for
earlier defences of Erasmus' remark.

tury, as most Lutheran authors did,[88] he could have established a neat parallel between cultural and religious history. But in Erasmus' view the corruption of religion and morality had started earlier and developed at a much slower pace than the degeneration of learning. Strikingly, he charged the early medieval authors with some intellectual shortcomings, but not with a lack of piety. The monastic age actually produced a number of saints who stood out as edifying examples of faith and charity. The most important among those were Benedict (c. 480–543), Bernard, and Francis (1182–1226). Strictly speaking, the life of Francis fell in the scholastic period, but Erasmus manifestly included him in an early medieval tradition of founders and reformers of religious orders and monastic life.

In Erasmus' perception, the foundation of religious orders at the dawn of "modern" times was in itself a sign of the moral degeneration of society: not because the orders themselves were corrupt, but because those who wanted to live religiously apparently needed rules. In the times of the fathers, the profession of monks like Jerome was nothing else "than the practice of the original, free, and purely Christian life"; they led an austere existence in contempt of the world but obeyed their bishops and performed the duties of the clergy.[89] The monks were merely "the purer part of laity"[90] and consisted of humble, devotional, charitable people without a rule; "to be a monk meant nothing more than to be a true Christian, and a monastery was nothing else but a congregation of men united in the true teachings of Christ".[91] The formulation of rules was symptomatic of the

---

[88] Luther and his followers dated the beginning of pontifical tyranny and the ensuing corruption of the (visible) church shortly after the pontificate of Gregory the Great, most often at 607, when Pope Boniface III obtained an edict from the Byzantine emperor Phocas which recognized Rome as the head of all churches. See Neddermeyer, *Das Mittelalter in der deutschen Historiographie*, 34ff.

[89] *Vita Hieronymi* CWE 61 29/Ferguson 146 (citation), scholia on *Ad Rusticum monachum*, *Vivendi forma* in Jerome, *Lucubrationes* I fol. 20r (antidotus); see also above p. 25 n. 93. Cf. *Colloquia* CWE 39 288/ASD I-3 292:120–3: "In the old days" girls devoted to God lived at home in chastity, having no other father than their bishop; CWE 40 641, 645/ASD I-3 486:598–9, 490:731–2: in olden days all bishops and canons were monks (this may refer to the age of Thomas Becket).

[90] *Colloquia* CWE 39 478/ASD I-3 397:312. Cf. *De vidua christiana* CWE 66 193/ LB V 729D–E: in 500 AD all Christians were called saints as well as brothers and sisters.

[91] *De contemptu mundi* CWE 66 173/ASD V-1 83:175–7. Cf. *Ecclesiastes* ASD V-4 378:266–7, V-5 32:514–5: the name of monastery was given to houses of bishops which at the time were "scholae pietatis", and even to any isolated place in towns

disappearance of this spontaneous devotion,[92] comparable to the definition of religious doctrine in reaction to heresies and the weakening of the evangelic spirit. This is not to say that Erasmus rejected monasticism as such, as some scholars have argued.[93] In the historical circumstances of the early Middle Ages, the formalisation of monastic life was actually the best solution for the general decline of religiosity—even if Erasmus once acknowledged that Benedict, by demanding the absolute obedience of his followers, had laid the foundation of the "tyranny" exercised by his late medieval successors.[94]

The original rules of the orders had still been quite simple. As Erasmus explained in the 1518 preface to his *Enchiridion militis christiani*:

> in ancient days the first origin of the monastic life was a retreat from the cruelty of those who worshipped idols. The codes of the monks who soon followed them were nothing but a summons back to Christ. The courts of princes were in old days more Christian in name than in their manner of life. Bishops were soon attacked by the disease of ambition and greed. The primitive fervour of the common people cooled. Hence the retreat aimed at by Benedict and Bernard after him, and then by many more. It was the banding together of a few men aimed at nothing but a pure and simple Christianity.[95]

The rules of Benedict and of Francis tried to preserve the ambition of the more loosely organised monks of earlier times: "to live with friends who joined them willingly a life according to the teaching of the gospel in liberty of spirit".[96] In their disgust over the wicked world, men like Patrick (c. 390–461), Benedict, Bernard, and Bruno withdrew to barely accessible places; only Francis preferred to live within society.[97] Erasmus' was willing to include Dominic (1170–1221)

---

or in the country; *Vita Chrysostomi* LB III 1333D: "monasteria vero, ni fallor, ea aetate dicebantur Episcoporum aedes, in quas se recipiebant a popularibus feriati negotiis".

[92] Cf. *Epistola contra pseudevangelicos* ASD IX-1 306:685–8: rules were introduced to check the lascivious behaviour of the religious.

[93] See notably Emile V. Telle, *Erasme de Rotterdam et le septième sacrement* (Geneva 1954) passim; Chomarat, *Grammaire et rhétorique*, 887–92.

[94] *Ecclesiastes* ASD V-4 378:287–303.

[95] CWE Ep. 858:539–47/Allen 508–15.

[96] Ibid. 549–51/Allen 517–9.

[97] Cf. *De ecclesiae concordia* ASD V-3 279:757–280:765 (mentioning Patrick, Benedict, Bernard, and Bruno "or whoever was the founder of the Carthusian order"), *Ecclesiastes* ASD V-4 383:419–384:430 (mentioning Benedict and Bernard; Francis did not opt for solitude, even if he fiercely despised the world).

among the saints who tried to preserve ancient monasticism, although he seems to have preferred Francis and the saints of an earlier age. He may have thought that the Dominican order, the first one to require that its members engage in systematic study and soon involved in inquisitiorial activity, was tainted from the outset by the spirit of disputation, even if he took pains in his writings to express respect for Dominic himself and for his early followers.[98]

In Erasmus' view, the orders initially succeeded in living up to the intentions of their founders, at least until the end of the twelfth century.[99] Basil, Jerome, Augustine, Benedict, Bruno, Francis, and Dominic had all tried to instruct their followers by their own examples, by sound teaching, by friendly warnings, and by brotherly corrections;[100] unlettered abbots had been very rare.[101] Erasmus took for granted the idea that learning had formed an ingredient of monastic life, even if he knew that Francis in particular had not held scholarship in high esteem[102] (but then Francis lived in the age of scholasticism). Nowhere did Erasmus give details about the organisation of intellectual or religious life in the monasteries in the period under consideration. He simply took them to be islands of learning and piety.

---

[98] Cf. CWE Epp. 948:151–2/Allen 146–7: the Dominicans once produced many men of learning, now many who expect to rule the roost; 1167:47–8/40–1: the Dominican order "always had, and I think still has, many men distinguished for learning and piety".

[99] Cf. *Institutio christiani matrimonii* CWE 69 284–5/LB V 646B–D: the rule that taking monastic vows annuls a non-consummated marriage was good in its time, when only the religious sustained the gospel in full vigour, whereas the nobility and the people were sliding back into paganism. The rule in question, *Decretales* X 3.32.2 (for citations from canon law cf. below p. 71 n. 40), was formulated by Pope Alexander III (1159–81); it would seem, then, that in the second half of the 12th c. monastic life was still exemplary, unless Erasmus thought that the rule dated from earlier times.

[100] CWE Ep. 447:671–81/Allen 606–15, cf. Allen Ep. 2523:55–9.

[101] Cf. *Colloquia* CWE 39 504/ASD I-3 407:152.

[102] Cf. *Colloquia* CWE 40 950/ASD I-3 663:368–70: Francis was a poor Latinist; CWE 40 1001/ASD I-3 688:78–82: Francis was not wise or learned by worldly standards, but most dear to God; *Ecclesiastes* ASD V-4 383:421–384:424: Francis did not care for learning himself and did not permit his followers to touch books if they had not studied before; *De libero arbitrio* CWE 76 18/LB IX 1219D–E: Dominic and Francis might have been "fools" to whom the Spirit revealed what he withheld from the wise. Cf. also *Colloquia* CWE 40 768/ASD I-3 540:110–2, *Responsio adversus febricitantis libellum* LB X 1680D, Allen Ep. 2205:249–50: Francis and Dominic had no affinity with scholastic theology and philosophy.

Erasmus not only praised the founders of monastic life (Francis in particular) on many occasions,[103] but suggested, notably in his controversies with Catholic critics, that he was actually a better disciple of them than many members of their orders. The founders of the mendicant orders in particular would not recognise as their true sons those who professed to be their followers.[104] Once Erasmus expressed the wish that his conflicts with contemporary Franciscans and Dominicans could be settled through the intervention of Francis and Dominic themselves, from whose examples Erasmus' adversaries had much degenerated.[105] Still more revealing is Erasmus' report of a dream in which Francis (without the cowl, the cord, and the stigmata attributed to him by the Franciscans) appeared to him, thanking him for denouncing the vices which he (Francis) had always shunned himself, and including Erasmus among the friends of his order. At his departure, Francis, extending his hand, said to Erasmus: "Fight bravely, soon you will be one of mine".[106]

Still, Erasmus believed that neither the religious orders nor the secular clergy had been exempt from corruption before the age of scholasticism. Bernard of Clairvaux was Erasmus' principal witness. An ardent defender of the pure faith (at least in this respect the equal of the ancients)[107] and a sharp critic of degenerated morals

---

[103] For praise of Francis cf. e.g. *Julius exclusus* CWE 27 175/Ferguson 81, *Enarratio in primum psalmum* CWE 63 39/ASD V-2 60:809–10, *Enchiridion* CWE 66 71–2/LB V 31D, *De immensa Dei misericordia* CWE 70 93/LB V 566A–B, Allen Ep. 1925:44–5. Erasmus' esteem of Francis was not exceptional. The first generation of Lutheran reformers likewise held Francis in high esteem, most notably Luther himself. Only from the second half of the 16th c. did a negative attitude toward Francis prevail among Protestant theologians. See Klaus Reblin, *Freund und Feind. Franziskus im Spiegel der protestantischen Theologiegeschichte* (Göttingen 1988), esp. 19–70.

[104] For this charge cf. *Enchiridion* CWE 66 79/LB V 36B (Augustine); *Supputatio* LB IX 615A (Francis); *Apologia adversus Sutorem* LB IX 797A, 803D, 804A (Bruno); *Responsio adversus febricitantis libellum* LB X 1683B and likewise Allen Ep. 2300:148–9 (Francis); see also *Apologia adversus rhapsodias Pii* LB IX 1147F (Benedict, Francis, Carthusians). For remarks on contemporary religious being a disgrace to the founders of their orders cf. also e.g. *Ciceronianus* CWE 28 386–7/ASD I-2 639:26–31 (Augustinians, Benedictines, Franciscans); *Modus orandi Deum* CWE 70 152/ASD V-1 124:109–12 (Franciscans, Dominicans); *Ecclesiastes* ASD V-4 326:959–61 (Franciscans), V-5 126:447–51 (Franciscans); CWE Ep. 967A:112–6/Allen Ep. 985:102–5 (Benedictines, Franciscans, Augustinians); Allen Epp. 1805:362–4 (Benedictines, Dominicans, Franciscans), 1967:132–3 (Franciscans, Dominicans); 2299:136–7, 143–4 (Franciscans).

[105] Allen Ep. 2094:76–80; cf. also *Supputatio* LB IX 587A (Erasmus claims support from Benedict and Francis).

[106] Allen Ep. 2700:37–53.

[107] Cf. CWE Ep. 858:544–5/Allen 513–4, *De praeparatione ad mortem* CWE 70

among the clergy, Bernard had insisted on strict rules for all clerics. When called to account for his attacks on the behaviour of church-men, Erasmus could therefore gleefully point to the example of Bernard, who had likewise denounced the corruption of the monks and even of the Roman curia, in the same way as Jerome had done before him. Notably Bernard's *De consideratione* would contain a much more acerbic critique of the clergy than one would be able to find in Erasmus' writings.[108] Erasmus generally liked to take sides with Bernard against his Catholic critics, while he protested when his adversaries tried to use Bernard's authority in favour of their views.[109]

In conclusion we must say that Erasmus' statements about the early and high Middle Ages do not perfectly sustain his general ideas about the historical development of Western Christendom any more than does his view of the ancient past. According to Erasmus, lit-erary and religious decay, which both germinated in the patristic period, did not break out simultaneously upon the arrival of mod-ern times. Literary culture underwent a severe setback in the monas-tic period, even if many authors had relative merits in the field of learning, something which Erasmus increasingly recognised after 1520. Religious culture, on the other hand, deteriorated much less in the period—or might we even say that it made progress? At any rate, religious life seems to have been, in Erasmus' eyes, less turbulent in the monastic age than in the days of the fathers. There were no serious threats by pagans and heretics any more. The most impor-tant case of heresy in the period Erasmus knew about, connected with Berengar of Tours, had actually been treated in an exemplary way, because of the calm and sound argumentation involved. Moreover, the early and high Middle Ages had produced a number of holy men who had tried to preserve the pure faith in the midst of the orders founded or reformed by them, and until the end of the twelfth

---

430/ASD V-1 374:850–4, *Ecclesiastes* ASD V-4 382:414–384:430, *In psalmum IV con-cio* CWE 63 246/ASD V-2 252:911–2, *De ecclesiae concordia* ASD V-3 279:757–280:765.

[108] Cf. *Colloquia* CWE 39 457/ASD I-3 384:315–6, *Lingua* CWE 29 380/ASD IV-1A 148:23–5; *Apologia ad blasphemias Stunicae* LB IX 358A, 360A; *Responsio ad epis-tolam Pii* LB IX 1102E, 1108C; *Dilutio* CWE 83 135/Telle 88; CWE Epp. 1173: 192–3/Allen 173, 1202:16–21/14–9, 1313:100/90–1, 1469:34–5/30–1. For a par-allel between Erasmus' and Bernard's complaints of the abuse of papal power in particular cf. *In epistola de delectu ciborum scholia* ASD IX-1 68:102–5, *Responsio ad epis-tolam Pii* LB IX 1105A.

[109] Cf. *Responsio ad notulas Bedaicas* LB IX 711E–F, likewise *In epistola de delectu cibo-rum scholia* ASD IX-1 70:158–60; *Apologia adversus Sutorem* LB IX 745F, 803D; see also *Apologia contra Latomi dialogum* CWE 71 72/LB IX 99E.

century their work had been quite successful. It would seem, then, that the downfall of the standards of learning in the monastic period had scarcely exercised a negative influence on religious life. Francis, who perhaps was Erasmus' favourite saint of the Middle Ages, had even dispensed with learning altogether. Thus Erasmus' own view of early medieval history implied a challenge to the reform programme of Christian humanism: learning and religion apparently did not need each other. But Erasmus seems to have been unaware of the challenge and hence did not worry about it.

Further, the degeneration of literary culture in the monastic period seems to have constituted for Erasmus a process beyond human grasp. It just happened; we do not see how it originated or who was responsible for it. Monastic authors who tried to preserve ancient knowledge were the victims rather than the instigators of literary decay; with a few exceptions (like Marcolphus) they were not to blame personally for the lowering of cultural standards. The fault lay rather with "the times they lived in". Intellectual decline seems to have originated and developed as an impersonal historical force which, almost as a Hegelian *Zeitgeist*, imposed itself irresistibly on the course of events. This observation is all the more remarkable since in *Antibarbari* Erasmus fiercely rejected all philosophies of history which tended to exclude the responsibility of human beings for the wrongs of the past, in particular for the loss of culture during the Middle Ages. Moreover, the notion of the inescapability of cultural decline would again seem to undermine Erasmus' programme of reform: if there is nothing one can do about the loss of culture, attempts to improve the situation must remain fruitless. In this case, however, Erasmus apparently perceived the lurking danger. In several writings he recognised in so many words that decline was inherent in all human institutions, in a couple of instances adding, however, that it was not impossible to turn the tide. In the preface (1516) to his New Testament edition he asserted that the Christian life, like anything else in human affairs, "naturally sinks back by degrees into something worse and seems to degenerate, unless we fight against this with all our might".[110] In a similar vein he wrote four years later in the preface to his *Paraphrases* on Peter and Jude that "human affairs tend always towards the worse unless we make great efforts

---

[110] CWE Ep. 384:27–9/Allen 25–6.

in the opposite direction".[111] Thus Erasmus did not succumb to fatalism. The faults of the past could be cured through strenuous efforts in the present. In addition, he held human beings personally responsible for the wrongs of the scholastic period of Christian history, when both intellectual and religious culture reached their nadir.

[111] CWE Ep. 1112:30–1/Allen 23–4. For other statements on the tendency of human affairs to decline cf. *Ratio* Holborn 303/LB V 136F (referring to scholasticism); Reeve 667 on 1 Tim. 1:17 "Soli deo" (cf. above p. 30 n. 115); *Epistola contra pseudevangelicos* ASD IX-1 300:491–3 (the mendicant orders), 304:596–7 (the early church), 306:661–2 (church music). See also below pp. 187–90.

CHAPTER THREE

MEDIEVAL HISTORY: THE SCHOLASTIC PERIOD

Beatus Rhenanus, a close friend of Erasmus and the most famous humanist historian of Germany, dated the rise of scholasticism (and hence the decay of theology) at "around the year of grace 1140", when men like Peter Lombard (1095/1100–1160), Peter Abelard (1079–1142), and Gratian († c. 1150) were active.[1] Erasmus, who cared relatively little about chronology, never gave such a precise indication, but one may assume that he did not disagree with Beatus, whose views may have directly influenced him. As we have seen, he believed that the fervour of the gospel had grown cold among most Christians during the previous four hundred years.[2] Although his statement pertained to public morality rather than to theology,[3] other passages from his work confirm that in Erasmus' eyes those four centuries represented the age of scholasticism. In his biography of Jerome, he complained that for the scholastics nobody "who had lived before the last four hundred years" was a theologian,[4] and in a work against Noël Bédier he pointed to a tradition of "four hundred years during which scholastic theology, gravely burdened by the decrees of the philosophers and the contrivances of the sophists, has wielded its reign".[5] In one other case he assigned to scholasticism a tradition of three centuries.[6] Thus by the second half of the twelfth century, Western Christendom, in Erasmus' conception, had entered the most distressing phase of its history, even though the

---

[1] See John F. D'Amico, "Beatus Rhenanus, Tertullian and the Reformation: A Humanist's Critique of Scholasticism", *Archiv für Reformationsgeschichte* 71 (1980), 37–63 esp. 42–7; idem, *Theory and Practice in Renaissance Textual Criticism: Beatus Rhenanus Between Conjecture and History* (Berkeley 1988), 152–7.

[2] CWE Ep. 1333:345–8/Allen 322–5. D'Amico, "Beatus Rhenanus", 48 shows that Erasmus' survey of history in Ep. 1334 (see above p. 40) was probably indebted to Beatus' views. Beatus may thus also have influenced Ep. 1333, which bears the same date as Ep. 1334.

[3] Cf. Erasmus' claim at *Divinationes ad notata Bedae* LB IX 481B.

[4] CWE 61 52/Ferguson 179.

[5] *Supputatio* LB IX 624C.

[6] *Adagia* IV v 1 ASD II-7 241:204–6; cf. also Reeve 270 on John 21:22 "Sic eum volo manere": the corruption of the passage in question seems to have become accepted during the last 300 or 400 years.

example of Francis shows that the traditions of the preceding monastic period had not expired immediately.

In Erasmus' view Peter Lombard, the compiler of the *Sententiae* (a textbook on which university teaching of theology was based and on which every advanced student had to write a commentary), stood at the beginning of the scholastic tradition of theology, even though he might not have been a full-fledged scholastic himself. Introducing Lombard in his annotations on the New Testament, Erasmus described him as a theologian who was far from despicable, honest, and learned with regard to the times he lived in. Lombard undertook his work with pious diligence, assembling all material relevant to his subjects without asking trifling questions. Unfortunately, his work was received by posterity in an altogether different spirit: an ocean of never ending questions had burst forth from it.[7]

The *Sententiae* epitomised the decline of literary culture which had accompanied the rise of scholasticism. Lombard's imperfections, Erasmus explained, had primarily to be blamed on his times. What could one expect from an author living in an age in which Greek, Hebrew, and, to a large extent, Latin as well were extinguished, and almost all ancient authors were forgotten, so that for all problems Isidore was treated as the ultimate authority? True enough, many authors made still use of commentaries by the Greeks that had been translated, as well as possible, into Latin. However—and here Erasmus repeated an accusation expressed earlier in his edition of Jerome— many scholastics concealed the names of the authors from whom they profited and even suppressed the works they consulted.[8] Thomas Aquinas quoted Greek authors like Theophylact in his *Catena aurea*, who afterwards had altogether disappeared, "which would hardly seem to have happened by chance".[9] Some commentaries on Acts

---

[7] Reeve 6–7 on Matt. 1:19 "Nollet eam traducere" (also advancing the possibility that copiers added much nonsense to Lombard's work); cf. CWE Ep. 1334: 168–71/Allen 158–61 where Lombard is praised for his care in reproducing the opinions of others instead of enforcing his own views (which Erasmus considered a scholastic habit). Erasmus' moderate judgement may again be due to Beatus Rhenanus, who had a much higher opinion of Lombard than of his followers. Nevertheless, Erasmus included Lombard among the scholastics at, e.g., *Responsio ad annotationes Lei* LB IX 187E, *Supputatio* LB IX 521B–C, Allen Ep. 2284:45–7, while he once disposed of Lombard as "coacervator Sententiarum", see Reeve 7 on Matt. 1:19 "Nollet eam traducere" (change of 1522).

[8] Reeve 7 on Matt. 1:19 "Nollet eam traducere", cf. above p. 38.

[9] Ibid. 142 on Mark 14:3 "Nardi spicati". In the 1527 edition Erasmus blamed Bede for not mentioning his source, in contrast to Thomas, who carefully mentioned

mentioned in that work were probably destroyed by those who collected them, for how else could one account for the loss of so many
texts?[10] Equally damaging had been the reverse procedure by which
late medieval scholars intertwined ancient texts with their own products in order to provide the latter with false authority. Thus the
works of Jerome had deliberately been spoilt by some "impostor",
presumably an Augustinian Eremite who had lived two hundred
years before Erasmus' day.[11] Even in their physical appearance, late
medieval books obscured the ancient literary heritage: Gothic script
was, according to Erasmus, clumsy, barbarous, hardly legible, and
inept for such ancient texts as those of Cicero or Jerome.[12]

The degeneration of letters, then, which had originated in late
antiquity as a seemingly independent phenomenon and had continued during the early Middle Ages despite the good intentions of the
monastic intelligentsia, was deliberately brought to completion by
late medieval authors who either annihilated their sources in order
to present their compilations as their own brainchildren, or distorted
old texts by dragging in inventions of their own making. Hence came
the question in *Adagia* about whether one should be grateful to late
medieval authors for their preservation of ancient texts or rather
blame them for what they had made disappear. In Erasmus' view,
the then current charge that the author of the *Sententiae* was responsible for the loss of theology, was, at any rate, "not far from the
truth".[13]

According to Erasmus, the extinction of ancient literature did not
affect theology alone. All fields of learning suffered from it. As a
result, religion and morality languished as well: in the scholastic
period, at least, intellectual and moral degeneration went hand in
hand. In this chapter we will inquire into Erasmus' view on the dis-

---

the authors and works he used; in 1535 he toned down his remark, supposing that
Bede had indicated his sources in the margins, but that copiers of his work had
failed to do the same thing—still preferring Thomas' method of mentioning his
sources in the text. For other references to translations from the Greek mentioned
by Thomas which later disappeared see ibid. 464 on 1 Cor. 7:17 "Nisi unicuique . . .",
529 on 2 Cor. 2:13 "Non habeo requiem spiritui meo", and next note.

[10] Ibid. 272 on Acts 1:1 "Primum quidem sermonem".
[11] *Edition of Jerome* CWE 61 83, 88–9/Jerome, *Lucubrationes* II fol. 189r, 189v–190r
(praefatio).
[12] Cf. *De recta pronuntiatione* CWE 26 390–1, 393/ASD I-4 34:655–7, 35:718–9;
CWE Ep. 396:185–9/Allen 170–4.
[13] *Adagia* III i 1 CWE 34 173/ASD II-5 30:191–4.

ruption of Christian civilisation during the four centuries preceding his own time.

The Breakdown of Learning

Antibarbari makes it clear that Erasmus regarded the decline of culture as a process that had reached its nadir in his own day. Christ had progressively disclosed his intellectual and spiritual gifts to humanity, but instead of using these gifts, Christians had increasingly been neglecting them. Rather than an accumulation of all good, the present displayed a combination of all that had gone wrong in the course of history.

The main theme of *Antibarbari* is literary culture. The dialogue reflects some of the young Erasmus' frustrations with his own education in the field. Strongly inclined to the classics from his earliest years, he was forced at school to study medieval linguistics instead of developing his literary gifts. To a certain extent, *Antibarbari* is his revenge. The protagonist of the dialogue is a humanist schoolmaster fulminating against the barbarians who spoil education and thus destroy the minds of the young, in particular because they favour inept books of grammar. Erasmus frequently attacked the books in question in his early writings—most often are mentioned *Mammetrectus, Catholicon, Floretus*, and the works of Alexander of Villedieu (1160/70–1240/50), Eberhard of Béthune († 1212), John of Garland (c. 1195–after 1272), and the modists, that is, those writing on *modi significandi*[14]—

---

[14] *Antibarbari* CWE 23 34, 36, 67/ASD I-1 58:10–2, 61:15–8, 89:19–90:2; *Conflictus Thaliae et Barbariei* LB I 892F; *Colloquia* CWE 40 834–5, 1103/ASD I-3 586:28–46, 588:89, 746:205–747:227; *De recta pronuntiatione* CWE 26 388/ASD I-4 32:587–91; *De conscribendis epistolis* CWE 25 17, 24, 40, 53, 54–5, 193/ASD I-2 219–20, 230, 248, 257, 283, 285, 494; *De pueris instituendis* CWE 26 345/ASD I-2 77:11–6, *Apophthegmata* LB IV 247D; *Ratio* Holborn 186, 268/LB V 80D, 121C; Reeve 317 on Acts 20:9 "De tertio coenaculo", 481 on 1 Cor. 8:4 "Quia nihil est idolum", 611 on Eph. 5:4 "Aut scurrilitas", 731 on Heb. 11:37 "In melotis"; scholia on *Ad Domnionem, Apologeticon* in Jerome, *Lucubrationes* III fol. 53r at "Et Carneadeum aliquid"; CWE Epp. 26:99–101/Allen 88–90, 30:30–1/28; 31:42–3, 54–5, 92–4/37, 47–8, 80–2; 56:37–40/32–4, 337:325–31/313–8, 447:103–5/98–9, 535:33/29–30, 1437:272–6/Allen I 48:34–6; Allen Ep. 1697:50–3. The names are not always identified correctly in CWE and ASD. *Floretus* is not a work of John of Garland (who wrote a *Compendium grammaticale*, a *Morale scolarium*, and a *Distigium sive Cornutus*) but an anonymous didactic poem from the 14th c. "Florista" refers to Ludolph de Luco (c. 1300), the author of *Flores (artis) grammaticae*. See A.G. Weiler, "Erasmus of Rotterdam's *Institutum hominis christiani*, a Substitute for the Mediaeval *Liber Floretus*",

and even continued to express his indignation in his later work, by
the time that, in his own country at least, the medieval grammarians
had vanished from the schools and been replaced by writings of,
among others, Erasmus himself.[15] It is important to note that the
medieval grammarians were typical exponents of scholastic learning.
Hence Erasmus could and did easily extend his criticism of contemporary school education to an attack on the intellectual tradition
of the whole scholastic period. He regarded the barbarians of his
own day as mere adepts of this tradition, something which they
would confirm by proclaiming themselves Albertists, Thomists, Scotists,
Occamists, Durandists and so on, ranking their heroes almost above
Christ.[16] Erasmus' retaliations against the barbarism of his own times
thus often involve a critique of the later Middle Ages. In a sense,
he held four centuries of scholasticism responsible for what he had
gone through as a schoolboy.

In Erasmus' view, grammar was the basis of all education, not
only chronologically, because school started with this subject, but
intellectually as well, because a due command of classical languages
was fundamental to all further study. The neglect of (good) grammar at the schools had caused, in his opinion, the loss of many good
authors and even of "whole departments of learning".[17] A great
decline of education had occurred, despite the care with which universities and lower schools had originally been founded by secular
and ecclesiastical authorities (Erasmus must be referring here to the
thirteenth century).[18] Instead of learning to speak and write prop-

---

Media latinitas: A Collection of Essays to Mark the Occasion of the Retirement of L.J. Engels,
ed. R.I.A. Nip et al. (Turnhout 1996), 359–63.

[15] The humanist reform of secondary education in the Low Countries seems to
have been completed by 1520. See R.R. Post, *The Modern Devotion: Confrontation with
Reformation and Humanism* (Leiden 1968), 557–75; P.N.M. Bot, *Humanisme en onderwijs
in Nederland* (Utrecht 1955), 28–43. For Erasmus' influence on English education see
Grafton and Jardine, *From Humanism to the Humanities*, 140–1.

[16] Cf. *Antibarbari* CWE 23 58, 67/ASD I-1 81:16–8, 90:8–10 etc.

[17] *De recta pronuntiatione* CWE 26 372/ASD I-4 17:130–2, cf. *Ecclesiastes* ASD
V-4 252:138–40, *Apologia contra Latomi dialogum* CWE 71 66/LB IX 96E.

[18] *De recta pronuntiatione* CWE 26 378ff./ASD I-4 23:316ff. Universities were founded
from the 13th c.; like many other humanists, Erasmus objected to their name (*uni-
versitas*), which would suggest that every discipline was taught in them (ibid. 378,
380/23:319–20, 24:357–8; in fact, the meaning of the term was "corporate body").
Lower schools had always existed, but their spread was stimulated by the Fourth
Lateran Council (1215), which decreed the foundation of schools by every church
having sufficient means. In the Low Countries every parish church seems to have
provided at least primary education, see R.R. Post, *Scholen en onderwijs in Nederland
gedurende de Middeleeuwen* (Utrecht 1954), 17–20.

erly, schoolchildren were trained in linguistics and dialectics and thus
educated as sophists, occupying themselves with trivialities and taking a fancy to obstinate disputation. Teaching was entrusted to incom-
petent and cruel men (and even to women) who had learned nothing
themselves and could only fill their pupils with a hatred for literature. Erasmus therefore urged public authorities to take their educational responsibilities seriously—after all, "the quality of its education
is the main factor in a country's progress or decline"[19]—and to
reverse, as it were, the medieval habit of leaving the care of learning to the monks: secular governments had to appoint able instructors in state-controlled schools and to suppress the institutions run
by the religious orders and the Brethren of Common Life, who had
no affinity with humane studies.[20] In fact, this was what actually happened in the Low Countries during Erasmus' life, so that in his later
writings he could present his criticism of medieval education as the
contemplations of an old man looking back on an unfortunate age
which he had known in his early years.[21]

Erasmus considered the troubles of higher education similar to
those in the lower schools. Inadequate study of languages and literature, along with excessive attention to logic, were the roots of all
evil. Although all higher studies were dependent on good letters,[22]
students were indoctrinated instead with confusing philosophical questions and concepts in the first phase of their studies, especially by
the arts faculty (instruction in the arts extended school education

---

[19] *De recta pronuntiatione* CWE 26 375–6/ASD I-4 20:237–8, cf. *Institutio principis
christiani* CWE 27 259/ASD IV-1 188:699–710.

[20] Cf. *Antibarbari* CWE 23 28–31/ASD I-1 50:27–55:18, *De pueris instituendis* CWE
26 325ff./ASD I-2 54:16ff. (declining female teachers); *De recta pronuntiatione* CWE
26 384–6/ASD I-4 28:476–30:544; see also *Institutio christiani matrimonii* CWE 69
417–8/LB V 713D (against schools of the Brethren), scholia on *Ad Laetam, De insti-
tutione filiae* in Jerome, *Lucubrationes* I fol. 24v at "Ne oderit studia" (bad and cruel
instructors). In the late medieval Low Countries, the urban parish schools were
already being taken over by local governments; the humanists supported this policy. Schools run by the orders and by the Brethren had never been numerous.
Female instructors played an important role in primary education, which was accessible to both sexes. See Post, *Scholen en onderwijs*, 45–55 (schools being taken over),
90–1 (participation of women), 163–4 (orders and Brethren); idem, *The Modern
Devotion*, 557–75.

[21] Cf. *De pueris instituendis* CWE 26 345/ASD I-2 77:11–78:1, *De recta pronuntiatione* CWE 26 388/ASD I-4 31:586–32:592; see also *De conscribendis epistolis* CWE
25 54–5/ASD I-2 285:11–4, Allen Ep. 2132:18–21.

[22] Cf. e.g. *Supputatio* LB IX 787F–788A, 788E–F, referring to all four faculties in
particular.

and partly overlapped it).[23] In the universities as well as in the monasteries[24] the young spent a bare three months on grammar before
being hurried on to sophistic and dialectic studies; after that, they
were taken straight into the midst of theology (or law or medicine,
as far as the universities were concerned), never coming into touch
with good letters and developing a hatred for them.[25] The result was
an oppressive barbarism.

Aristotle in particular held sway in the faculties of liberal arts.
There can be no doubt that Erasmus regretted the ascendancy that
the Greek philosopher had gained over more literary authors from
the ancient world, even though some modern commentators claim
that Erasmus opposed the purported distortion of Aristotle by the
scholastics rather than Aristotelian influence in itself. Certainly,
Erasmus maintained that the scholastics did not know the genuine
Aristotle: even if the Greek philosopher had understood Latin, he
would have been unable to recognise the translations of his work
used by Thomas Aquinas.[26] But this does not imply that Erasmus
would have approved of an arts education based on Aristotle if the
organon was read in the original Greek. The truth is that Aristotelian
philosophy, in Erasmus' view, contributed little to wisdom—a simple-
minded fool might display more wisdom than trained academics[27]—
let alone to the *philosophia Christi* which was the aim of all study. He
therefore left only modest room for it in his own educational programmes,[28] asking time and again what Aristotle (or his Arabian
commentator Averroes) had to do with Christ.[29]

---

[23] At *Responsio ad febricitantis libellum* LB X 1680C–D Erasmus claims that he studied most subjects of Aristotelian philosophy as a schoolboy, cf. also *Appendix respon-
dens ad Sutorem* LB X 810A–C. In the late Middle Ages, school education in the
Netherlands consisted of (Latin) grammar, dialectics, and music, see Post, *Scholen en
onderwijs*, 92–7.

[24] In the Low Countries many young men took vows after having finished (public) school, pursuing higher studies, especially theology, in their monasteries, see
Post, *Scholen en onderwijs*, 162.

[25] Cf. *Antibarbari* CWE 23 70/ASD I-1 93:16–9, *De recta pronuntiatione* CWE 26
380/ASD I-4 24:356–68; CWE Epp. 337:325–31/Allen 313–8, 447:103–5/98–9.

[26] Reeve 7 on Matt. 1:19 "Nollet eam traducere".

[27] Cf. *Adagia* III iii 1 CWE 34 266/ASD II-5 166:124–31, *De praeparatione ad mortem*
CWE 70 441/ASD V-1 384:114–24, *Concio de puero Jesu* CWE 29 65/LB V 605E.

[28] Cf. *De ratione studii* CWE 24 673/ASD I-2 120:12–3, *De recta pronuntiatione* CWE
26 387/ASD I-4 30:556–31:570, *Institutio principis christiani* CWE 27 214/ASD
IV-1 144:263–145:268, CWE Ep. 393:18–28/Allen 17–26.

[29] Cf. e.g. *Paraclesis* Holborn 148/LB V 143D–144A, VI *4; *Ratio* Holborn 191–2,
297ff./LB V 82E, 83A–D, 133Ff.; *In psalmum IV concio* CWE 63 242, 244/ASD

The neglect of literary studies in favour of (Aristotelian) logic had been pernicious, according to Erasmus, in every higher discipline. In terms of medicine, Erasmus never really substantiated this statement. He welcomed and personally stimulated the renascence of ancient authors who had written on medical subjects,[30] but never alleged that the neglect of these authors had been responsible for the emergence of bad physicians. Erasmus might have agreed with the obvious truth that a physician well versed in ancient literature in his field would make a better scholar, but not necessarily a more competent medical practitioner.

As for the study of civil and canon law, which by its nature was more bookish than medicine, Erasmus was less reluctant with his accusations. In his *Moria* he depicted lawyers as self-satisfied men who liked to make everything seem difficult, endlessly quoting from as many laws and commentaries as possible.[31] The parallel with his criticism of quibbling scholastics growing old over thorny trifles is clear. As far as civil law is concerned, Erasmus suggested that famous medieval commentators like Bartolo of Sassoferato (1313–57), Baldo de Ubaldis (1327–1400), and, to a lesser extent, Accursius (c. 1185–1263) had obscured rather than clarified the ancient imperial decrees (preserved for a great part in the codifications of the Byzantine emperor Justinian, dating from the sixth century but considered by Erasmus a product of the ancient world).[32] They had often gone "madly and hideously astray",[33] and Erasmus made sport of their followers, who sometimes would go so far as to put more trust in

---

V-2 248:800–249:802, 250:834–6; Reeve 664 on 1 Tim. 1:6 "In vaniloquium"; CWE Epp 337:422–35, 733–42/Allen 402–13, 697–705; 1581:590–2/530–3. Cf. also scholia on *De quadringentaduabus mansionibus* in Jerome, *Lucubrationes* IV fol. 23v (antidotus): "Neque dubito quin si diuus Hieronymus hanc uidisset theologiam, Aristotelicis sententiis ac legibus undique contaminatam, uel obrutam potius, tota libertate in rem tam indignam detonuisset". See also above pp. 38–40.

[30] Cf. CWE Epp. 542:31–50/Allen 27–43, 862:20–4/16–9; see also Reeve III Appendix A [555] on 1 Thess. 2:7 "Sed facti sumus paruuli", *Edition of Jerome* CWE 61 85–6/Jerome *Lucubrationes* II fol. 189r–v (praefatio), CWE Ep. 541:60–3/Allen 54–7, Allen Ep. 2274:18. Personal contributions are Erasmus' translations of Plutarch (1512–3) and Galen (1526).

[31] CWE 27 125/ASD IV-3 142:348–53.

[32] Cf. e.g. CWE Epp. 143:219ff./Allen 201ff., 1126:224/203; Allen Ep. 2750:95–102.

[33] *Apologia contra Latomi dialogum* CWE 71 48/LB IX 86A; cf. ibid. 39/80D, *Apophthegmata* LB IV 360A. At CWE Epp. 134:29–33/Allen 25–8, 1469:265/246 Erasmus suggests that their Latin was bad. CWE Ep. 134:30–1n. identifies Accursius as Francesco Accorso; the latter figure, however, is one of Accursius' sons who likewise became civil lawyers, without equalling their father's reputation.

Bartolo and Baldo than in Christ,[34] much like the theologians for whom the great scholastics of the thirteenth century were the supreme authorities of religion.

Erasmus showed even more overt contempt for canon lawyers, especially for Gratian. Around 1140 this monk of Bologna produced a compilation of ancient and early medieval canonical texts, modelled on the codification of Justinian. His collection was far more complete than the works of his predecessors and quickly gained universal acceptance as an authoritative handbook, becoming known as the *Decretum Gratiani*. According to Erasmus, however, the *Decretum* was a setback in juridical studies. In the prefatory material to his Jerome edition, he seriously contended that Gratian or Crassian, "whoever he was", deliberately supplanted ancient collections of decrees with a new one in order to enhance the reputation of Isidore (whom, astoundingly, Erasmus called Gratian's "contemporary") and other *recentiores*.[35] As for his use of Jerome's work, Gratian, "born as he was in a barren age that produced little or nothing, was utterly lacking in the discipline and knowledge of ancient literature" and therefore omitted anything he did not understand, including passages relevant to his subject. Moreover, he frequently ascribed the same text to different authors. Finally, the *Decretum* contained contradictory views (a correct observation: Gratian himself called his work *Concordia discordantium canonum*, considering it his main task to bring different legal opinions together in one system). Commenting on the work's reception, Erasmus pointed out that the *Decretum* had never been officially approved but had rather been usurped by the schoolmen (among whom he included Gratian himself);[36] some theologians attached extraordinary importance to it, but most experts simply accepted the parts which suited them while disregarding the rest.[37]

---

[34] Cf. *In psalmum IV concio* CWE 63 242/ASD V-2 248:800–249:802; see also CWE Ep. 1469:105–9/Allen 100–3; Allen Epp. 2604:31, 2682:4–8.

[35] Perhaps "Isidore" does not refer to Isidore of Sevilla (who is, however, regularly cited by Gratian) but to the so-called Pseudo-Isidorian Decretals, an early medieval mixture of genuine and spurious church decrees. Some pieces enhance papal jurisdiction. About ten percent of the *Decretum Gratiani* is drawn from this work.

[36] Cf. CWE Ep. 1581:601–2/Allen 542–3.

[37] *Edition of Jerome* CWE 61 81, 93–4/Jerome *Lucubrationes* II fol. 4r (praefatio), 190v–191r (praefatio). Cf. also *Antibarbari* CWE 23 88–9/ASD I-1 108:16–109:16 (scorn of Gratian's method and style), ibid. 90/110:9–11 (use of suitable parts only), *Apologia contra Latomi dialogum* CWE 71 41/LB IX 81F (the *Decretum* has come into

Erasmus' lack of respect for the *Decretum* reveals itself also in his careless treatment of the work, which contrasts sharply with the philological diligence he demanded of himself and of others with regard to the ancient literary heritage. Once he quoted a passage from Augustine contained in the *Decretum* as if it were a decree. His critic Jacobus Latomus corrected him, scoring a cheap point according to Erasmus, since the whole work carried the title "Decrees of the Popes".[38] In a later work he insisted himself that not every opinion cited in the *Decretum* had the force of law. Actually the opinions of the ancient authorities often conflicted with each other and were sometimes even heretical.[39] Nevertheless Erasmus once expressed the wish that the ancient regulations codified in the *Decretum* as well as the *Decretales* had been preserved by popes and bishops instead of being abrogated or forgotten.[40]

Erasmus' charge that many jurists accepted canon law only insofar as it suited them would also seem to apply to himself. Although he considered quotations from civil or canon law normally out of place in erudite discourse,[41] he occasionally used canonist arguments in order to justify his own activities and opinions. Thus he referred with approval to the opinion quoted in the *Decretum* that the Latin text of the New Testament had to be checked against Greek manuscripts.[42] Likewise he defended his philological approach to Scripture by pointing out that the *Decretales* condemned documents with obvious linguistic faults as spurious,[43] while still another compilation of decrees,

---

use without official approval). The latter observation is correct: the *Decretum* was a scholarly work, but functioned as a source of law.

[38] *Apologia contra Latomi dialogum* CWE 71 40/LB IX 81D. The passage in question is D. 9 c. 6 (actually a quotation from Jerome, wrongly attributed to Augustine by Gratian and hence by Erasmus). "Decrees of the Popes" (*Decreta Pontificum*) is neither a usual nor an appropriate title for the *Decretum* and would rather refer to (a collection from) the *Decretales*.

[39] *Responsio de divortio* CWE 83 168/LB IX 961A.

[40] *Apologia adversus rhapsodias Pii* LB IX 1183A. *Decretales* refers to *Decretales Gregorii IX* or *Liber extra* (1234; usually abbreviated as X) and five minor collections of papal decretals which, together with the *Decretum*, make up the *Corpus iuris canonici*. Our citations are from *Corpus iuris canonici*, ed. Aemilius Friedberg 2 vols. (Leipzig 1879–81).

[41] At *Parabolae* CWE 23 232/ASD I-5 252:499–504 and CWE Ep. 1211:72–5/Allen 66–8 he criticises orators who interlard their texts with such and other quotations. Cf. *Ecclesiastes* ASD V-4 260:290–3: canon law is hardly a fitting source for a preacher.

[42] Cf. *Apologia in Novum Testamentum* Holborn 170/LB VI **2v, *Ratio* Holborn 183/LB V 78E, *Capita argumentorum* LB VI ***2, CWE Ep. 843:389–91/Allen 350–2. The reference is to D. 9 c. 6 (Jerome, but attributed to Augustine, see above n. 38).

[43] Cf. *Apologia contra Latomi dialogum* CWE 71 45/LB IX 84B–C, CWE Ep.

the *Clementinae*, would call for university instruction in the ancient languages.[44] In several writings Erasmus quoted commentaries from medieval canonists like Hostiensis (Henry of Segusio, c. 1200–71), Johannes Andreae (c. 1270–1348), and Panormitanus (Nicholas de Tudeschi, 1386–1445) to sustain his seemingly novel views, for instance in favour of the possibility of divorce. In a couple of instances he provided his canonist digressions with an excuse, explaining that he did not like to dwell on authors who offered a variety of human reasonings without a solid base, but that their precedent at least justified his own undertaking in the eyes of those who set great store by their authority.[45] On the other hand, Erasmus took canon law to be the source of regulations unknown to the early church, such as the current practice of confession.[46]

In the field of theology, the neglect of good letters and the addiction to logical disputation had had their most devastating effects. In countless passages Erasmus deplored the catastrophic downfall of theological studies under the influence of scholasticism. In most of these passages he caricatured scholastic theology, depicting its practitioners as petty quarrellers growing old over irrelevant thorny problems. He may thus not have given a fair representation of the discipline—which, contrary to what many commentators believe, he came to know only slightly as a student during his stay in Paris between 1495 and 1501[47]—but surely revealed his own concerns. His most famous

---

843:109–10/Allen 97–8. Erasmus mistakably refers in the first passage to X 2.26.13; he would be more likely to mean X 1.3.11 (Lucius III) (and not *Decretum* D. 9 c. 3–6 as is said at CWE Ep. 843:109n.).

[44] Cf. *Apologia contra Latomi dialogum* CWE 71 41–2/LB IX 82A–C; CWE Epp. 149:50–9/Allen 43–51, 182:205–8/180–4, 337:733–5/697–8, 843:273–84/244–53. The reference is to Clementinae 5.1.1 decreed at the Council of Vienne (1311–2) and promulgated in 1314. As Erasmus' critic Jacobus Latomus pointed out, the decree actually demanded chairs of Arabic, Hebrew, and Chaldaic (Syriac) at the universities of Paris, Bologna, Oxford, and Salamanca. The reference to the decree was commonplace among humanists, cf. Erika Rummel, *The Humanist-Scholastic Debate in the Renaissance and Reformation* (Cambridge MA 1995), 114–6.

[45] Cf. Reeve 469–71 on 1 Cor. 7:39 "Liberata est a lege" (excuses at 469, 471), *Responsio ad annotationes Lei* LB IX 267B–269D (excuses at 269D). Also the first half of *Institutio christiani matrimonii*, which discusses legal impediments to marriage, has many quotations from the decretalists. For an acid comment on canon lawyers who pile up various contradictory statements and leave their readers in confusion see *Antibarbari* CWE 23 90–1/ASD I-1 111:1–7.

[46] Cf. CWE Ep. 1300:21–4/Allen 19–22, referring to *Decretales* X 5.38.12 (Innocent III).

[47] James K. Farge, "Erasmus, the University of Paris, and the Profession of

descriptions are probably those contained in his preface to the 1518 edition of *Enchiridion militis christiani* and in his *Ratio verae theologiae*, which was composed in the same year.[48] On the basis of these and other writings, we will summarise the most important tenets of Erasmus' critique of scholastic theology.[49] One should keep in mind that the primary targets of his critique were always the scholastics of his own day. But for Erasmus, these scholastics were continuing a tradition which had started with Peter Lombard and had produced its greatest masters in the thirteenth century. As in the case of literary studies, the whole scholastic period carried responsibility for the wrongs of the present.

Of course theology suffered, in Erasmus' view, from an inadequate knowledge of languages. Having no Greek or Hebrew, scholastic theologians were unable to study the Bible and the Greek fathers in the original, while their Latin had turned into barbarous speech. This was true for all other academics as well, but in the case of the theologians the situation was all the more distressing because their

---

Theology", *Erasmus of Rotterdam Society Yearbook* 19 (1999), 18–46, argues that Erasmus did not take a theological degree in Paris and cannot have intended to do so. His stay was too short to earn even a first degree, especially since he should first have followed the arts curriculum—something which he did not do, as he never registered in the English-German nation. Moreover, theological degrees were never granted to candidates of illegitimate birth. Erasmus merely attended a few classes of theology in the Franciscan studium and was otherwise occupied with tutoring and finding his way as a humanist author. Important developments in academic theology with relevance to his later programme of Christian humanism seem to have escaped him. For the nature of his doctorate in theology awarded by the University of Turin in 1506 after a stay of two weeks see Paul F. Grendler, "How to Get a Degree in Fifteen Days: Erasmus' Doctorate of Theology from the University of Turin", *Erasmus of Rotterdam Society Yearbook* 18 (1998), 40–69.

[48] The 1518 preface to *Enchiridion* is Ep. 858; for *Ratio* (an expansion of the 1516 *Methodus*) see Holborn 175–305/LB V 75–138. Other good examples are Epp. 108 (to Colet), 337 (defence against Dorp), 1062 (preface to *Paraphrase on Ephesians*), 1581 (to Bédier). For an older assessment see Christian Dolfen, *Die Stellung des Erasmus von Rotterdam zur scholastischen Methode* (Osnabrück 1936), 51–64 (general discussion based on *Ratio* and the annotation, now at Reeve 662–5, on 1 Tim. 1:6 "In vaniloquium"), 82–94 (discussion of Erasmus' attitude to individual scholastic authorities).

[49] Our concern is with Erasmus' critique of scholasticism as an intellectual system. The question of whether the humanist critique of scholasticism was really at the heart of the numerous controversies between humanist and scholastic authors around 1500—a question which has notably been answered in the negative by James H. Overfield, *Humanism and Scholasticism in Late Medieval Germany* (Princeton 1984) and has since been forcefully re-addressed by Rummel, *The Humanist-Scholastic Debate*; see also Charles G. Nauert, "Humanism as Method: Roots of Conflict with the Scholastics", *Sixteenth Century Journal* 29 (1998), 427–38—is irrelevant to our discussion.

tedious, frigid, and artificial style so patently contrasted with the literary qualities of the church fathers. The replacement of the brilliant patristic writings by the insipid products of the *sordidum scriptorum genus*[50] of the scholastic age probably constituted in Erasmus' eyes the most lamentable event in Western cultural history. Bad Latin made the voluminous commentaries of the theologians highly unattractive, while their frenetic dissections of their material rendered their works practically unintelligible.[51]

Further, scholastic theologians displayed a double arrogance. First, they investigated everything, obstinately subjecting even the hidden mysteries of the faith to their scrutiny. In Erasmus' perception, not all of religion could be grasped by the intellect: in certain matters it was more pious to remain ignorant. The scholastics, however, thought themselves capable of resolving any problem, precisely because they lacked knowledge of languages and religion—a knowledge that had made the ancients more modest. Their indiscreet discussions on matters which were not for our knowing had even caused schisms. In one instance Erasmus acknowledged that the unwholesome curiosity of scholasticism had its origins in antiquity, adding however that at present it had reached intolerable proportions.[52] Second, the scholastic theologians intended to lay down the law for others. They never arrived at clear and sound conclusions, but meanwhile took their definitions for decrees. The trivial human fantasies that they worked out were put on a par with the articles of the faith, so that the yoke of Christ, which was light in itself, was burdened with numerous regulations unknown to the early church and oppressive to Christian liberty. Whereas in ancient days the church consoled the believers against pagan attacks, it now suffered from a tyranny imposed by its own members.[53]

---

[50] Scholia on *Catalogus scriptorum ecclesiasticorum* in Jerome, *Lucubrationes* I fol. 138r (Erasmus . . . lectori pio).

[51] For this last charge cf. e.g. *Ratio* Holborn 191/LB V 82E–F, *Ecclesiastes* ASD V-4 306:407–12 (mentioning Lyra, Thomas' Bible commentaries, and Gerson in particular).

[52] Cf. Reeve 54–5 on Matt. 11:30 "Iugum meum suave" ("haec pronuncianda temeritas a veteribus orta nunc longius progressus est, quam ut ferri possit"), *Annotationes in Novum Testamentum* CWE 56 27/Reeve 341 on Rom. 1:5 "Ad obediendum fidei", Reeve 662–4 on 1 Tim. 1:6 "In vaniloquium"; *Apologia contra Latomi dialogum* CWE 71 49, 74/LB IX 86D, 100F; CWE Ep. 337:441–4/Allen 417–20, Allen Ep. 1877:207–30.

[53] Cf. e.g. *Enarratio in primum psalmum* CWE 63 26–7/ASD V-2 50:488–513, Reeve

The dependence of theology on logic had had some more negative consequences. Theology had degenerated into mere sophistry.
The scholastics occupied themselves with sterile, hair-splitting subtleties which were irrelevant to the faith. They never touched the
Bible or the church fathers, but studied only Aristotelian philosophy
and, above all, the scholastic authorities of the thirteenth century
and their followers—or rather the authority of their taste: their logical and dialectical training had given them a zest for arguing which
had led to their division into several conflicting schools. *Eruditio* and
pietas, happily combined in the patristic tradition, had thus separated
again.[54] The theatrical quibbles of the schoolmen titillated the intellect without contributing to the inner force of Christians; they rather
destroyed all spiritual and moral life. As a consequence, scholastic
theology was not only unable to cure heretics or convert pagans,
but exercised a pernicious influence on Christian civilisation itself.
Tyranny, superstition, greed, iniquity, ambition, the lack of charity,
war[55]—in sum, the moral degeneration of Christendom—was to a
large extent the result of modern theologians clogging the gospel
teaching.

A feature of Erasmus' critique which deserves special attention is
his belief that the methodological doubt of scholastic theology led to
real uncertainty in matters of faith. Trained as they were in dialectics, the scholastics discussed every theological issue in the form of
questions, formulating arguments pro and con before expounding

---

54–5 on Matt. 11:30 "Iugum meum suave", *Apologia ad blasphemias Stunicae* LB IX
369E–F.

[54] Cf O'Malley, "Introduction", CWE 66 xii: "In Erasmus' view, the scholastics
created a dichotomy between spirituality and theology, and that fact is fundamental in explaining his consistent and sometimes fierce antagonism to the "recent theologians". His opposition did not spring from disagreement . . . but from dissatisfaction
with the scholastic enterprise as such".

[55] Sometimes Erasmus suggested that war was a phenomenon typical of the later
Middle Ages which should be eradicated with the aid of humanism, cf. CWE Epp.
542:27–31/Allen 22–6, 858:401–2/378–9, 1225:244–7/225–8 and below p. 104;
see also Allen Ep. 1815:12–8: for many centuries, conservative theologians are
responsible for the discord among the Christian princes. Erasmus was especially
concerned with peace in his own country. At *Panegyricus* CWE 27 63–4/ASD IV-1
82:808–43, dedicated to Philip the Fair, he cautiously blames the bellicose men-
tality of Philip's forebears Philip the Good and Charles the Bold. James D. Tracy,
The Politics of Erasmus: A Pacifist Intellectual and His Political Milieu (Toronto 1978)
explores the ties between Erasmus and the "Burgundian national party" which sus-
pected the Habsburg rulers of sacrificing the interests of the Low Countries to wars
which served their dynastic policy.

their own views. In fact, Erasmus complained, there was nothing in their disputations which was not called into doubt. Thomas, Gratian, and Scotus in particular discussed even the most approved articles, like the sacramental status of the Eucharist, on both sides with equal probability. Especially Scotus' arguments opposing the truth had sometimes more strength than those in favour. With his over-subtle arguments Scotus even endangered the church, undermining her dogmas and giving a handle to the heretics.[56] These accusations, sustained by Erasmus in a steadfast manner, contradict the idea that he consistently favoured a rhetorical approach to theology aimed at discussing the truth without providing definite answers, as did the scholastics.[57] Writing against his critic Luis de Carvajal (1529), Erasmus contrasted the rhetorical and the dialectical method in exactly the opposite way:

> He says that the rhetoricians treat both sides with equal probability, the doctors not at all. But this charge applies rather to the dialecticians than to any other persons. For what else are they doing, Thomas, Durandus, and Scotus, when they are disputing on both sides even on the most accepted subjects, Scotus meanwhile being more forceful on the rejected side?[58]

---

[56] Cf. *Antibarbari* CWE 23 88–9/ASD I-1 108:19, 109:13–6 (mentioning Gratian), *Ratio* Holborn 299/LB V 134F–135A (Scotus), *Annotationes in Novum Testamentum* CWE 56 151/Reeve 372–3 on Rom. 5:12 "In quo omnes peccaverunt" (Scotus); *Responsio ad annotationes Lei* LB IX 263B–D (Thomas, Gratian), 266E (Thomas); *Responsio ad collationes gerontodidascali* LB IX 1002D–E (Scotus), *Hyperaspistes I* CWE 76 194–5/LB X 1290B (Thomas); see also above p. 50 n. 69 for similar misgivings about the *Glossa ordinaria*. But cf. *Hyperaspistes I* CWE 76 245/LB X 1312F: "Thomas asks whether the Eucharist is a sacrament of the church, and he gives arguments on both sides. Does that mean he has doubts on the matter he is arguing about?"; *Dilutio* CWE 83 121/Telle 74, *Appendix Clichtove* CWE 83 113–4/LB IX 813B: the arguments listed by Thomas should not be confused with his own views.

[57] Cf. Manfred Hoffmann, *Rhetoric and Theology: The Hermeneutic of Erasmus* (Toronto 1994), 18: scholars agree that Erasmus' theology as well as his literary studies are marked by "an attempt to achieve consensus by discovering elements of truth on either side of an issue". Hoffmann agrees with this view and expands on it in his treatment of Erasmus' theology, see esp. 22–5 where Erasmus' alleged relativism and scepticism are opposed to the dialectical method of the scholastics; cf., however, Hoffmann's reservation with regard to Erasmus' scepticism at 126. For an assessment of Erasmus' scepticism in theological discussions see Marjorie O'Rourke Boyle, *Rhetoric and Reform: Erasmus' Civil Dispute with Luther* (Cambridge MA 1983), 17ff. and the discussion below pp. 162–3.

[58] *Responsio adversus febricitantis libellum* LB X 1680D–E. Durandus is probably the theologian Durand of St Pourçain (c. 1275–1334) rather than the canonist William Durand (c. 1235–96).

In reality, Erasmus' attitude with regard to the essential truths of Christendom was anti-philosophical. Instead of proposing other ways of arguing than the scholastics, he rejected the idea of inquiry altogether, not in order to respect the loose nature of truth but lest established truths be challenged at all. Erasmus did favour loose definitions of truth in unessential questions concerning religion, questions he felt the scholastics had been answering with too much assertion, turning their inventions into dogmas. As for real and undisputed dogmas, however, Erasmus' position was fideist. The scholastics, he argued in his *Ratio*, should not challenge with their disputations what God does not want us to discuss, but to believe.[59] Accordingly, in *De praeparatione ad mortem* (1534) he created as opponents a philosopher and a simpleton, assigning the former to hell because of his doubts on Christian dogma, but admitting the latter to heaven.[60] In fundamental religious questions, Erasmus was as much opposed to rationalism, scepticism, relativism, or freethinking as to scholasticism.

Time and again Erasmus stressed that he did not condemn scholastic theology as such, but only its excesses. In his own esteem, his critique had always been gentle. He had only advocated moderation and discretion in order to purify scholastic theology, not to abolish it; the introduction of good letters he aimed at would reinforce rather than replace existing theological and philosophical studies.[61] But Erasmus' programme of *ad fontes revocare*[62] was more radical than that. Often he described the project of restoring theology in negative terms: the stains of scholasticism had to be washed off, the entanglements of a later age had to be removed.[63] The *philosophia Christi* had to be drawn from the New Testament and its earliest commentators. To this end theologians had to learn languages, not logic, and to study

---

[59] Holborn 299/LB V 134F–135A: "Videtur enim subhaesitare, qui tam sollicite tamque curiose rationes contrahit, quibus vel impugnet vel tueatur quod nobis traditum est, ut credamus, non ut discutiamus".

[60] CWE 70 441/ASD V-1 384:114–24. On Erasmus' fideist position see also Chomarat, *Grammaire et rhétorique*, 34.

[61] Cf. e.g. *Ratio* Holborn 191ff., 303/LB V 83Aff., 136E–137A; Reeve 664–5 on 1 Tim. 1:6 "In vaniloquium", *Apologia contra Latomi dialogum* CWE 71 38/LB IX 79D–80B, *Divinationes ad notata Bedae* LB IX 476F–477C; *Supputatio* LB IX 521B–C, 624D; *Declarationes ad censuras Lutetiae* LB IX 919C, *Apologia adversus rhapsodias Pii* LB IX 1168B–C; CWE Epp. 541:132–9/Allen 118–25, 950:16–20/14–6, 1002:11–20/8–16, 1062:65–72/59–65, 1111:14–21/9–17, 1124:14–7/12–4, 1127:10–20/6–10, 1581:121–8/113–9; Allen Epp. 1747:96–100, 1856:37–8, 1877:228–30, 2136:192–4.

[62] For this expression cf. Allen Epp. 1672:140, 1700:38–9, 1744:153–4, 1891:186–7.

[63] Cf. e.g. CWE Ep. 108:62–5/Allen 56–8, Allen Ep. 2899:27–30.

the Bible and the fathers, not modern authors or pagan philosophers.[64] Had the apostles ever read Scotus or Aquinas?[65] In fact,
Erasmus wished to preserve the study of theology ("scholastic" in a
broad, literal sense, that is, being taught in the schools), but not its
scholastic character ("scholastic" in a narrow sense, that is, as it had
actually been taught in the schools of the later Middle Ages).[66]
Essentially the scholastic theologians, in his view, had nothing to
offer. They had merely enveloped in darkness what ancient thinkers
had cleared, and reading too much in their works might make one
as frigid and disputatious as they. One could compare the fathers
to the scholastics as golden rivers to shallow rivulets, oracles of eter-
nal truth to futile human commentators, safe harbours to whirlpools,
fruitful gardens to barren thorn-bushes, majesty to triteness, "to
abstain for the moment from a comparison of morality".[67] In piety,
learning, style, and interpretations the ancients were far superior, so
that one should read their work in preference to the moderns.[68]
Erasmus' favourite comparison of ancients (including the apostles)
and moderns to fountain-heads and muddy pools[69] suggests what his
Ratio states in so many words: scholastic theology was to a great
extent superfluous.[70] Still, in his defence against Jacobus Latomus

---

[64] Cf. e.g. *Enarratio in primum psalmum* CWE 63 31/ASD V-2 54:604–7: "Without skill in the three languages, Holy Writ cannot be understood at all, but it can
be understood without Aristotle's *Physics* and *Metaphysics* . . . anyone who wants truly
to be a theologian must be familiar with the original sources"; CWE Ep. 541:
157–61/Allen 141–5: "I could wish that those frigid sophistries could either be quite
cut out or at least were not the theologians' only concern, and that Christ pure
and simple might be planted deep into the minds of men; and this I think could
best be brought about if, aided by the support of the three tongues, we drew our
philosophy from the true sources".
[65] Cf. *Apologia contra Latomi dialogum* CWE 71 75/LB IX 101C; see also *Paraclesis*
Holborn 148/LB V 143D, VI *4 (what can one find in Scotus or Thomas, in spite
of their erudition and the latter's sanctity, which is comparable to the apostolic
epistles?); *Ratio* Holborn 191/LB V 82E–83A.
[66] Cf. CWE Ep. 948:97–8/Allen 92–3: "scholastic authorities—as the word 'scholastic' is now understood".
[67] *Ratio* Holborn 189–90/LB V 82A–B.
[68] Cf. *Enchiridion* CWE 66 34–5/LB V 8D–E.
[69] Cf. *Parabolae* CWE 23 239/ASD I-5 262:692–3, *Apologia contra Latomi dialogum*
CWE 71 39/LB IX 81A, *Apologia adversus Sutorem* LB IX 772F; CWE Epp.
373:176–9/Allen 161–3, 529:77–8/70–1, 805:38–9/32–4, 1002:18–20/14–6,
1007:21–3/19–21, 1062:45–6/41–2; Allen Ep. 1805:24–6. Cf. also *Colloquia* CWE
39 522/ASD I-3 412:22–5 (the fountain of the Muses contrasted to the frog's pond
of Scotus), CWE Ep. 1062:40–1/Allen 36–7 (the scholastics choke the springs of
the gospel with Philistine sawdust).
[70] Holborn 298/LB V 134E ("bona scholasticae theologiae pars . . . supervacanea"),
cf. ibid. 296–7/133C–E.

(1518) Erasmus alleged that he had never sought to dissuade any-one from reading scholastic authors, challenging his adversaries to cite "a single passage even in some comical work of mine where I have written that the time spent on authors like Scotus is time wasted".[71] Taking up the challenge would not have been too difficult.[72] Even in the same work, Erasmus later mentions Pico della Mirandola's regret, repeated by "the best theologians" after him, at "wasting all his time" during six years on the study of Thomas, Scotus, and Albert the Great.[73]

As we have said, Erasmus' revulsion from scholastic theology was first of all directed against its representatives in his own time, with whom in *Antibarbari* he has even less patience than with the great scholastics of the thirteenth century. But basically the scholastic tra-dition was for him inferior in its entirety. Of course not every sneer at the Thomists or the Scotists necessarily implies a sneer at Thomas or Scotus themselves: Erasmus also attacked the Franciscans without deprecating Francis. However, what Erasmus thought wrong about the Franciscans was that they did not follow Francis, whereas his problem with Thomists and Scotists was that they followed Thomas and Scotus as closely as possible. Whereas monasticism had devel-oped from good to bad, scholasticism had developed from bad to worse.[74] Essentially, all theologians of the scholastic period were birds of a feather for Erasmus (trying to distinguish between their styles was no easier than "to see the difference between one broom and another broom or between one piece of metal and another piece").[75]

---

[71] *Apologia contra Latomi dialogum* CWE 71 39/LB IX 81A (in fact, Erasmus refers to scholastic theologians in general, not to Scotus in particular).

[72] Cf. *Colloquia* ASD I-3 38:213–39:217, 83:205–10, CWE 39 121/ASD I-3 187:2034–188:2040 (theologians dream—about Scotus, as Erasmus added in 1522—without ever coming to their senses); CWE Ep. 421:115–7/Allen 106–8: "And noth-ing seems to me a greater waste of time (*nugacius*) than to go on discussing the worthless questions which make so many theologians fancy themselves gods". For similar passages from later writings cf. e.g. *Colloquia* CWE 39 192/ASD I-3 252:626–7 (cf. CWE Ep. 1341A:377–9/Allen I 11:22–4), CWE 40 1098/ASD I-3 741:23–5; *Apologia adversus rhapsodias Pii* LB IX 1167E, CWE Ep. 1581:587–92/Allen 528–33.

[73] *Apologia contra Latomi dialogum* CWE 71 77/LB IX 102E.

[74] Cf. *Adagia* IV v 1 ASD II-7 241:204–6: scholastic learning started three hun-dred years ago and has gone from bad to worse ever since. Cf. also O'Malley, "Introduction", CWE 66 xvii: "When Erasmus criticized others, the ground of his complaint was that they did a good thing poorly. When he criticized the scholas-tics, he was saying, despite his disclaimers, that they were doing a bad thing all too well. Their very enterprise was wrong-headed".

[75] *Edition of Jerome* CWE 61 77–8/Jerome, *Lucubrationes* II fol. 3v (praefatio). Cf. ibid. 218/scholia on *Ad Paulinum* in Jerome, *Lucubrationes* IV fol. 4v at "Captus a

As a consequence, Erasmus often blamed the *recentiores*, the *vulgus theologorum*, or the *scholae* in general for their inept comments, without feeling the need to specify the object of his criticism. But even when he did mention medieval theologians or schools by their names, his remarks were not always aimed at them in particular. It has rightly been observed that in his sneers at Scotus the latter often seems to stand for scholasticism in general. Erasmus' criticisms of specific Scotist views are indeed rare (as are the instances where he takes sides with Scotus against his Catholic critics), although he did think that Scotus, more than other scholastics, had mixed theology not only with gentile philosophy but with inventions of his own.[76] Perhaps Erasmus' experiences during his years in Paris, where the few theological courses he attended were apparently dominated by Scotus, made him choose the British Franciscan as the principal butt of his anti-scholastic fulminations.[77]

Among the theologians of the scholastic period, Thomas Aquinas and Jean Gerson stand out as those whom Erasmus, if he did not admire them, at least considered worthy of scholarly attention, as our discussion below will make clear. For the biblical commentators Nicholas of Lyra († 1349) and Hugh of St. Cher he showed overt contempt, although he used their work extensively on behalf of his

---

piratis" (also CWE Ep. 337:710–8/Allen 676–84): confronted with the Jerome commentary of Guillaume le Breton (13th c.), Erasmus had not recognised it—"dolt that I was, I had thought that this little commentary was the work of Lyra".

[76] Cf. CWE Ep. 1581:95/Allen 86–7, Allen Ep. 1679:34–5. For discussions of specific Scotist views see e.g. CWE Ep. 447:720–1/Allen 651–2 ("Scotus' fancy that a monk's vow is indissoluble because it is taken before God through men"), Allen Ep. 2443:230–4 (against Scotus' view that images should be adored in the same way as the objects they represent) and esp., concerning free will, *De libero arbitrio* CWE 76 28ff./LB IX 1223Aff.; *Hyperaspistes I* CWE 76 164, 279, 284/LB X 1277B, 1327D–E, 1329E–F; *Hyperaspistes II* LB X 1369E, 1457B, 1472B; CWE Ep. 1342:1040/Allen 944.

[77] Cf. Craig R. Thompson, "Better Teachers than Scotus or Aquinas", *Proceedings of the Southeastern Institute of Medieval and Renaissance Studies* 2 (1966), 114–45 esp. 128; Jean-Claude Margolin, "Duns Scot et Erasme", *Erasme: le prix des mots et de l'homme* (London 1986) [III] 89–112; Marjorie O'Rourke Boyle, "Fools and Schools: Scholastic Dialectic, Humanist Rhetoric; from Anselm to Erasmus", *Medievalia et Humanistica* 13 (1985), 173–95. Boyle relates Erasmus' dislike of Scotus to his ill feelings with John Mair or Major (1469–1550) in particular: the Scotsman ("Scotus") Major taught logic at Montaigu College where Erasmus lived; in the early 16th c. he was the most prominent master of arts in the University of Paris, and in 1527 he was commissioned by the Sorbonne to examine Erasmus' *Paraphrases* on the New Testament. For Erasmus' experiences as a student exposed to Scotist theology see esp. Ep. 64.

New Testament studies. For the rest, Erasmus' confession, in a letter
to Bédier, that he tried to keep away from scholastic theology as
much as possible[78] would seem to reflect the truth. Theologians and
philosophers like Bonaventure (1217–74), Albert the Great (c. 1200–80),
and William of Ockham (c. 1285–1349), whose works were absent
from his personal library, were more often the object of his ridicule
than of his scholarly criticism;[79] likewise, he never discussed the views
of Averroes (1126–98), the famous Arabian commentator of Aristotle,
but frequently cursed the man as a blasphemer.[80] A good illustra-
tion of Erasmus' disregard of scholastic authors is offered by a letter to him from Ulrich Zasius. Zasius had sent Erasmus the works
of the Franciscan theologian Alexander of Hales (c. 1185–1245).
Apparently the gift had appalled Erasmus (his letter is not extant),
for in his reply Zasius offered him his apologies, stating that Alexander,
as a man *ex veteri barbarie*, was of course useless to Erasmus. Zasius'
limited talents, however, would only permit him to enlarge Erasmus'
knowledge of rejectable things, not of what had value.[81]

In order to justify his wilful neglect of scholastic authors, Erasmus
frequently pointed to the real or supposed disagreements among them
(ignoring the fact that the fathers had disagreed on many points as
well). As he wrote to Bédier, every generation since the early thirteenth century had had its own heroes. Alexander of Hales, Albert
the Great, Thomas Aquinas, Duns Scotus, and Jean Gerson had all

---

[78] CWE Ep. 1581:134–9/Allen 125–6, likewise Reeve 614 on Eph. 5:18 "In quo
est luxuria". Cf. also Reeve 559 on 2 Cor. 11:23 "Ministri Christ sunt": "Cum
antiquis potius nobis res est".

[79] For references to Bonaventure see above p. 5 n. 10; to Albert: *Responsio ad
annotationes Lei* LB IX 187F–188B; Occam is mentioned (from hearsay?) as an adversary of papal supremacy in *Apologia ad conclusiones Stunicae* LB IX 388B, *Responsio ad
epistolam Pii* LB IX 1105A. For the library see Husner, "Die Bibliothek des Erasmus".

[80] Cf. *Lingua* CWE 29 333, 336/ASD IV-1A 101:476–9, 104:563; *Capita argumentorum* LB VI ***2; *Apologia contra Latomi dialogum* CWE 71 59/LB IX 92C, also
61/93F ("something worse than a pagan"); *Supputatio* LB IX 517B (yet "utiliter legi
potest"), *Apologia adversus rhapsodias Pii* LB IX 1168D; see also *Ratio* Holborn 191/LB
V 82E ("impium"), CWE Ep. 868:34–5/Allen 31–2 ("that thrice-cursed atheist").
At Allen Ep. 2465:99 Erasmus blames his Italian critic Agostino Steuco for criticising Averroes too harshly; Steuco points to Erasmus' hypocrisy at Allen Ep.
2513:745–7.

[81] Allen Ep. 2857:2–6; possibly Erasmus even returned the gift, since Alexander's
work was absent from his library, see Husner, "Die Bibliothek des Erasmus". Cf.
also *Declarationes ad censuras Lutetiae* LB IX 911C: many people would laugh at the
Sorbonne for including Gratian, Alexander of Hales, William of Paris, Lyra, and
Thomas Waldensis among those who breathed the vigour of the gospel.

replaced their predecessors as reigning authorities; likewise, the nominalists had dethroned the realists. At present the various schools waged war on each other. How should Erasmus take refuge in doctrines which changed with time and party? One should better study the scholastics historically, taking into account by whom, when, and in what circumstances their ideas were produced.[82] Moreover, the scholastics, and even the popes in their decrees, had occasionally diverged from orthodoxy.[83] This fact cannot have bothered Erasmus a great deal, since he thought that no author, ancient or modern, was free from error. But the fallibility of the scholastics provided him with a welcome argument against his Catholic critics. First, it was evident that one could not take the work of the scholastics as an absolute standard; second, those who accepted the authority of scholastics in spite of their errors had no reason for being upset when they found unorthodox views in ancient authors or contemporary ones like Erasmus himself.

In spite of his usual disregard of scholastic theologians, Erasmus admitted that "one is sometimes compelled to cite those who lacked elegance of style" like Bonaventure, Thomas, and Scotus.[84] For this compulsion we can adduce several reasons.

First, Erasmus sometimes wanted to demonstrate what kind of flaws were the result of the insufficient attention to letters which he considered typical of late medieval education. This holds for his edition of the New Testament in particular. In his annotations he had "pointed out the passages where Augustine, Aquinas, Hugh [of St. Cher], and Nicholas of Lyra had obviously gone wrong to prevent people from saying that my work had been unnecessary".[85] Correcting

---

[82] CWE Ep. 1581:640–57, cf. 701–3/Allen 577–92, 631–3; see also *Apologia contra Latomi dialogum* CWE 71 72/LB IX 100A.

[83] Cf. e.g. *Enarratio in psalmum XXXVIII* ASD V-3 196:948–197:978, *Capita argumentorum* LB VI ***2v, Reeve 473 on 1 Cor. 7:39 "Liberata est a lege", *Apologia invectivis Lei* Ferguson 278; CWE Epp. 1033:49–51/Allen 44–5; 1581:603–4, 643–8/ 544–5, 581–4.

[84] *Vita Hieronymi* CWE 61 57/Ferguson 184.

[85] *Apologia contra Latomi dialogum* CWE 71 58/LB IX 91E–92A (CWE wrongly mentions Hugh of St. Victor instead of Hugh of St. Cher, as also happens at 49); cf. *Loca obscura* LB VI *6r–v (the full title is: *Loca obscura, et in quibus lapsi sint magni nominis interpretes, ex innumeris pauca decerpta, ut sit ad manum quod objiciatur eis, qui dicunt superfuisse, quod nostris annotationibus foret explicandum*), *Capita argumentorum* LB VI ***2, *Apologia adversus Sutorem* LB IX 776A–C (mentioning the same four men); *Apologia in Novum Testamentum* Holborn 171–2/LB VI **3, *Ratio* Holborn 183/LB V 78E–F (mentioning Augustine and Thomas).

the mistakes of his scholastic predecessors (and of their champion Augustine, who did not have Greek) was an excellent means of stressing the usefulness of his own work as well as the necessity of a literary education, since the lack of Greek and (for the late medieval authors) an imperfect knowledge of Latin were chiefly responsible for their faulty interpretations of the Bible text.

Second, Erasmus felt compelled to quote scholastic theologians for the same reason as he occasionally cited canon lawyers: "some will more willingly believe a modern".[86] Defending, for instance, his reading of *sermo* instead of *verbum* at John 1:1, he adduced support not only from the fathers but from the *Glossa ordinaria*, Thomas, Lyra, and Hugh of St. Cher, excusing himself for the unpleasant effect this would have on readers accustomed to better authors: Erasmus was dealing with those among whom their authority carried weight.[87] Siding with the scholastics, Erasmus could neutralise in advance possible reproofs that he was a heretic or a revolutionary. Accordingly, he often quoted various late medieval theologians in his writings against his Catholic critics. Repeatedly he even pretended to have not only a better knowledge of medieval theologians but more respect for them than his adversaries who boasted of their orthodoxy. For instance, in his dispute with Jacques Lefèvre d'Etaples on the interpretation of Heb. 2:7, Erasmus tried to blame his adversary for a lack of esteem for Thomas, thus flinging back the same accusation Lefèvre had cast at Erasmus first.[88] Likewise, he stated that his critic Nicolaas Baechem should better have read the fathers, Thomas, and the *Glossa ordinaria* before taking up his pen.[89] In his controversy with Edward Lee, Erasmus countered the accusation of having scorned modern theologians in his New Testament edition by maliciously interpreting Lee's defence of them. Lee had said that Thomas and especially Lyra, having no Greek, had done what they could according to their

---

[86] *Annotationes in Novum Testamentum* CWE 56 226/Reeve 388 on Rom. 8:29 "Quos praescivit".

[87] *Apologia de "In principio erat sermo"* LB IX 116D. Cf. *Responsio ad annotationes Lei* LB IX 262B–C: the author of *Fasciculus temporum* is lowly in some people's eyes, but not in the eyes of those with whom Erasmus is dealing.

[88] *Apologia ad Fabrum* CWE 83 18–20/ASD IX-3 98:369–100:424, ASD IX-3 234:238–41 (= Reeve 711 on Heb. 2:7 "Minuisti eum paulominus ab angelis"), cf. 226:22–9 (= Reeve 707). In fact Erasmus does not even follow Thomas in his own interpretation, cf. Jean-Pierre Massaut, "Erasme et Saint Thomas", *Colloquia Erasmiana Turonensia* 2 vols. (Paris-Toronto 1972), 581–611:603.

[89] *Apologia de "Omnes quidem resurgemus"* LB IX 435C–D.

tenuous understanding of the Bible text. Although Erasmus, in his calmer moments, endorsed the same view,[90] he inferred from Lee's words that his English opponent apparently had a low opinion of the abilities of Thomas and Lyra, whom Erasmus himself would have quoted with diligence and respect, more often indulging them than not (a manifest falsehood).[91] Also Diego López Zúñiga, who charged Erasmus with heaping ridicule on Lyra, would in fact have less regard for Lyra than Erasmus himself.[92] Much in the same vein, Erasmus accused his critic Pierre Cousturier of never having seriously studied the Bible, the fathers, canon law, Lombard, Thomas, and Scotus; moreover, Erasmus denied him the right to treat Lyra as a barbarian, since Cousturier himself was incapable of writing good Latin.[93] It is ironic that in these passages Erasmus set himself up as a defender of Lyra especially, an author who in his view, as he stated three times, did not deserve respect.[94] In a letter against his adversary Agostino Steuco, Erasmus even put forward the charge that his opponent, in his Italian arrogance, had belittled Lyra because he came from Lower Germany like Erasmus himself. In his reply Steuco claimed he did not know that Lyra was German (which indeed he was not: Lyra was born in Normandy) and rightly pointed out that Erasmus' own criticisms of Lyra were not conspicuous for their courtesy.[95]

In his writings against Protestant adversaries, Erasmus had a third reason to quote late medieval authors. Not only could he accentuate his own orthodoxy in the eyes of his Catholic readers, but siding with the scholastics served his strategy of isolating the Protestants with regard to the traditions of the church. If he could demonstrate

---

[90] Cf. e.g. the following remark on Lyra, Reeve 759 on 2 Pt. 1:16 "Virtutem et praescientiam": "Non quod illos insecter, qui quod potuerunt praestiterunt, sed quod miserandos existimem, qui coacti sint tractare sacras literas, non satis instructi literis, sine quibus, ut dignum est, illae tractari non queunt".

[91] *Responsio ad annotationes Lei* LB IX 221D–E, 240B, 244C–F; cf. *Apologia invectivis Lei* Ferguson 287.

[92] *Apologia ad Stunicam* ASD IX-2 138:568–73, cf. 132:459–65, 248:386–250:401, 260:565–262:572.

[93] *Apologia adversus Sutorem* LB IX 741A, 795D; on Lyra: 741C–D, 742D, 743C, 743F, 782D.

[94] *Capita argumentorum* LB VI ***1v; CWE Epp. 843:591–4/Allen 536–40, 1171:81–2/76–8.

[95] Allen Epp. 2465:77–81 (Erasmus' letter); 2513:121ff., 555–9, 750–2 (Steuco's reply). As is suggested in *La correspondance d'Erasme*, ed. A. Gerlo et al. 12 vols. (Brussels 1967–84) IX 289n.11, Erasmus may have thought that Lyra came from Lier in Brabant. See also above n. 80.

that the Protestants diverged from the opinions dominating the early church as well as in all later periods of ecclesiastical history, it would become clear that they were not reformers but dangerous innovators. For this reason citing Thomas and other late medieval authors against Martin Luther could be useful, even though scholastic arguments in themselves must have impressed Luther even less than Erasmus.[96] In addition, Erasmus frequently associated Luther with late medieval heretics like Peter Waldo († before 1218), Jan Hus (1370–1415), and especially John Wyclif (c. 1330–84), probably following general opinion[97] rather than his own insights, since he denied having any familiarity whatsoever with late medieval heterodox movements.[98]

The difficult entry of the humanities in the faculties of theology may also have encouraged Erasmus to cite scholastic authorities. After the spread of the Reformation, conservative theologians looked upon humanism with even greater suspicion than before. In order to appease them, Erasmus frequently insisted that he aspired to a conjunction of traditional learning and good letters.[99] His increasing attention to scholastic theology (and, as we have seen in the previous chapter, to early and high medieval authors) in his own writings after 1520 may have partly stemmed from a wish to display benevolence.

A last (and probably the least cogent) reason for Erasmus to delve into scholastic writings was his occasional scholarly interest in them. After all, the Spirit had distributed its gifts to every existing century.[100] Thus it did happen, though not very often, that late medieval

---

[96] Erasmus knew that Luther did not attach much importance to Thomas (CWE Ep. 1033:161–2, 243–4/Allen 146–7, 222–3) but claimed that he had the same right as Luther to quote (scholastic) authorities in his favour (*Hyperaspistes II* LB X 1369E). At Allen Ep. 2143:67–9 he observes not without amusement that the English king Henry VIII even reads scholastics like Thomas, Scotus, and Gabriel Biel to defeat the Protestants. See also below p. 170ff.

[97] As Erasmus knew, the Sorbonne had pointed to the precedent of Wyclif and Hus in its condemnation of Luther, cf. e.g. *Apologia ad prodromon Stunicae* LB IX 378B; *Apologia adversus rhapsodias Pii* LB IX 1128E, 1133E. See also Ludwig Borinski, *Wyclif, Erasmus und Luther* (Hamburg 1988).

[98] Denial of any familiarity with the Waldensians: *Declarationes ad censuras Lutetiae* LB IX 834D, 835F. With the Beghards: ibid. LB IX 860B–861B, 911F–912A; CWE Ep. 843:681–6/Allen 620–4 (or the Turlupins). With the Wycliffites: *Declarationes ad censuras Lutetiae* LB IX 927C, *Apologia ad blasphemias Stunicae* LB IX 365B, *Apologia ad conclusiones Stunicae* LB IX 383D (or the Hussites), Allen Ep. 1708:36–8.

[99] See below p. 161.

[100] Cf. above p. 22 with n. 80.

theologians had something to offer which Erasmus could not denounce as a deformed version of an idea taken from ancient authors. In such cases he could use their insights as additional arguments, or even as a main argument. The best example would be *De taedio, pavore, tristitia Jesu* (1503), where Erasmus defended the views of the *recentiores* on Christ's agony in the garden of Gethsemane against his friend John Colet.[101]

Thomas Aquinas is the scholastic theologian Erasmus cited and, as he asserted himself, appreciated most.[102] As a matter of fact, many scholars have described Erasmus' attitude to the angelic doctor in positive terms, playing down his criticisms as much as possible—as if Erasmus would become less Catholic, or Thomas less erudite, if we would admit what appears to be the truth: that Erasmus was highly critical of Thomas. Jean-Pierre Massaut has elucidated this truth in a most outspoken manner, but unfortunately his assessments, for all their frankness, have been ignored or misunderstood by many a commentator after him,[103] which allows us to reopen the case.

Erasmus' praise of Thomas was hardly ever straightforward, and his criticism was often circumspect. Being a circumspect critic, however, was opportune; being a reluctant eulogist was not. As Erasmus

---

[101] For a discussion of Erasmus' treatment of patristic and medieval views on the subject see James D. Tracy, "Humanists among the Scholastics: Erasmus, More, and Lefèvre d'Etaples on the Humanity of Christ", *Erasmus of Rotterdam Society Yearbook* 5 (1985), 30–51 esp. 30–42.

[102] Cf. *Apologia in Novum Testamentum* Holborn 171/LB VI **3 ("inter recentiores doctissimum"), *Ratio* Holborn 183/LB V 78E–F ("neotericorum omnium . . . diligentissimus"), *Annotationes in Novum Testamentum* CWE 56 10/Reeve 336 on Rom. 1:4 "Qui praedestinatus est" ("there is no recent theologian, at least in my opinion, who is equal in diligence, more distinguished in ability, more solid in learning"), *Apologia contra Latomi dialogum* CWE 71 78/LB IX 103B. Erasmus claimed to have studied Thomas already before he was twenty years old: *Supputatio* LB IX 694D.

[103] Cf. Massaut, "Erasme et Saint Thomas"; according to Margolin, "Duns Scot et Erasme", 94 Massaut tries to demonstrate that Erasmus recognised Thomas' greatness! For earlier references to Erasmus' purported benevolence to Thomas cf. Dolfen, *Die Stellung des Erasmus*, 86–8; Ernst-Wilhelm Kohls, *Die Theologie des Erasmus* 2 vols. (Basel 1966) e.g. I 59, 193–4. For later examples cf. the assertion at CWE 23 67:6n. that Erasmus' criticism of authors of summae can hardly refer to Thomas, "whom he admired as far as he could admire a 'modern' theologian without Greek" (which repeats Erasmus' own statement at Reeve 547 on 2 Cor. 8:8 "Vestrae charitatis ingenium bonum"). CWE 56 480 indexes some passages from the annotations on Romans where Thomas is criticised for his careless or irrelevant comments (CWE 56 86–7/Reeve 355–6 on Rom. 2:24 "Blasphematur", 302/405 on Rom. 11:11 "Ut illos aemulentur") under the heading: "[Thomas as an] assiduous exegete". See also below nn. 121, 131.

knew, "no one can praise St Thomas enough to please the Dominicans"·
who set him almost above the gospel and called anyone who disagreed with him a heretic.[104] Moreover, Thomas was a saint. Erasmus
had therefore many more reasons to exaggerate his positive than his
negative sentiments. The lukewarm quality of his compliments, then,
already indicates that he did not include Thomas among his favourites.
Upon closer inspection, even some of his seemingly benevolent comments turn out to be rather disparaging. Erasmus stated, for instance,
that he did "not wholly disapprove" of the precepts of Scotus and
Thomas (whose names he often mentioned in the same breath)[105]
and that it was not his intention to drive them out of the universities.[106] He did not think that their works "should be rejected in their
entirety", for they "wrote for their own age, and they passed on to
us much that was drawn from the books of the ancient Fathers and
examined with some discrimination".[107] Few scholars could bear the
thought of being praised in such a way. Likewise, in his biographical sketch of John Colet, Erasmus related that years ago he paid
tribute to Thomas in Colet's presence "as no negligible figure among
recent philosophers, because he did seem to have read both sacred
literature and the old authors . . . and showed some sensibility in what
he wrote". Even this faint praise was more than Colet would hear,
since he started to fulminate against Thomas' arrogance and his
defilement of Christ's teaching with gentile philosophy. After this
incident Erasmus began to read Thomas again, and formed a lower
opinion of him than before.[108]

The fact that Erasmus appreciated Thomas best "among the moderns" cannot count as a serious commendation either, given what
Erasmus thought of modern theologians in general. We have seen
that he preferred Bernard of Clairvaux to any of the scholastics, and
any of the fathers to Bernard. Small wonder, then, that according
to Erasmus one would not find "as much true theology in the works

---

[104] CWE Epp. 1140:14–5/Allen 14; 1033:161–2, 243–4, 259/147–8, 222–3, 236.

[105] Cf. Margolin, "Duns Scot et Erasme", 93–4; Rummel, *Erasmus' Annotations*,
76–7, 80. Massaut, "Erasme et Saint Thomas" affirms that normally Erasmus did
not single out Thomas from the other scholastics in a positive way (cf. e.g. 585:
"Au total donc, Thomas est bien pareil à Scot!"). Cf. *Ratio* Holborn 296 (not in
LB): Thomas is "dilucidior", Scotus "excussior".

[106] CWE Epp. 952:50–1/Allen 45–6, 1002:11–5/8–12.

[107] CWE Ep. 1334:955–8/Allen 915–7.

[108] CWE Ep. 1211:467–83/Allen 429–44.

of Aquinas and Albert the Great as in any one of the early theologians".[109] At one point Erasmus admitted that Thomas had deviated less from the ancients than other scholastics because he had taken Augustine as his model, but he added immediately that Augustine had deviated from all other fathers.[110] Generally speaking, for Erasmus Thomas was an exponent, though perhaps not the worst exponent, of the degenerated theology of the later Middle Ages. It was through the mingling of theology with human philosophy by "Thomas and others like him" that the queen of sciences had fallen into decay.[111]

As a Latin author Thomas was certainly no better in Erasmus' mind than the other scholastics of his age, who had set forth their ideas without attention to their style, so that readers might remain untouched by their discourse or even be deterred from it.[112] Erasmus

---

[109] *Apologia contra Latomi dialogum* CWE 71 79/LB IX 103C.

[110] Allen Ep. 1844:26–8.

[111] *Declarationes ad censuras Lutetiae* LB IX 919E (also mentioning the contrivances introduced by Scotus, "ne quid commemorem de caeteris"). The term "human philosophy" would first of all refer to Aristotle. At *Moria* ASD I-4 165:498/CWE 27 130 Thomas is called ἀριστοτελικώτατος.

[112] Cf. *Ciceronianus* CWE 28 414/ASD I-2 661:7: Thomas is "impassive in his writing, concerned only to inform the reader"; *De vidua christiana* CWE 66 246/LB V 760A: authors like Thomas and Scotus simply teach and do not affect people's emotions; *De contemptu mundi* CWE 66 170/ASD V-1 80:100–01: Thomas, Albert, and similar authors offer a simpler style than the fathers and a square meal; *Edition of Jerome* CWE 61 78/Jerome, *Lucubrationes* II fol. 3v (praefatio): "Never does Jerome let his writings deteriorate to the point of becoming less polished than St Thomas even at his most rhetorical"; *Ecclesiastes* ASD V-4 268:473–4: Thomas had some talent for rhetoric, but he only exercised his powers of argumentation; ibid. V-5 16:195–200: like many others in his age, Thomas quoted the Bible abundantly and without necessity in his commentaries on Paul, impeding a smooth reading of his texts; *Apologia de "In principio erat sermo"* LB IX 116B: Erasmus does not object to quoting Thomas, being by no means deterred by the simplicity of his style; *Declarationes ad censuras Lutetiae* LB IX 866D: Thomas discussed the authenticity of some Bible books "adeo frigide" that he should better have kept silent about them; CWE Epp. 379:6–9/Allen 5–8 (to Zasius, commenting on a draft of *De origine iuris*): "Not but what by citing Thomas you have somewhat spoilt the brilliance of your style. But I know for whom you did it, and accept it; otherwise I would prefer the flow and colour of your style to remain unbroken"; 1196:177–81/163–6: ascribing eloquence to Thomas while denying it to Erasmus is absurd, like comparing an ant and a camel; see also ibid. 488–9/451–3: "out of the same block of wood you will find it easier to make two distinguished Thomists than one tolerable poet or orator". At CWE Ep. 1334:139–46/Allen 129–37 he includes Thomas among the most distinguished Christian authors because of his work on the Eucharist (perhaps *Officium de festo Corporis Christi*, *Opera omnia*, ed. R. Busa 7 vols. (Stuttgart 1980) VI 580–1), but he states at *Ciceronianus* CWE 28 414/ASD I-2 661:9–10, referring to the same work, that Thomas "reveals the least command of language precisely when he makes an attempt at fluency and fine writing".

thought Thomas' *Secunda secundae* in particular too lengthy and intricate to be practical, although it offered useful examples of virtue.[113] Moreover, even though Erasmus (in his own words) recoiled from proclaiming himself wiser than Thomas, the fact that the angelic doctor "knew only Latin, and not very precisely" made him inferior to Erasmus as an exegete.[114]

Erasmus' reception of Thomas' exegetical writings became particularly extensive in his New Testament edition. Erasmus made ample, though not indiscriminate, use of Thomas' *Catena aurea* as a reference work.[115] As for Thomas' own opinions, Erasmus' negative assessments dominate. He claimed the right to disagree respectfully with the fathers or with those like Thomas who "perhaps" had earned respect as well.[116] Dissenting from Thomas now and then would not do any harm to his deserved reputation as a scholar and a saint;[117] Thomas would even have been grateful for Erasmus' corrections of his views.[118] Meanwhile Erasmus' reprimands were not always as gentle as he pretended them to be.[119] Moreover, he quoted Thomas chiefly to expose his faults, not to subscribe to his views. Erasmus' frequent use of deferential formulas does not alter this fact. Correcting

---

[113] Cf. *Copia* CWE 24 636/ASD I-6 259:541–260:546, *Ecclesiastes* ASD V-5 336:496–7, CWE Ep. 858:64–8/Allen 57–60.

[114] *Apologia in Novum Testamentum* Holborn 172/LB VI **3; cf. Reeve 6 on Matt. 1:19 "Nollet eam traducere", where Lombard's knowledge of languages is disqualified with the same phrase. For Erasmus' avoiding to proclaim himself wiser than Thomas cf. also Allen Ep. 2172:39–41.

[115] For a critical judgement cf. Reeve 270 on John 21:22 "Sic eum volo manere": "Quin et in Catena quum multi frustulatim citentur, tamen bonus aliquis casus uno loco servavit integram lectionem . . .". For his appreciation of Thomas' mentioning his sources see above n. 9.

[116] *Capita argumentorum* LB VI ***1v; likewise *Apologia ad Stunicam* ASD IX-2 174:178–9, *Apologia contra Latomi dialogum* CWE 71 82/LB IX 105B; CWE Epp. 843:586–94/Allen 532–9, 1171:76–82/72–8 (esp. 79–81/75–6: "towards Thomas I have a more open mind than commends itself to many excellent and learned men").

[117] Cf. *Apologia ad Fabrum* CWE 83 18–9/ASD IX-3 100:387–96, *Apologia invectivis Lei* Ferguson 249, *Apologia adversus rhapsodias Pii* LB IX 1168B.

[118] CWE Epp. 456:129–35/Allen 117–22, cf. CWE Ep. 809:82–90/Allen 70–8.

[119] Cf. e.g. *Soloecismi* LB VI *5v (Thomas and his followers "foedissime lapsi sunt"), *Loca obscura* LB VI *6v (Thomas "miserabiliter lapsus est", "insigniter hallucinatus est"), Reeve 677 on Eph. 5:11 "Quum enim luxuriatae fuerint in Christo" ("Equidem non possum non admirari, quid accideret ei viro, tum *ut opinor*, pio, tum *ut habetur* erudito, ut ad hanc modum lascivere voluerit in Paulinis literis, quasi in re ludicra versaretur, praesertim post tot egregios ac probatos interpretes. Denique sic ista tractat, ut non addubitet, sed mera decreta nobis praescribat"; my italics). On Erasmus' use of Thomas in his New Testament edition see also Massaut, "Erasme et Saint Thomas", 597–603; Rummel, *Erasmus' Annotations*, 77–80.

Thomas' mistakes, he often stressed that "otherwise" Thomas did much better, but as he hardly gave any examples of Thomas' usual probity, his readers may have wondered why the angelic doctor would deserve respect at all except for being a saint.[120] Actually Erasmus did not want to stress Thomas' sanctity too much: in 1522, he deleted in many instances the epithets *divus, sanctus,* or *beatus* which he had put before Thomas' name in earlier editions.[121]

Studying Erasmus' criticism of Thomas' exegesis more closely, it is possible to discern some typical features. The most striking one is that Erasmus did not think Thomas to be diligent in the normal sense, but overly assiduous and therefore predisposed to superfluous reasoning. Thomas tended to give multiple interpretations of New Testament passages which were in fact unambiguous, heaping up irrelevant comments and artificial distinctions. By twisting (*torquere*) the meaning of Scripture in every direction, he tried to satisfy all authorities known to him lest he should make a clear choice himself. The main reason for this was his ignorance. Having an insufficient understanding of many questions, he evaded the difficulties involved in them and preferred to keep all options open.[122] Moreover, his

---

[120] Cf. Massaut, "Erasme et Saint Thomas", esp. 597: "Que saint Thomas soit *eruditus*, les Annotations s'acharnent à l'infirmer sans le dire, ou même en disant le contraire"; ibid. 598: Erasmus' excuses for Thomas are in reality "des coups de chapeau, annonciateurs de coups purs et simples".

[121] See Reeve 336 on Rom. 1:4 "Qui praedestinatus est", 17 on Rom. 1:4 "Per spiritum sanctificationis" (both instances have been overlooked in CWE 56 10, 17); CWE 56 118/Reeve 362 on Rom. 4:17 "Quia patrem multarum gentium posui te", 226 on Rom. 8:29 "Quos praescivit" (overlooked in Reeve 388), 302/405 on Rom. 11:11 "Ut illos aemulentur", 322n.5/410 on Rom. 12:1 "Rationabile obsequium", 399/428 on Rom. 15:10 "Laetamini gentes cum plebe eius", 433/436 on Rom. 16:25 "Ei autem qui potens"; Reeve 439 on 1 Cor. 1:11 "Ab his qui sunt Chloes", 464 on 1 Cor. 7:17 "Nisi unicuique...", 481 on 1 Cor. 8:4 "Quia nihil est idolum", 491 on 1 Cor. 11:10 "Velamen habere", 539 on 2 Cor. 6:1 "Adiuvantes autem exhortamur", 547 on 2 Cor. 8:8 "Vestrae charitatis ingenium bonum", 548–9 on 2 Cor. 8:19 "Destinatam voluntatem", 602 on Eph. 3:15 "Omnis paternitas", 677 on Eph. 5:11 "Quum enim luxuriatae fuerint in Christo". In some additions from after 1522 he used the epithets again: Reeve 155 on Luke 1:29 "Quae cum audisset" (1527), 209 on Luke 22:36 "Sed nunc qui habet sacculum" (1527), 396/CWE 56 262 on Rom. 9:19 "Quid adhuc queritur" (1535), 501 on 1 Cor. 13:1 "Charitatem non habeam" (1535), 613 on Eph. 5:14 "Et illuminabit te" (1535). Germain Marc'hadour, "Erasmus, Annotator of Romans", *Moreana* 33 (1996), 65–80:70–1 suggests that the suppression of the epithets points to Erasmus' having grown as intimate with Thomas as with the fathers for whom he did not use these epithets either. However, Erasmus did use similar epithets for the fathers for and after 1522, also in his New Testament edition.

[122] Cf. CWE 56 10/Reeve 336 on Rom. 1:4 "Qui praedestinatus est", 86–7/355–6

inadequate knowledge of the ancient languages prevented him from a thorough study of source texts, so that his interpretations were often no more than guesswork.[123] Erasmus therefore indignantly rejected the legend that Paul had appeared to Thomas to tell him that he was the first one to understand Paul's epistles.[124] Erasmus toned down his critical remarks in later editions in only in a few instances.[125] In some other instances he tried to find excuses for Thomas, pointing to the infelicity of the times in which he had been living, or blaming his faults on the translator of the Vulgate or on Thomas' own interpolators.[126]

---

on Rom. 2:24 "Blasphematur", 171/375 on Rom. 5:17 "Abundantiam gratiae . . .", 302/405 on Rom. 11:11 "Ut illos aemulentur", 313/407 on Rom. 11:31 "In vestram misericordiam", 318/409 on Rom. 11:36 "Quoniam ex ipso et per ipsum"; Reeve 437 on 1 Cor. 1:6 "Sicut testimonium", 438–9 on 1 Cor. 1:10 "In eadem scientia" ("detorquet sensum"), 439 on 1 Cor. 1:11 "Ab his qui sunt Chloes" ("ambigit"), 446 on 1 Cor. 3:12 "Foenum, stipulam" ("torqueri"), 454 on 1 Cor. 5:10 "Debueratis ex" ("pro uno sensu multos producit, ut est foecunda ignorantia"), 481 on 1 Cor. 8:4 "Quia nihil est idolum", 497 on 1 Cor. 12:27 "Membra de membro", 501 on 1 Cor. 13:4 "Benigna est", 509 on 1 Cor. 14:27 "Secundum duos . . .", 517 on 1 Cor. 15:51 "Omnes quidem resurgemus", 539 on 2 Cor. 6:1 "Adiuvantes autem exhortamur" ("torquet sese"), 607 on Eph. 4:16 "Secundum operationem" ("Thomas ita moderatur interpretationem, ut uideatur utrunque sensisse"), 618 on Eph. 6:13 "Et in omnibus perfecti stare", 634 on Col. 1:15 "Primogenitus omnis creaturae", 638 on Col. 2:9 "Divinitas corporaliter", 639 on Col. 2:15 "Traduxit" ("non opus erat hic geminis interpretationibus pro unica"), 647 on 1 Thess. 1:5 "In plenitudine" ("duas adducit interpretationes, sed quarum neutra scopum attingat"), 665 on 1 Tim. 1:10 "Plagiariis" ("prudens dissimulat, satis ipso silentio confitens, vocem sibi parum intellectam fuisse"), 669 on 1 Tim. 2:9 "In habitu ornato", 693 on Tit. 1:2 "Ante tempora secularia", 699 on Tit. 2:13 "Magni dei et salvatoris" ("torqueri"), 700 on Tit. 3:4 "Et humanitas", 731 on Heb. 12:1 "Circunstans nos", 733 on Heb. 12:21 "Moyses autem dixit" ("torquet"), 733 on Heb. 12:23 "Et spiritum", 734 on Heb. 13:2 "Placuerunt quidam etc.".

[123] Cf. CWE 56 87/Reeve 356 on Rom. 2:24 "Blasphematur" (the remark that among the modern theologians Thomas alone was accustomed to consult the original texts, was excised in 1522, which has been overlooked in Reeve), 118/362 on Rom. 4:17 "Quia patrem multarum gentium posui te", 313/407 on Rom. 11:31 "In vestram misericordiam"; Reeve 547 on 2 Cor. 8:8 "Vestrae charitatis ingenium bonum", 548–9 on 2 Cor. 8:19 "Destinatam voluntatem", 549 on 2 Cor. 8:23 "Gloriae christi", 639 on Col. 2:15 "Traduxit", 733 on Heb. 12:23 "Et spirituum".

[124] Cf. Reeve 485 on 1 Cor. 9:13 "Qui altario deserviunt", 486 on 1 Cor. 9:26 "Sic pugno", 669 on 1 Tim. 2:15 "Si permanserit".

[125] Cf. ibid. 511 on 1 Cor. 15:10 "Non ego autem . . ." (addition of 1527 neutralising Valla's criticism), 517 on 1 Cor. 15:51 "Omnes quidem resurgemus" (sarcastic clause excised in 1522).

[126] Times: cf. *Apologia in Novum Testamentum* Holborn 172/LB VI **3, *Annotationes in Novum Testamentum* CWE 56 10/Reeve 336 on Rom. 1:4 "Qui praedestinatus est", Reeve 549 on 2 Cor. 8:19 "Destinatam voluntatem", but cf. also below n. 131. Translator: CWE 56 302/405 on Rom. 11:11 "Ut illos aemulentur". Suggesting

Despite his rather consistent disapproval of Thomas, Erasmus eagerly used his authority against his own adversaries, including the Protestants among them. Thomas is by far the most quoted scholastic doctor in Erasmus' polemical writings. Not only did Erasmus justify his opinions and attitudes whenever he could by pointing to the precedent of Thomas,[127] but he boldly set himself up as Thomas' advocate. As we have seen, he tried to charge Lefèvre and Lee with disrespect for Thomas, while he urged Baechem and Cousturier to study Thomas with more attention. Especially against Lee he asserted that he, and not his English opponent, had Thomas on his side.[128] Similarly, he charged his Spanish adversary Juan Ginés de Sepúlveda with criticising Thomas without necessity,[129] and pointed out that the Louvain Dominican Vincentius Theoderici, for all his slavish devotion to Thomas, did not have a better understanding of the angelic doctor than Erasmus himself;[130] moreover, Theoderici had foolishly twisted Erasmus' appreciative words on Thomas.[131] Once Erasmus

---

interpolations: Reeve 506 on 1 Cor. 14:11 "Et qui loquitur mihi", 719 on Heb. 5:11 "Et interpretabilis ad dicendum", 731 on Heb. 11:37 "In melotis". Massaut, "Erasme et Saint Thomas", 602 with 610n.116 suspects that Erasmus merely raised the suggestion to increase the irony of his attacks. But since Erasmus made his suggestion three times (Massaut only mentions the first instance) and made similar suggestions with regard to several other medieval authors (see above nn. 7, 9 and p. 43 n. 35, p. 49 n. 63) it would seem that he was serious. Moreover, he may have been right! Thomas' commentary on Paul is only fully authentic up to 1 Cor. 7 inclusive. From 1 Cor. 9 we only have at our disposal notes by Raynaldus de Piperno, who added and reworked many passages. See Thomas Aquinas, *Super epistolas S. Pauli lectura*, ed. R. Cai 2 vols. (Turin 1953) I vi–vii.

[127] Cf. e.g. *Apologia ad prodromon Stunicae* LB IX 379E, *Apologia ad conclusiones Stunicae* LB IX 383E, CWE Ep. 1236:174–8/Allen 156–60: Thomas' work contains as many parallels with Luther as Erasmus' work; CWE Ep. 1571:45–7/Allen 41–3: if Erasmus is a heretic because he departs from the Vulgate, Thomas (and Bede and Lyra) are heretics too.

[128] See esp. CWE Ep. 843: Lee ascribes spurious writings and statements to Thomas, and misunderstands his genuine work (218–20, 245–50, 522–6/Allen 193–5, 218–22, 471–7), whereas Erasmus has the same authorisation for his work on the New Testament as Thomas had (491–3, 544–8/444–5, 491–6) and introduces no more novelties than Thomas did (644–5/586–7).

[129] Allen Ep. 2905:25–30.

[130] CWE Epp. 1126:345ff./Allen 311ff.; 1196:70ff., 211ff., 293–7/62ff., 194ff., 272–5.

[131] Cf. CWE Epp. 1126:289–301/Allen 261–72, 1196:45–51/40–5, Allen Ep. 2045:111–5. Theoderici had attacked Erasmus for calling Thomas unworthy ("indignus"). Erasmus responded that he had called Thomas unworthy of his times, thus indicating that Thomas was worthy of a happier age. Massaut, "Erasme et Saint Thomas", 599–600 refutes Erasmus' defence. First, Erasmus did call Thomas unworthy, without reference to his times, at Reeve 501 on 1 Cor. 13:4 "Benigna

even raised the complaint that not only the fathers, but also Thomas and Lombard, were rarely defended among contemporary theologians.[132] His lamentation in later years that nobody emulated Eccle- *— Chrysostom* siastes whereas Thomas and Scotus had countless followers[133] would *the preacher* seem a more accurate representation of his concerns.

Apart from Thomas, the exegetes Nicholas of Lyra and Hugh of St. Cher are regularly mentioned in Erasmus' works, albeit with much less consideration. Erasmus did not think that the two men deserved a respectful treatment,[134] although he once acknowledged a debt to Lyra.[135] In his annotations on the New Testament, he cited their Bible commentaries principally to show to what kind of enormities their ignorance of languages and patristic scholarship had led. Whereas he presented most of Thomas' flaws as exceptions to the rule, he quoted those of Lyra and Hugh as representative examples of their stupidity and arrogance. Looking in the works of Hugh in particular for passages to criticise, Erasmus asserted, was "a foolish waste of time"; he had noted only a few especially absurd statements in his annotations as warnings to those who put blind confidence in Hugh's work.[136] Even in the few cases where he did not depart from the views of the two men, he mentioned them without sympathy. Many of his criticisms were accompanied by stinging or even scurrilous remarks, some of which he removed after 1520, in an effort— we have observed its existence before—to display a more benevolent attitude toward medieval authorities.[137] We have also seen that Erasmus

---

est". Second, if he had wished to say that Thomas deserved to live in a better age, he should not have said that Thomas was unworthy of his times, but that his times were unworthy of him. Unfortunately CWE Ep. 1126n.38 does not refer to Massaut's pertinent argument.

[132] CWE Ep. 843:638–40/Allen 580–2, cf. for Lombard Allen Ep. 2037:175–6.

[133] Allen Ep. 2359:73–5. *pref to Froben Chrysostom, 1530*

[134] *Capita argumentorum* LB VI ***1v, CWE Epp. 843:591–4/Allen 535–40, 1171:76–82/72–8. For Erasmus' use of Lyra and Hugh in his New Testament edition see also Rummel, *Erasmus' Annotations*, 80–4.

[135] CWE Ep. 1171:82/Allen 78. Cf. CWE Ep. 165:13–4/Allen 10–1: on behalf of his commentary on Paul, Erasmus wants to use all previous commentators, including Lyra.

[136] CWE Ep. 456:136–41/Allen 123–8. Cf. Reeve 667 on 1 Tim 1:18 "In illis": in the work of authors like Hugh it is easier to find than to avoid errors. Hugh is also severely attacked in Erasmus' scholia on several of Jerome's prefaces to his Old Testament translations, see Jerome, *Lucubrationes* IV fol. 5v–10r.

[137] Suppression of caustic passages: for Lyra cf. Reeve 324 on Acts 23:15 "Notum facite tribuno" (passage excised in 1522), 751 on 1 Pt. 3:7 "Honorem impartientes" (1527); for Hugh: ibid. 675 on 1 Tim. 4:15 "Haec meditare" (1522), 750 on 1 Pt.

tried to parry the attacks on his criticism of Lyra in particular by pretending that he actually held Lyra in higher esteem than did those who tried to vindicate him. In addition, he came to admit after 1520 that the works of Lyra and Hugh were possibly mixed up with additions of their even more silly followers.[138] Yet he never overcame his revulsion for the two men. Strikingly, he not only charged Lyra with scholarly incompetence but insinuated that he was morally depraved. Lyra was never canonised, Erasmus empha- sised in a tract against Lyra's confrère Luis de Carvajal (1529), and nobody knew that he had led a holy life; in fact, many Franciscans were familiar with biographical details of a quite different order. The possibility that Lyra was burning in hell could therefore not be excluded.[139]

One late medieval author whom Erasmus quoted with an apparent sympathy is Jean Gerson (1363–1429). The Paris theologian did not appear in Erasmus' writings until 1518, and almost all references to his work can be found in the apologies. Provoked to a renewed study of medieval theologians by his Catholic critics (in 1526 Noël Bédier, syndic of the Sorbonne, urged Erasmus to read Gerson in particu- lar),[140] Erasmus found in the works of Gerson some welcome prece- dents for his own opinions, especially for his critical attitude toward the proliferation and strictness of ecclesiastical regulations. Erasmus' comparatively frequent references to Gerson in his later work do not seem to have been merely dictated by opportunism: he appears really to have valued Gerson's relative open-mindedness. In addition, he

---

2:24 "Cuius livore" (1527). Erasmus also attenuated some criticisms with regard to content; for Lyra cf. ibid. 244 on John 7:38 "Qui credit in me . . ." (modification of 1522), 324 on Acts 23:15 "Notum facite tribuno" (1519), 356/CWE 56 91n.6 on Rom. 3:2 "Illis eloquia" (1527); for Hugh: Reeve 249 on John 8:57 "Quinquaginta annos" (1535), 254 on John 12:35 "Adhuc modicum lumen" (1519), 466 on 1 Cor. 7:35 "Quod honestum est . . ." (1527), 542 on 2 Cor. 6:16 "Sicut dixit deus" (1535).

[138] For Lyra cf. ibid. 454 on 1 Cor. 5:9 "Commisceamini fornicariis" (1522), 665 on 1 Tim. 1:10 "Plagiariis" (1522); for Hugh cf. ibid. 333 on Acts 28:11 "Cui erat insigne castrorum" (1522), 689 on 2 Tim. 3:2 "Seipsos amantes" (1522). In his scho- lia on *Praefatio in Paralipomenon* in Jerome, *Lucubrationes* IV fol. 8v at "Iuxta Ismenium" Erasmus suggests that a work so weighty as Hugh's can scarcely be the product of one man.

[139] *Responsio ad collationes gerontodidascali* LB IX 1014C–1015B. Cf. also *Capita argu- mentorum* LB VI ***1v: Lyra and Hugh do not deserve a respectful treatment "neque doctrinae neque sanctimoniae nomine".

[140] CWE Ep. 1579:185–90/Allen 159–66; for Erasmus' reaction cf. CWE Epp. 1581:90ff., 601ff./Allen 82ff., 542ff.; 1596:20–2/17–9.

referred with approval to Gerson's questioning of papal supremacy and his complaints about the degeneration of scholastic theology. This is not to say that Gerson became one of Erasmus' favourite authors. Notwithstanding his scholarship and piety, for which Erasmus frequently expressed his esteem, Gerson remained in the eyes of Erasmus a representative of scholastic theology. Erasmus criticised especially Gerson's views on the creed (as expressed in a work which nowadays is no longer ascribed to him).[141] Moreover, he considered Gerson overly scrupulous in intellectual as well as moral questions, and had little patience with his deficient style. But with regard to Gerson's shortcomings Erasmus advanced the same excuse as for the flaws of Thomas Aquinas: his times had worked against him. In a more prosperous intellectual climate, Gerson's mind would have developed more happily.[142] Although it is difficult to weigh Erasmus' sympathies for late medieval scholars against each other, it would seem that he actually was more inclined to Gerson than to Thomas. His citations of Gerson are free of the irritation which pervades many of his references to the angelic doctor. This may partly have resulted from the fact that Thomas, unlike Gerson, had many head-strong supporters: Erasmus' treatment of Thomas contains an element of debunking for which there was no need in the case of Gerson.

Erasmus took far less interest in the literary culture of the later Middle Ages than in the development of the scholarly disciplines in the period. He had little affinity with vernacular literature in par-ticular. Romance languages were to him corrupt forms of what used to be Latin, whereas the other European vernaculars were products inherited from the barbarians who had destroyed the Roman empire. For Erasmus, the rise of the vernaculars was a deplorable turn of history, which had caused—along with bad education, of course—the downfall of Latin literary culture.[143] Some specimens of vernac-ular literature, like chivalrous romances, he explicitly rejected.[144] On

---

[141] The work in question is the first tract, *De articulis fidei*, of Simon of Hinton, *Compendium theologiae breve et utile* or *Speculum iuniorum* (c. 1255).

[142] Cf. *Copia* CWE 24 318/ASD I-6 50:487–8; *Supputatio* LB IX 568D, 648C. For a detailed study of Erasmus' reception of Gerson see my "Erasme explore le moyen âge".

[143] Cf. e.g. *Ecclesiastes* ASD V-4 262:348–52. For Erasmus' attitude to vernacu-lar languages see Chomarat, *Grammaire et rhétorique*, 79–150.

[144] *Institutio principis christiani* CWE 27 250/ASD IV-1 179:427–180:430. At CWE Ep. 843:653–5/Allen 595–7 Erasmus condemns the *Ovide moralisé* (early 14th c.).

the other hand, he encouraged preachers to read the best authors in their mother tongue in order to develop their eloquence, naming, for Italy, Dante and Petrarch in particular.[145] He did not show much interest in medieval Latin literature either. In his discussion of Latin literary history in *Ciceronianus*, Erasmus did not even mention other late medieval authors than the scholastics, whom he collectively condemned.[146] Only incidentally did he praise some authors who had produced valuable work in spite of the times in which they had lived, or reject some others.[147] As we have seen in Chapter One, this holds true also for the genre of historiography.

The Breakdown of Piety

In Erasmus' perception, the intellectual decline of the later Middle Ages was chiefly responsible for the moral degeneration of the Christian world in the same period. As medieval scholarship had suffocated the gospel message, neither teachers nor preachers were able to uphold a model of good and spiritual life to the common people (who, as Erasmus took for granted, had a natural tendency to corruption if left to themselves). As a result, the world had become prey to base instincts. Governmental rule provided at best a negative check to depravity by punishing crimes. But in the absence of positive examples, the mass of believers had hardly any possibility of fol-

---

[145] *Ecclesiastes* ASD V-4 264:395, cf. V-5 14:146; see also CWE Ep. 1211:306–8/Allen 277–9 (the English have authors comparable to Dante and Petrarch). Erasmus did not comply with the request of Mercurino di Gattinara (Ep. 1790A) to prepare an edition of a Latin work of Dante, *De monarchia*, perhaps—as Allen Ep. 1790A headnote thinks—because he had little sympathy with Dante's idea of universal imperial rule. Petrarch was for Erasmus the "leader in the rebirth of eloquence in Italy", but his Latin suggested "the lack of polish of an earlier age" (*Ciceronianus* CWE 28 414/ASD I-2 661:16–20).

[146] CWE 28 414/ASD 661:2–13.

[147] He praised Geoffrey of Vinsauf for his *Poetria nova* (c. 1210) (CWE Ep. 27:44–7/Allen 42–5), and Boccaccio for his *De genealogia deorum*, written "with more elegance than one would expect from the age in which he lived" (*De ratione studii* CWE 24 674/ASD I-2 123:8–10). He thought the style of Dionysius the Carthusian (1402–71) simple and inelegant, but clear (CWE Ep. 1332:8–13/Allen 6–11). The generation of preachers following on the great scholastics (who were to be avoided as models: *Ecclesiastes* ASD V-4 260:288–90, 306:407–12, V-5 370:157–60) with men like Jordan of Quedlinburg (c. 1300–80), Jacobus a Voragine (1226–98), and Robert of Lecce (c. 1425–95), fitted perhaps in their age but showed great ignorance; fortunately they had been forgotten (ibid. V-4 268:475–80).

lowing Christ as they should. Bereft of spiritual leadership, the church had fallen to decline along with its helmsmen.[148]

The late medieval clergy, however, lacked not only the capacities but also the will to instruct their flocks properly. In the climate of moral inertia into which the world had been lulled by the schoolmen, the pope and especially the monastic orders had been able to establish their "tyranny".[149] In his later years Erasmus developed an almost obsessive hatred of the "tyranny" of the monks, doubtless because the majority of his adversaries came from their ranks. He abhorred the mendicants in particular, although he occasionally tried to assure Franciscan and Dominican critics alike that he had always preferred their respective orders to all others because they had suffered less from degeneration.[150] His question in *Colloquia* about how the church had run when the mendicant orders did not exist, and how it ran when there were one and later three,[151] clearly suggests that in his view the development of the orders had not been profitable to ecclesiastical life.

Erasmus' most frequent charges against the religious pertained to ignorance, pride, idleness, luxury, and superstition. As for their ignorance, he sometimes blamed them for being inimical to all sorts of higher learning, even traditional (scholastic) university education,[152] but more often for opposing humanist studies. Many scholastic theologians belonged to the religious orders, and in numerous instances Erasmus attacked "the monks and theologians" in one breath or referred to scholastic theology as "the learning of the monks". Accordingly, he held the religious in particular responsible for the decline

---

[148] The same thing had already happened in patristic times, see e.g. *Vita Chrysostomi* LB III 1334B: "Clerici et Episcopi ad mundanos mores degenerarant, unde factus est talis populus qualis sacerdos". Cf. also *Apologia contra Latomi dialogum* CWE 71 66/LB IX 96E: the main responsibility for "Christendom's being reduced to its present straits . . . lies in the personal faults of those who govern the Christian community".

[149] Cf. e.g. *Ratio* Holborn 206–8/LB V 90C-91C; CWE Epp. 1313:23ff./Allen 21ff., 1333:342–8/319–25, 1581:784–91/704–10. Also worldly princes had profited from the situation to extend their power, cf. *De bello turcico* ASD V-3 78:39–47. For a definition of tyranny see *Responsio ad annotationes Lei* LB IX 250D: "Tyrannidem appellavi, si quis sua doceat, non quae sunt Christi, et ad haec eos vi cogat, cum persuadere non possit".

[150] Franciscans: Allen Ep. 1823:6–8, cf. 1891:22–6; Dominicans: CWE Ep. 1196:293–5/Allen 272–3, cf. 1173:142/127.

[151] CWE 40 769/ASD I-3 541:152–3.

[152] Cf. e.g. *Antibarbari* CWE 23 75/ASD I-1 97:3–26, *Colloquia* CWE 39 502/ASD I-3 404:40ff.

of learning in the later Middle Ages.[153] In the monastic age, when
the religious had devoted themselves to learning without the subtleties of scholasticism, the name of monk had still been honourable;
now the bad habits of some had caused all to be detested.[154]

The pride of the monks made them think themselves superior to
all other people, Erasmus believed, but especially to religious of a
different stamp. They were more attached to their orders, which
were granted special papal privileges, than to the gospel, and they
put the founders and the famous members of their orders above
Christ. The rivalries between the orders resembled those between
the theological schools and sometimes coincided with them: the
Franciscans, for instance, stuck firmly to Scotus and Lyra, whereas
the Dominicans did not suffer any deviations from Thomas or Hugh
of St. Cher, according a greater authority to them than these had
claimed for themselves.[155] The rules of the orders likewise upset
Erasmus. The simple original rules had increased with papal approval
into a wide variety of petty and superstitious precepts, much the way
the definition of a small number of doctrines in patristic times had
degenerated into the proliferation of scholastic trifles. Little remained
of the humility of an earlier age. Whereas Benedict, Francis, and
Dominic refused the honour of priest, their followers did not shrink
from the dignity of cardinal or pope, and offered kings their feet to
kiss.[156] In his *Colloquia* Erasmus twice stated, echoing Pope Alexander
VI, that it was actually safer to offend a king than a mendicant
friar.[157]

The idleness and the luxury of many religious likewise afforded a
stark contrast to the monasticism of former days. Previously the
monks had devoted themselves to manual labour and to study; later
monastic life became "a kind of idleness", a development which was

---

[153] See above pp. 38, 63–64. Cf. also *Ecclesiastes* ASD V-5 30:480–91: the orders
"with dubious founders" (Erasmus mentions Eliah, Bridget, Augustine, and Bruno)
caused the loss of Greek and the corruption of Latin.

[154] Allen Ep. 2771:22–5.

[155] Cf. *Querela pacis* CWE 27 298/ASD IV-2 67:178–68:184, *Ratio* Holborn 205/LB
V 90A, *Capita argumentorum* LB VI ***1v; Reeve 73 on Matt. 17:5 "Ipsum audite",
93 on Matt. 23:16 "Debitor est", 167 on Luke 2:35 "Et tuam ipsius animam", 237
on John 5:2 "Quae cognominatur Hebraice Bethsaida", 667 on 1 Tim. 1:18 "In
illis".

[156] *Colloquia* CWE 40 950/ASD I-3 663:374–8. As for Dominic, Erasmus was
mistaken: Dominic was a priest.

[157] Ibid. 952, 1012/665:450–2, 698:426–8.

fostered by the proliferation of orders and monasteries in the later Middle Ages.[158] With the passage of time, wealth and ceremonies had destroyed the original piety of men like Bernard and Francis. Once a refuge from the world, many monasteries were now in the heart of it, being no more than "breeding places of impiety" or outright brothels.[159] For the majority of the monks, religion consisted of the superstitious observance of ceremonies and exterior practices, and especially in the care of their cowls, whereas Benedict, Francis, Dominic, and other founders of orders had modelled their garb on that of poor men and farmers of their native countries, without a wish to devise something special.[160]

The result of these developments was that the piety, erudition, and sanctity of monastic life had been replaced by mere tyranny. Some religious in Erasmus' day still preserved a *vestigium* of evangelical life,[161] but they were a tiny minority: "the religious fervour of the earlier monasteries, and the reputation for it to which those houses owed their rise in the first place, are now no more".[162] Most professed followers of Basil, Jerome, Augustine, Benedict, Bruno, Dominic, and Francis were monks in name only, and had no wish for improvement.[163]

Corruption had also affected the episcopal hierarchy, especially the papacy. The skit *Julius exclusus* not only contains the most outspoken details on the subject, but puts them into a historical perspective. The degeneration of the curia, which culminated in the papacy of Julius II, is represented as a phenomenon of the last few centuries in particular, even if it probably had set in already during the reign of Constantine the Great. "I have managed affairs so well", boasts Julius, "that the church, and Christ himself, owe more to me than any previous pope, even the more recent ones, to say nothing

---

[158] Cf. *De recta pronuntiatione* CWE 26 386/ASD I-4 30:527–44, *Colloquia* CWE 40 768–9/ASD I-3 540:113–23, *Institutio principis christiani* CWE 27 267/ASD IV-3 198:962 (citation), CWE Ep. 966:18–23/Allen 15–20.

[159] Cf. *De contemptu mundi* CWE 66 173/ASD V-1 84:181 (citation), *Enchiridion* CWE 66 79/LB V 36A, CWE Ep. 858:581–91/Allen 549–59. Brothels: *Supputatio* LB IX 588F, *Dilutio* CWE 83 135/Telle 88. For charges of debauchery see also *Colloquia* CWE 39 385, 471–2/ASD I-3 341:87ff., 389:3ff.

[160] Cf. e.g. *Colloquia* CWE 39 481, CWE 40 720/ASD I-3 400:393–7, 401:426–9, 535:1488–536:1494.

[161] Cf. *Colloquia* ASD I-3 393:145/CWE 39 474 ("survival").

[162] *Adagia* II viii 65 CWE 34 76/ASD II-4 192:923–4.

[163] Cf. CWE Ep. 447:671ff./Allen 606ff., Allen Ep. 2037:179–91.

of the early ones who, in my opinion, were popes in name only".[164]
The use of force to obtain the papacy has been current "for hun-
dreds of years"; in the early church, when bishops had no other
rewards than hardship, vigils, fasting, study, and death, the situation
was different, but now popes "can get a kingdom and tyrannical
power".[165] As Julius' adversaries on earth had done, Peter constantly
reaches back to the days of early Christianity in order to remind
Julius of his duties, but for the latter the ancient church is no point
of reference: since the first centuries "time has changed everything
for the better".[166] Julius' depravity, then, not only resides in his deeds,
but also in the bewildering view of history which Erasmus ascribes
to him. The fact that he dares to present the Middle Ages as an
era of progress demonstrates that he is a scoundrel through and
through.

On the degeneration of the lower secular clergy Erasmus was
much less explicit, although he did believe that their moral standards had fallen as well. We have seen that in his view priests were
fewer in the early church, but more pious and hence more respected.
In later times the priesthood had become an ordinary profession, as
Erasmus explained in the preface of his edition of Alger of Liège
(1530). New forms of liturgy were introduced, partly for the sake of
gain, and finally many opted for the priesthood with the sole object
of making their living.[167]

In Erasmus' opinion, the corruption of learning and the moral
degeneration of the clergy at all levels had produced lamentable
effects on Christian society at large. As a result of the general neglect
of educational and pastoral responsibilities, very few people respected
the commands of Christ or lived according to the teaching of the
gospel. Religion had been reduced to ceremony and superstition,
while the inner moral and spiritual force of common believers had

---

[164] CWE 27 172/Ferguson 73.

[165] Ibid. 175–6/82–3; cf. ibid. 171/71, *Moria* CWE 27 139/ASD IV-3 172:792–3:
performing miracles is out of date for the pope.

[166] CWE 27 192/Ferguson 117. For other references to the corruption and the
tyranny of the curia cf. e.g. *Moria* CWE 27 137ff./ASD IV-3 170:739ff.; *Spongia*
ASD IX-1 173:180–1, 174:193–8; CWE Ep. 1332:84–6/Allen 76–8, Allen Ep.
2177:11–5. At *Epistola ad fratres Inferioris Germaniae* ASD IX-1 372:972–3, however,
Erasmus feigns not to know whether the curia suffered from corruption.

[167] Allen Ep. 2284:147–61, cf. above p. 25 n. 91. Erasmus situated the introduction of new forms of liturgy in the later Middle Ages, cf. Reeve 164 on Luke
2:14 "Hominibus bonae voluntatis" where he adduces evidence from Peter Comestor.

been annihilated. We cannot investigate here all of Erasmus' criticisms of contemporary society. But we should keep in mind that there was little he did not think wrong, and that almost all of what was wrong was the outcome, in his perception, of the processes of decline during the later Middle Ages which we have described in this chapter.

De profundis

For Erasmus the goal of history was the combination of God's gifts to humanity, notably classical learning and the Christian faith, into a perfect synthesis. What should have developed after the first days of Christendom was a Christian culture with the gospel teaching as its centre and secular learning in a subservient role. The literary and intellectual upbringing of the faithful should have helped them to enter the realm of the spirit. After fifteen hundred years of Christian history, however, this ideal had been not realised but perverted: corrupt learning went hand in hand with degenerate morals. The later Middle Ages had been crucial in this development. Before, in the patristic and monastic periods, intellectual and religious culture had already suffered from neglect; in the age of scholasticism, learning and morality were consciously distorted. A wide variety of ancient texts, from papal decrees to Bible commentaries translated from the Greek, were suppressed on purpose. Surviving texts were often deliberately spoilt with interpolations. This had even happened to the writings of late medieval authors themselves (Lombard, Thomas Aquinas, Hugh of St. Cher), writings which already represented a decline in comparison to the products of an earlier age. Moreover, Christian doctrine and religious practice suffered from wilful distortion. The teaching of Christ was mixed with heathen philosophy and with the inventions of the scholastics. Countless human regulations burdened the yoke of Christ. The spirit of contention which pervaded theology suffocated true virtue. In short, Christian society had strayed far away from the gospel through the activities of malevolent men. Many of those men were monks, unchecked or even stimulated by ecclesiastical and public authorities.

Of course this view of history lacks nuance, to say the least. But Erasmus was not interested in the past for its own sake. His concerns were with the present. His view of late medieval history lent support to his project of reform: given his clear-cut survey of what

had gone wrong in the recent past, one could easily guess what measures had to be taken in order to secure a better future. The recovery and study of the pagan and Christian literature from ancient
times, which had all but expired in the scholastic period, were a key
to any future improvement.

More problematic is the fact that Erasmus' view of the scholastic
period is not perfectly in accord with his view of the more remote
past. Had he believed that the intellectual and moral decline of
Western Christendom set in with the rise of scholasticism, he would
have had good reason to think that, once scholasticism had been
replaced by humanist studies, degeneration would cease to exist. We
have seen, however, that Erasmus placed the beginning of decline
much earlier in Christian history. Not only had evil never been
absent from any period, but the spirit of contention, typical of scholasticism, had originated already in the patristic era, most notably in
the writings of Augustine. In fact, scholasticism had germinated from
the seeds sown by the later fathers, with the early Middle Ages as
a sort of incubation period. The decline of literature had likewise
started in the patristic age, albeit slightly, and had become full-scale
in early medieval times. All this suggests that the scholastic period
represents only the final phase of the degeneration of Western
Christendom, not its roots. Even if Erasmus had been able to extirpate the period from history, he would merely have destroyed evil's
most recent outgrowths.

A related problem concerns the question, introduced in the previous chapter, of whether history was subject to human control.
Erasmus thought that late medieval scholars had destroyed culture
on purpose. But could scholars with better intentions rebuild it? In
earlier times, cultural decline had occurred in spite of good intentions, Erasmus maintained, and even men like Thomas Aquinas and
Jean Gerson had to be considered the victims rather than the instigators of the low cultural standards of their age. Theoretically, the
deliberate destruction of culture could be stopped, but combating
the phenomenon of cultural decline as a whole was a different matter. Still more important, there was no guarantee, from a historical
point of view, that a restoration of literary and intellectual standards
would lead to moral improvement. In view of the fact that learning
and religion had developed and declined apart from each other earlier in history, their joint downfall in the scholastic period might
seem a mere coincidence. Was it true even for the scholastic period

that the loss of letters had generated bad morals? Was it not rather the existing depravity of the learned which had made them neglect, corrupt, or destroy humane studies?

The weak spots in his view of the Western past do not seem to have bothered Erasmus. Normally he did not trace back the barbarism of his times any further than to the scholastic period, thus limiting his scope to the centuries in which human beings consciously provoked the decline of letters and religion. Accordingly, he affirmed that cultural and religious reform was a matter of facing one's responsibilities. History had brought Christendom down to where it was, but it also offered inspiration for improvement to those who were prepared to turn the tide. No period of history had been favourable in all respects, but the most valuable products of antiquity in particular—classical civilisation, the teaching of Christ and the apostles, patristic scholarship—had to be picked up like "jewels from a dungheap"[168] in the present and to be combined so as to fulfil the plans of Providence.

---

[168] *Institutio principis christiani* CWE 27 251/ASD IV-1 180:464 (see above p. 15 n. 50), with respect to pagan history; CWE Ep. 1000:169–70/Allen 164–5, with respect to Cyprian's use of Tertullian despite the latter's separation from the church.

CHAPTER FOUR

RESTORING A GOLDEN AGE

As the previous chapters have shown, Erasmus knew and increasingly insisted in his later years that ideal historical epochs had never existed. No period had been entirely dominated by a perfect synthesis of classical learning and Christian religion. Yet he never gave up the idea that his programme of reform was aimed at restoration. Throughout his life he continued to argue for an historical legitimation of humanism: by eradicating the faults of the medieval past, humanism would be able to revive the erudition and the piety of older and better times.

In this connection Erasmus frequently employed the famous classical metaphor of a return of the golden age. In numerous passages from his letters and works he stated that a golden age was near or had already begun. He associated this age first of all with the establishment of universal peace in the Christian world, thanks to which studies and religion would flower again—suggesting that the warlike attitude of the prevailing age of iron had caused the decline of civilisation. The majority of the references date from Erasmus' happiest years, between 1515 and 1520, but even after the Reformation he still hoped for a return of golden times.[1] Of course Erasmus knew

---

[1] Cf. *Panegyricus* CWE 27 48, 59, 64/ASD IV-1 68:330–3, 78:707, 83:867–9 (Philip the Fair turns the age of iron into a golden age); CWE Epp. 335:80/Allen 76–7 (when Leo X became pope "at once that age of worse than iron turned into an age of gold"), 533:18–21/15–7 (if we have peace we shall see a return of "a sort of golden age", with a flowering of religion, good laws, and liberal arts), 566:38–45/34–40 ("this age of ours . . . has good hopes of becoming an age of gold", for Erasmus foresees the restoration of true Christian piety, the study of the humanities, and peace and harmony in the Christian world, "the fountain and parent of religion and learning"), 964:84–6/76–8 (Henry VIII is restoring a golden age), 966:43–7/38–42 (Erasmus perceives the dawn of a new golden age, which he may not live to see), 967:18–9, 43–4/13–4, 36–8 (Wolsey is turning England's bronze age into gold), 1418:68–9/63–4 (Erasmus prays that Christ makes Clement VII "the champion and founder of a new golden age" of peace), 1599:20–1/18–20 (rumours promise a golden age, but Erasmus is pessimistic); Allen Epp. 2091:262–4, 611–3 (Erasmus hopes that our age of iron will be followed, if not by a golden age, at least by a happier one); 2393:1–6 (thanks to honest men like Nicholas Olah, the golden generation of mortals may revive), 2423:49–54 (peace is responsible for

that he was alluding to literary fiction rather than to historical reality: apart from his doubts about the existence of the golden age in the past, he was aware that this age did not stand for the flowering of classical civilisation but for its absence in archaic times.[2]

The next two chapters concentrate on Erasmus' idea of restoration. It is this idea which connects his view of the past to his perception of the present and the future. In this chapter we will try to determine—from Erasmus' perspective—to what extent civilisation had been or was being restored in the Christian world of his day, and what was or had been his own role in this development. We will ask in particular whether in Erasmus' view intellectual culture and piety did progress, as they should, hand in hand. In the following chapter we will ask whether Erasmus' contributions to the reform of civilisation can really be encompassed within the idea of restoration. To this end we will analyse in some detail Erasmus' most important and ambitious enterprise: his edition of the New Testament.

Paving the Way

By the time Erasmus began to compose his first writings, humanism already had a history behind it, not only in Italy but also in Erasmus' own environment. Erasmus acknowledged the fact, as his writings attest. The young Erasmus did not think of himself as an isolated figure, but as an active member of a small group of men who advanced the cause of learning in the German world, taking Italy as their model and embracing Rudolph Agricola (1444–85), the first Northern humanist, as their shining example. Not a few men followed the tracks of antiquity, as Erasmus asserted in a letter of 1489 to Cornelis Gerard; he could see "countless well-schooled writers of

---

a revival of studies in Italy and France; if Germany would follow, a golden age would return), 2452:32–4 (if God puts an end to Germany's troubles without bloodshed, one may hope for a golden age), 2453:27–8 (idem); see also *De recta pronuntiatione* CWE 26 368/ASD I-4 13:15–6. For references to a prevailing age of iron cf. also *De contemptu mundi* CWE 66 150–1/ASD V-1 56:471–58:502, Reeve 46–7 on Matt. 10:9 "Nolite possidere"; CWE Epp. 269:96–8/Allen 88–91, 333:11/7.

[2] Doubts: cf. CWE Epp. 566:38–40/Allen 34–5, 964:84–6/77–8. Absence of civilisation: *Adagia* I v 22 CWE 31 401/ASD II-1 494:492–4, *Moria* CWE 27 107/ASD IV-3 110:727–111:739; see also *Encomium medicinae* CWE 29 43–4/ASD I-4 176:245–50, *In hymnos Prudentii* CWE 29 186/LB V 1344C, *Oratio de pace* LB VIII 548A.

the present day who approach quite closely the ancient ideal of eloquence", in Italy as well as in Germany.[3] Like the mechanical arts,
eloquence had been restored in its ancient splendour after centuries
of shameful distortion and neglect, first of all by the Italians, who
had kindled the flame in Northern Europe too.[4] True enough, bar-
barity still dominated the world, but her days were numbered now
that the Muses were reborn, as Erasmus averred in his *Conflictus
Thaliae et Barbariei*. Humanism, then, was not a movement which the
young Erasmus believed he initiated, not even in his own country.
The rebirth of ancient literary culture had already got into its stride;
Erasmus, in his own estimation, went along with existing tendencies
which he energetically tried to amplify in a rather favourable climate. A sign that he had the wind behind him was that in the late
1480s he wrote his paraphrase of Valla's *Elegantiae linguae latinae* at
the request of a schoolmaster from Holland, who apparently wished
to make his pupils familiar with the Latin of antiquity. As early as
1499 Erasmus could write that bad manuals of letter-writing, which
had circulated for a long time in the grammar schools, had vanished in recent days as mists before the rising sun, "when a more
polite kind of literature began to flower again".[5] Thus the Northern
Renaissance, in Erasmus' perception, had become a matter of fact
before 1500, as humanists were winning the day in the field of education and Latin literary culture.

The young Erasmus limited his scholarly scope to Latin literature
and his geographical radius of action to Northern Europe, and these
two facts are logically connected. As a Latinist, Erasmus had important contributions to make to his own part of the world, but not to
Italy, where the rebirth of classical eloquence had begun much earlier (inaugurated by Petrarch, as Erasmus would later recognise)[6] and
had already been brought to perfection. In his view, men like Ermolao
Barbaro, Giovanni Pico, and Angelo Poliziano, eager "to challenge
Antiquity on its own ground", actually did better than a great many
of the ancients themselves.[7] Erasmus' role, then, could only be to

---

[3] CWE Ep. 23:54–80/Allen 52–77, cf. CWE Ep. 32:45–55/Allen 41–50. On
Erasmus' adherence to "Germany" see my "Erasmus Becomes a Netherlander".
[4] Cf. CWE Epp. 23:81–111/Allen 77–106, 26:117–21/105–8.
[5] CWE Ep. 117:30–3/Allen 26–8.
[6] Cf. *Ciceronianus* CWE 28 414/ASD I-2 661:16–7.
[7] CWE Ep. 126:151–5/Allen 129–32.

help the diffusion of classical eloquence north of the Alps—as a local branch manager, so to speak, of Italian humanism. His own Holland and its neighbouring regions, often reviled by Erasmus as particularly boorish,[8] had to be civilised in the Italian mode by Erasmus and his humanist companions.

After 1500 Erasmus observed with much satisfaction that the cultural emancipation of Northern Europe was making steady progress. His stay in Italy from 1506 to 1509 may have convinced him that Transalpine Europe was not doing that badly. In the 1508 edition of his *Adagia*, he praised Holland for the first time for its level of scholarship.[9] This is not to say that from now on he thought his fatherland a model of classical civilisation. But when in later years he wanted to single out Holland or the Low Countries for their rudeness, he did so by contrasting those regions not to Italy, but to the whole rest of Europe, especially to other Northern European countries like England, Germany proper, or France.[10] By 1516, these three countries, according to Erasmus (whose opinion was shared by other Northern humanists), had equalled or even surpassed Italy's level of scholarship and would progress still further in the future.[11]

---

[8] Early references are *Carmina* 5:23–9 CWE 85 43/ASD I-7 116; CWE Epp. 32:45–8/Allen 41–4, 47:10/8; 49:29–31, 129–34/24–6, 112–5; 113:65–6/54–5, 118:2–8/1–6, 144:4–10/3–8, 157:7–10/5–8; 159:6–7, 63–8/4–5, 57–62; 296:114–5, 221–6/108–9, 205–11. In later years Erasmus occasionally called himself a (coarse) Batavian, cf. e.g. CWE Epp. 996:45/Allen 43, 1331:38/35–6, 1629:11–2/9, 1635:9–10/6; Allen Epp. 1840:85–7, 2088:52–3, 2290:2–4, 2604:33–5, 2795:37–8, 2809:8–9, 3064:24–5; see also below n. 24. But he became angry if others did the same, cf. CWE Ep. 1216:46–52/Allen 45–51 = *Apologia ad Stunicam* ASD IX-2 68:152–7.

[9] In *Auris Batava*, *Adagia* IV vi 35 ASD II-8 36:427–44:477; see also Ari Wesseling, "Are the Dutch Uncivilized? Erasmus on the Batavians and His National Identity", *Erasmus of Rotterdam Society Yearbook* 13 (1993), 68–102.

[10] Cf. CWE Epp. 483:18–20/Allen 15–7 (still including the Italians), 886:52–4/50–1, 894:3–9/1–7, 928:24–30/19–24, 968:14–22/11–8, 969:11–6/8–13; 970:16–7, 23–5/13–4, 20–1; 1003:19–31/15–25, 1060:46–8/37–8. See also my "Erasmus versus Italy", *Mediaevalia et Humanistica* 24 (1997), 123–45 esp. 127–8.

[11] For England cf. CWE Epp. 185:14–6/Allen 13–5, 188:17–22/13–7, 211:18–9/15, 396:406–13/381–7. For France: CWE Epp. 421:34–5/Allen 31–2, 480:105–7/100–02, 529:30–4/25–8, 531:45–52/39–46. For Germany: CWE Epp. 305:218–22/Allen 214–6, 307:17–20/13–6, 397:24–6/20–3. See also Reeve 650 on 1 Thess. 2:7 "Sed facti sumus parvuli" with Appendix A [555]. In some instances Erasmus was more critical, cf. CWE Epp. 408:12–3/Allen 10: Zasius "seems to me the only German who knows how to express himself"; 843:86–9/78–80: Lee's claim that Paris, Germany, England, and Scotland have many men skilled in Latin and Greek, while of Italy he says nothing, is absurd. For claims by other Northern humanists see e.g. David O. McNeil, *Guillaume Budé and Humanism in the Reign of Francis I* (Geneva

Addressing himself in these years to the humanists in the German world, whose leader he had become by universal acclamation, Erasmus kept insisting that the Italians had nothing to offer which could not be found in Northern Europe as well.[12]

A second reason for Erasmus to distance himself from Italian humanism was that around 1500 the scope of his scholarly attention broadened considerably. Apart from Latin literary culture, he came to champion the restoration of Christian religion, the sources of which—the New Testament and the patristic writings—had, in his estimation, been corrupted and cast aside while the trifles of the scholastics reigned supreme, with all its consequences for society at large. Assuming the role of Western Christianity's teacher,[13] he tried from now on to redirect Christian history toward a new, perfect harmony of *eruditio* and *pietas*—step by step, accommodating himself to historical circumstances, as once Christ himself had done.[14]

Erasmus' new project was not just a matter of broadening his scholarly interests to include sacred literature. It amounted rather to a transition from an aesthetic to an ethical orientation of his activities. As a young scholar, he had primarily been concerned with good Latin as an end in itself; his main goal had been to invest the world with literary beauty. Embellishing the world, however, was not the same thing as working at its moral and spiritual improvement. By 1500, Erasmus adopted the latter task as his proper ambition, and came to conceive the revival of good letters as a means to it.[15] He did not abandon his high literary standards, but invested them

---

1975), 32–4: especially in *De asse* (1515) Budé asserted France's equality with Italy in the Republic of Letters, uttering (like Erasmus) misgivings about the moral character of Italian humanists.

[12] Cf. my "Erasmus versus Italy", 127–8. In his *Epitoma rerum Germanicarum* (1505) Jakob Wimpfeling had already made a similar assertion, see Jacques Ridé, "Les humanistes allemands et le moyen âge", *L'histoire au temps de la Renaissance*, ed. M.T. Jones-Davies (Paris 1995), 131–45:137.

[13] The title of Jean-Claude Margolin, *Erasme: précepteur de l'Europe* (Paris 1995) is indeed accurate. Pabel, *Conversing with God*, 8 rightly points to the spiritual dimension of Erasmus' teaching: "much of Erasmus' scholarship constituted a pastoral ministry to all western Christendom, a ministry exercised through the printing press".

[14] Both Chomarat, *Grammaire et rhétorique*, 658–65 and O'Malley, "Grammar and Rhetoric", 97–8 draw a parallel between Erasmus' perception of Christ's activities and of his own role in society.

[15] Cf., among many other assessments, Jozef IJsewijn, "Erasmus ex poeta theologus sive de litterarum instauratarum apud Hollandos incunabulis", *Scrinium Erasmianum*, ed. J. Coppens 2 vols. (Leiden 1969) I 375–89.

with ethical value. This new moral emphasis may have made it easier to pursue his literary tastes in the cultural climate of Northern
Europe, where a penchant for beauty is still easily seen as a sign of
decadence. Making use of this bias, Erasmus in his later years repeatedly accused the Italian humanists of the aestheticism he had adhered
to in his youth, depicting them as frivolous and irreligious people
merely interested in rhetoric while he had been the first to make literary studies serve Christian ends[16] (as if Lorenzo Valla had not written annotations on the New Testament, first published in 1505 by
no other than Erasmus himself).

Erasmus' renewed project of reform necessitated the study of Greek,
the language of the New Testament and of the best and earliest
Church fathers. Italy had been the cradle of a humanist interest in
Greek studies, but its achievements in the field had been wanting,
as Erasmus noted not without some delight.[17] Thus in Greek scholarship, Transalpine Europe could catch up relatively quickly: its cultural emancipation by 1516 included, in Erasmus' view, the study
of both ancient languages.[18]

Erasmus' Christian humanism and, to a lesser extent, his achievements as a scholar of Greek, enabled him to conceive of himself as
a scholar of world-wide importance. His project of restoring the
sources of Christianity, which in 1516 yielded major results in the
form of the New Testament edition and the edition of Jerome, was
profitable not just to his country or to Northern Europe, as his contributions to Latin literary culture had been, but to the whole Christian
commonwealth. As he put it in a letter from 1521:

> In all my work my sole object has been to resuscitate the humanities,
> which lay almost dead and buried *among my own people*; secondly to
> arouse *a world* which allowed too much importance to Jewish ceremonial

---

[16] For this last claim cf. *Apologia adversus Sutorem* LB IX 751D, CWE Ep.
1581:124–6/Allen 115–7; Allen Epp. 1753:19–22, 1805:64ff., 2127:24–6. For his
treatment of the Italians see my "Erasmus versus Italy", 128ff.

[17] CWE Ep. 188:41–50/Allen 34–43.

[18] Cf. CWE Epp. 185:14–6/Allen 13–5, 428:42–5/37–40. At CWE Ep.
211:76–7/Allen 62–3 (preface to the *Adagia* edition of 1508) he still explains to have
translated the Greek passages as an "allowance for the times in which we live".
But cf. CWE Epp. 1341A:241–2/Allen I 8:11–2 (1523): "when the knowledge of
Greek began to be widely shared, as happened most successfully in our part of the
world", there was no need any longer for his translations of Lucian; 1558:196–7/180–2:
"the study of Greek has made such progress everywhere that many men no longer
need the help of a translator".

to a new zeal for the true religion of the Gospel; and finally to recall to its sources in Holy Scripture the academic theology in our universities, too deeply sunk in the quibbling discussion of worthless minor problems.[19]

Claiming only a local reputation as a promoter of letters was something which Erasmus continued to do in his later years,[20] presenting himself as the bearer of refined learning to a country which, untouched by Italian humanism, had scarcely had any commerce with the Muses before[21]—obscuring the fact that, in his own youthful experience, humanism had been a successful collective enterprise which he had joined, not initiated.[22] Fighting barbarism had been a lonely struggle, Erasmus claimed with regard to his early years, but a fairly rewarding one. Posterity would recognise that "in an unpromising age, and in a part of the world where liberal studies had been quite extinct and were resented, I have fought a long and unpopular fight against the most obstinate opponents of the humanities".[23] Fortunately, "at least among our own barbarians and at a very

---

[19] CWE Ep. 1183:38–44/Allen 35–40 (my italics).

[20] Cf. CWE Epp. 1634:30–2/Allen 27–9: "In the subjects which I have tackled, I think I have acquitted myself tolerably well, especially if you bear in mind that I am a barbarian writing for barbarians"; 1635:11–4/8–10: "I had fair success in Germany in arousing interest in languages and polite letters . . . remember, the show was not intended for Italian ears"; Allen Epp. 3032:464–7: "Itaque pro mea quantulacunque portione conatus sum iuuentutem ab inscitiae coeno ad puriora studia excitare. Neque enim illa scripsi Italis, sed Hollandis, Brabantis ac Flandris. Nec omnino male successit conatus meus"; 3043:38–40: "illa non scripsimus Italis, sed crassis Batauis ac rudibus Germanis, idque seculo non perinde felici atque nunc est". Ironically, he had jeered at Cornelis Gerard and Willem Hermans in those allegedly unpropitious years for contenting themselves with a local reputation, cf. CWE Epp. 26:127–9/Allen 113–4, 178:20–1/18–9.

[21] Cf. CWE Epp. 1110:4ff./Allen 2ff.; 1341A:31–43, 87/Allen I 2:20–30, 3:36; 1437:272–6/Allen I 48:34–7; Allen Ep. 3032:190–7, 462–4.

[22] This youthful experience is corroborated by the facts as recorded in Jozef IJsewijn, "The Coming of Humanism to the Low Countries", *Itinerarium Italicum: The Profile of the Italian Renaissance in the Mirror of Its European Transformations*, ed. Heiko A. Oberman and Thomas A. Brady (Leiden 1975), 193–301. According to IJsewijn, the period of incidental and often superficial contacts with humanism in the Low Countries lasted until 1455/60. In the period from 1455/60 to 1485/90 (covering only Erasmus' very first activities) some aspects of Italian humanism became definitely incorporated. The following "Erasmian" age was a period of consolidation, self-confidence, and the development of independent characteristics.

[23] CWE Ep. 935:66–9/Allen 63–6. At CWE Ep. 853:45–7/Allen 40–3 he had still claimed to be no general, but a dutiful soldier in the restoration of humane studies in the Low Countries. For the insufficient recognition from his homeland cf. Allen Epp. 1885:58–60, 2329:22–3.

unpromising time I have advanced the cause of liberal studies not wholly without success".[24] As far as the intellectual climate in the Low Countries was concerned, Erasmus took credit personally for putting an end to the Middle Ages.

After 1516 Erasmus sometimes even referred to himself as the initiator of humanism in all of Northern Europe. No one could deny that he had become the prime leader and organiser of Northern humanism, but his own claims went further than that. Forgetting that he had not been a pioneer but an adept follower of an existing movement, he increasingly pretended to have been the first to arouse the interest for humane studies in an age of utter barbarism. Strikingly, he often presented his alleged role of initiator as a cross which he had to bear, suggesting that his groundbreaking work had provoked universal resistance and brought him personal suffering. "In promoting the study of the humanities no one did more, and great was the unpopularity he had to suffer in return for this from barbarians and monks", he said of his lot in his *Compendium vitae* (1524).[25] All enemies of good letters hated him personally,[26] not just as a contributor to the revival of letters, as he had asserted earlier,[27] but as its originator, "a charge which I neither can nor wish to repudiate entirely".[28] It was by standing up all by himself against the hatred of the barbarians that Erasmus claimed to have made his most important contribution to civilisation. His unremitting defence of literary culture against its adversaries had prepared the world for the fruits of humanism which were to come after him. "I enjoyed

---

[24] CWE Ep. 1482:27–9/Allen 24–5. Cf. Allen Epp. 1753:19–20: Erasmus exerted himself "vt nostra Batauia mitesceret commercio bonarum litterarum"; 2299:105–8: "Quod si quis conferat seculum quod fuit ante triginta sex apud nos, cum hoc quod nunc est, intelliget an aliquid litteris contulerit Erasmus"; 2419:6–8: "Rudi seculo fortassis excitauimus iuuenum studia, praesertim apud Cimbros et Batauos"; 2443: 138–40: Erasmus' old enemies believe that he in particular revived good letters among his compatriots; 2449:4–5: Erasmus was one of the first, if not the first, to reduce the hatred of literature in his country to silence; 2466:58–74: while declining the title "Batavian Hercules" (but see 2468:45–8), Erasmus admits that thirty years ago he underwent severe attacks in his country because he urged the young to study the classics.

[25] CWE Ep. 1437:398–400/Allen I 52:147–8.

[26] Cf. e.g. CWE Ep. 905:44–6/Allen 43–4: Erasmus' recovery from illness is "a great disappointment . . . to those who hate to see the resurgence of a better sort of studies"; Allen Epp. 1697:24–5: in Louvain and Paris there are "deuotissimi bonarum litterarum hostes, et *ob has* mei quoque" (my italics).

[27] Cf. CWE Epp. 541:80–4/Allen 72–5; 967:55–8, 73–5/48–52, 66–7.

[28] CWE Ep. 1635:34–5/Allen 28–9; cf. CWE Ep. 1219:12–4/Allen 10–1.

paving the way for others who had greater projects in hand", he asserted in a letter published in 1517, so that those others might have an easier job than he.[29] Especially with regard to the restoration of sacred literature Erasmus claimed to have taken the first difficult step. "The shock of the first encounter . . . I have supported myself", he assured in the same letter;[30] it was up to others now to bring to perfection what he had begun.

Setting himself up as the father of Northern humanism (and of Christian humanism all over the world), Erasmus naturally interpreted the progress of learning in Northern Europe from 1516 as the fruits of his own efforts[31] and considered the humanists of a younger generation his own offspring—*post me ergo propter me*, so to speak. Being born in a happier age than Erasmus (since he had removed many obstacles for them), they had more opportunities to develop their talents than Erasmus, who in his youth had nobody to stimulate him.[32] It was especially to the young, then, that Erasmus desired "to hand on the torch":[33] they should continue his work and preferably surpass it. From 1517 Erasmus often expressed the hope that men like Juan Luis Vives or Christophe de Longueil would eclipse him some day, and later in his life he recognised that this was actually happening—stressing, however, that his juvenile superiors owed their success to his pioneering work.[34] If many youngsters were putting his name in the shade, "this is not surprising, since I absorbed the first hostility and I paved the way, since I took it on

---

[29] CWE Ep. 541:86–9/Allen 76–9.

[30] Ibid. 140–1/125–6. For similar claims to have "paved the way" for others with his New Testament scholarship cf. *Apologia ad Stunicam* ASD IX-2 78:363–5; CWE Epp. 373:161–2/Allen 147–9, 1137:24–7/21–5.

[31] Cf. e.g. CWE Epp. 413:31–5/Allen 28–31 ("I am delighted to know that my labours, such as they are, find some favour with men of good will. Many are taking this opportunity to read the Scriptures who would never read them otherwise . . . many people are beginning to take up Greek, or rather, this is now common"), 943:9–16/8–13, 1124:9–11/8–9.

[32] Cf. e.g. Reeve 650 on 1 Thess. 2:7 "Sed facti sumus parvuli" with Appendix A [556], CWE Ep. 1341A:31ff./Allen I 2:20ff.

[33] For this metaphor see *Adagia* III i 1 CWE 34 180/ASD II-5 38:428–9; CWE Epp. 541:105–9/Allen 94–8, 796:11–2/10–1, 948:253–4/247–8, 1597:20–1/16, 1600:17–9/14–5; Allen Ep. 2250:26–7.

[34] Cf. *Apologia invectivis Lei* Ferguson 270, *Spongia* ASD IX-1 142:499–500; CWE Epp. 531:91–5/Allen 82–6, 905:23–5/21–3 (Longueil), 935:61–5/58–62 (Longueil), 943:9–10/8, 967:51–5/46–8, 1107:9–10/7–8 (Vives), 1112:83–7/71–4, 1146:21–9/18–26, 1309:41–3/36–8, 1479:85–7/74–6; Allen Epp. 1805:14–9, 2305:39–40, 2315:101–4, 2419:8–10, 2517:9–11, 2773:116–7, 2880:18–21, 2892:88–90.

me to develop new ground. Actually, I regret that there are not more people who surpass me. For to this end I have been sweating".[35] The young were standing on Erasmus' shoulders, and they were well aware of it: many of them would acknowledge a debt to him, which assured him that in their memories "the name of Erasmus [would] somehow live, in return for what he [had] done for them".[36]

One can even point to passages in Erasmus' writings where he unreservedly presented the entire humanist movement as his own work, no longer distinguishing between Italy and the North or between beginnings and later achievements:

> It is I, as cannot be denied, who have aroused the study of languages and good letters. I have brought academic theology, too much subjected to sophistic contrivances, back to the sources of the holy books and the study of the ancient orthodox authors; I have exerted myself to awaken a world slumbering in pharisaic ceremonies to true piety.[37]

L'humanisme, c'est moi! Small wonder that the struggle with the medieval past was vital to Erasmus. Contrary to what the above passage suggests, however, Erasmus did not think that this struggle had come to an end in his lifetime.

Happy Days are here Again

Presenting his alleged introduction of humanism to the North as an act of altruism for which he had suffered greatly, Erasmus believed that he was entitled to the gratitude of his contemporaries. In 1519 he could observe that "[a]ll men everywhere express their gratitude to me" for his efforts to promote honourable studies and the advancement of religion; only some theologians remained resentful, but for the most part his audience was growing more well disposed.[38] Early in his life Erasmus was already convinced that his fame would come slowly, but last for a long time.[39] After the successes of Northern

---

[35] Allen Ep. 2299:102–5. Cf. *Capita argumentorum* LB VI ***2v: "juvenibus potissimum hic desudat labor. Nec dubito quin ventura sit aetas, et jam fortassis exoritur, qua videbuntur haec magna ex parte supervacanea".

[36] CWE Ep. 966:46–7/Allen 41–2, likewise *Apologia invectivis Lei* Ferguson 270.

[37] Allen Ep. 1700:36–40; for similar, slightly less boastful statements cf. Allen Epp. 1744:150–8, 1891:185–95.

[38] CWE Ep. 967:59–61, 203–7 (citation)/Allen 42–4, 185–8.

[39] Cf. CWE Ep. 139:45ff./Allen 38ff.

humanism from 1516, he maintained that the best of his contemporaries appreciated him, but that general praise would only come from posterity.[40]

Erasmus' estimations of his own popularity were directly related to his expectations of the development of Western civilisation. Having appropriated Northern humanism as his own brainchild, he saw the fate of the movement and his personal destiny as two sides of the same coin. His idea that posterity would be more favourable towards him than the present generation stemmed from his conviction that humanism could and would make important progress in the future, until it had reshaped the complete intellectual and religious culture of Christendom. Erasmus believed, as we have seen, that he had laid the foundations for the reform of the Christian world, having accomplished some important first steps; posterity should finish the job, taking the baton (or "the torch", as he liked to put it himself) from where he had carried it and bringing the race of humanism to a victorious end. Erasmus never thought that humanism could rest on its laurels yet. Even in his most successful years, between 1515 and 1520, he interpreted the universal breakthrough of humanism in a climate of peace not so much as the mark of a glorious present but as the announcement of a better future, insisting that there was still much work to do. "I wish we might see even now the success which I believe awaits the humanities in the near future", as he wrote to Guillaume Budé.[41] Time was running in favour of the young, as he repeatedly exclaimed: "In heaven's name, what an age will soon be upon us! How I wish I might be young again!";[42] "What riches, if only one could be young again! I count this gen-

---

[40] Cf. CWE Epp. 456:285–90/Allen 255–60, 507:30–1/23–4, 530:31–3/26–7, 749:41–3/36–7, 757:31–3/26–9, 794:85–6/78–9, 942:23–4/19–21; Allen Epp. 1805:333–4, 2046:378–9. Cf. also CWE Ep. 471:28–31/Allen 25–6 (predicting a similar fate to Reuchlin). Our evaluation of Erasmus' view of his own significance accords rather well with the unflattering picture of his narcissist character by Nelson H. Minnich and W.W. Meissner, "The Character of Erasmus", *American Historical Review* 83 (1978), 598–624. See esp. 622: "His life appears to have been an incessant seeking for recognition, acceptance, and adulation from his fellow man". For an assessment of Erasmus' orchestration of his fame, marked by the (supposedly conscious) confusion of his personal appeal and the programme of Christian humanism, see Lisa Jardine, *Erasmus, Man of Letters: The Construction of Charisma in Print* (Princeton 1993).

[41] CWE Ep. 531:91–2/Allen 82–4.

[42] CWE Ep. 534:62–4/Allen 61–2.

eration fortunate, even though I cannot include myself".[43] All was activity everywhere; "gifted minds bestir themselves to take up interrupted tasks", giving life again to all branches of learning.[44] The last few monks and theologians resisting the fresh bloom of humane studies would soon be silenced when, with the passage of time, truth would win the day.[45] In a famous letter from 1517 to Wolfgang Faber Capito, Erasmus set forth his view of an approaching golden age in some detail:

> I feel the summons to a sure and certain hope that besides high moral standards and Christian piety, the reformed and genuine study of literature and the liberal disciplines may be partly reborn and partly find new lustre; the more so, since this object is now pursued with equal enthusiasm in different regions of the world . . . [i.e. by Leo X at Rome, Ximénes in Spain, Henry VIII in England, Charles "in our country", Francis I in France, and Maximilian I in Germany]. So it is to their piety that we owe the spectacle of the best minds everywhere rising as though at a signal given and shaking off their sloth, as they set themselves in concert to restore the humanities. How else can one describe the way in which so many good scholars are attacking this splendid programme . . . so that we have the almost certain hope of seeing every subject come forth into the light of day reformed and purified?[46]

Continuing his letter, Erasmus listed what humanism had achieved thus far. The results were most splendid in the field of literary culture. Even Scots, Danes, and Irishmen studied and absorbed "that elegant literature which has so long been reduced almost to extinction". Medicine, too, had many champions all over Europe, while civil law and mathematics were being restored in several places in the North. One field of learning, however, was lagging behind: "the science of theology was rather more of a business", Erasmus confessed, because its teachers were as a rule obstinate opponents of the humanities who defended their ignorance under the cloak of piety. But Erasmus had good hopes: "Here too I am confident of success, as soon as knowledge of the three tongues proceeds to secure public

---

[43] CWE Ep. 643:29–30/Allen 27–8.
[44] CWE Ep. 542:21–8/Allen 18–23.
[45] Cf. CWE Epp. 868:49–57/Allen 43–51, 966:13–7/10–4, 974:8–11/6–8, 979:8–11/5–8.
[46] CWE Ep. 541:37–58/Allen 32–52.

recognition in the universities, as it has already begun to do".[47] If the princes, priests, and schoolmasters took up their proper duties, he wrote in his *Paraclesis* (1516), a true and pure sort of Christians would emerge soon enough.[48]

It was especially in the field of theology, then, that humanism had not completed its course. "Physicians embrace, lawyers value, and philosophers accept whatever leads to the renewal of their disciplines", Erasmus wrote in his *Apologia in Novum Testamentum* (1516). "We theologians alone stubbornly protest and hate what is good for us".[49] In 1518 Erasmus repeated this message in a letter to Boniface Amerbach. Again he started with a eulogy. Literature and scholarship had made so much progress that Erasmus could describe their renascence in the form of a historical narrative:

> we must continually count our generation fortunate . . . those humane studies, which for so many centuries had been almost buried, now flourish once more the whole world over and are so prosperously multiplied. Eighty years ago, more or less, . . . grammar itself, mistress of correctness in language, and rhetoric, the guide to abundance and brilliance of expression, lisped with a wretched, sorry sound, and the arts which had in the old days been so well equipped with languages then spoke Latin only, and bad Latin at that. Thereafter, as noble studies slowly increased, Italy alone had the gift of self-expression, and even there no science used it except rhetoric. But now, in every nation in Christendom, all branches of study (under the favour of the Muses) marry useful learning with splendour of expression.[50]

When humanist Latin crossed the Alps and began to be applied in higher studies (the innuendo is clear: Italian humanists had been mere literary aesthetes), the academic disciplines could breathe again. Medicine, philosophy, and civil law had been restored already, but not theology:

> Yet somehow, I know not how, equal success in this department still eludes the theologians, although there may be some with a keen desire to write well. I hope however that we shall soon see this profession, like the others, shake off the dust and reassert its ancient brilliance. Hitherto, those who wrote with some attempt at polish were excluded from the ranks of the learned . . . But soon, if I am not mistaken,

---

[47] Ibid. 58–76/52–68.
[48] Holborn 144/LB V 141C, VI *3v.
[49] Holborn 164/LB VI **2 (wording of 1516).
[50] CWE Ep. 862:5–19/Allen 2–15.

things will be very different: none will be admitted to the roll who do not reproduce these ancient fountain-heads of learning in language still more elegant than their own, nor will it be thought right for any man to lay claim to wisdom unless it is accompanied by eloquence.[51]

Erasmus had not always been so confident: as early as 1515 he referred to the restoration of theology with sighs of despair.[52] Yet this restoration was essential to his programme of reform. In Erasmus' view, scholastic theology was chiefly responsible for the degeneration of Christian morality. Restoring the teaching of the gospel, the sole source of Christian piety and virtue, by removing additions and distortions of a later age, was the core of Christian humanism and the only possible way envisaged by Erasmus to create a better world. At the dawn of the Reformation, however, scholastic theology was far from being dead, and the revival of true Christendom was therefore not assured. True, Erasmus could point to some important contributions to a better sort of theology (including his own editions of the New Testament and Jerome) as well as to well-intentioned rulers and hopeful signs of progress in different parts of Europe,[53] including his own country.[54] But the battle was not over yet. Whereas the other disciplines had given way to humanism, theology was, at best, engaged in a war on an equal footing.

---

[51] Ibid. 35–49/29–41.

[52] Cf. CWE Ep. 337:453/Allen 428–9: "there is no hope even of recalling the world to the old true Christianity".

[53] Cf. *Ratio* Holborn 303/LB V 137A (in Cambridge and Louvain a better sort of theology is arising), Reeve 650 on 1 Thess. 2:7 "Sed facti sumus parvuli" (the study of secular and Christian literature in Latin and Greek has made great progress in Britain); CWE Epp. 396:406–13/Allen 381–7 (in England humane studies and religion are making great progress), 384:23ff./20ff. (Leo X is rebuilding Christian life, cf. also 446:92–4/87–9, 1007:131–2/121–2), 456:253–82/228–53 (in thirty years the university of Cambridge has developed into a humanist place of learning, and its present theologians put the earlier generation in the shadow), 541:76–80/68–72 (Lefèvre d'Etaples and some others have introduced humane studies into theology), 821:7–11/6–9 (in England "under the favour of princes the humanities hold sway and the love of honour flourishes, while the painted mask of false piety and the useless and tedious learning of monks are alike exiled and overthrown"), 964:61–2/54–6 (Henry VIII restores religion and discipline in all men and especially in the monks and clergy, cf. 967:29ff./24ff.), 1003:22–8/18–23 (the Sorbonne "returns from time to time to the pure springs of Holy Scripture"; the Paris bishop Etienne Poncher is "a man designed by heaven for the revival of humane studies and true religion"), 1013A:20–1/Ep. 660:17–8: "a Christian spirit wins the day everywhere").

[54] Cf. CWE Epp. 758:24–5/Allen 21–2 (wonderful progress in learning and piety could be made if the country had more benefactors like Philip of Burgundy); 853:41–3, 64–6/37–9, 60–2 (Charles V is inclined to promote and spread Christian

The Reformation: A Serious Setback?

It is often stated that as a consequence of the Reformation Erasmus turned from an optimist into a pessimist, substituting his happy announcements of a better future for depressing assessments of his times.[55] There seems to be ample evidence to substantiate this statement. After 1520 the number of passages in his work welcoming an approaching golden age decreased considerably. The depiction of his own century as a fierce and troublesome epoch, if not the most abominable age of history, became clearly dominant, although before Martin Luther had declared war on the Catholic church, Erasmus had already referred on occasion to the darkness of his times.[56] Moreover, Erasmus repeatedly averred that the Reformation had spoilt his work. His careful and promising attempts to restore civilisation had been upset by the Lutheran fury; it was the Wittenberg reformer who had held back Erasmus (and so Christian humanism) from a triumph all over the world of Christendom.[57]

Still, the view that Erasmus became a pessimist lacks nuance. In his eyes, the Reformation did not challenge the results of humanism achieved before 1520, but only complicated the task which had been left unfinished: the restoration of theology and, consequently, of Christian piety. As Erasmus put it in a letter of 1521:

> The classical languages and liberal studies have almost reached a stage at which we may hope that their future is secure, though even now there is active opposition from the champions of ancient ignorance. If

piety and scholarship; if there were many men like Le Sauvage, the world would soon blossom with liberal studies, high standards of conduct, and peace), cf. also 421:148–57/136–44. But see CWE Epp. 887:11–2/Allen 8–9 (Le Sauvage being dead, there is no hope for the Low Countries), 1003:29–31/24–5 ("We are the only country that cannot yet congratulate itself on any movement of the kind [i.e. the restoration of humane studies and true religion]. But yet we have good hopes").

[55] See e.g. Gilmore, "Fides et Eruditio", 109; Bietenholz, *History and Biography*, 32–5. Bietenholz adds, however, that Erasmus occasionally gave expression to a "new optimism", believing that a turn for the better depended on God's favour. See for this latter idea below p. 125. Bietenholz's observation that Erasmus no longer used the phrase "golden age" after 1520 (33, 35) is mistaken; see above n. 1.

[56] Cf. CWE Epp. 786:18–9/Allen 17–8 ("an age like ours, the most lawless for many centuries"), 978:18–9/14–5 ("the thick darkness of our times").

[57] Cf. CWE Epp. 1238:63–5/Allen 57–8, 1596:26–9/22–5; Allen Epp. 1672:138–46 (claiming, however, a reasonable success for his personal contributions: the editions and paraphrases of the New Testament, and the editions of the fathers), 1753:19–25, 1805:20–50, 1976:13–25.

only we had the same hope of seeing the teaching of the Gospel restored to its purity and simplicity! But here a bloody battle rages still. Yet we have a good hope of victory, if Christ will help us . . .[58]

As this passage indicates, Erasmus' assessment of his age became twofold after 1520. In the domain of literary culture the Renaissance had passed the point of no return. Erasmus' frequent remarks in his later years that he was being outstripped by the young is a clear sign of his belief in the steady progress of humane studies in the Reformation era. Moreover, Erasmus repeatedly affirmed in the late 1520s that eloquence had reached its pinnacle, not only as happily as he had hoped, but much earlier than he had expected.[59] The remark in many of his letters that learning would tumble into ruin, and civilisation with it, as a result of the Reformation[60] must have struck his contemporaries as an overstatement. As soon as discord or war surfaced anywhere, Erasmus moaned that the end of civilisation was near; but as soon as the threat was over, he cheerfully welcomed the joyful blossoming of true culture.[61] In his perception, the flowering of the humanities had stood the test of time. Under its influence times themselves had changed, giving way to a new and happy epoch in which princes and nobles turned to humane studies after several centuries of neglect, and even women showed competence in Latin.[62] Not only had the products of medieval literature become unsaleable as a result of the rebirth of letters,[63] but Erasmus

---

[58] CWE Ep. 1181:36–41/Allen 30–5.

[59] Allen Epp. 1805:14–9, 1976:17–8.

[60] Cf. e.g. CWE Epp. 1445:12–5/Allen 10–3, 1584:21–5/18–21, 1591:60–3/52–6, 1635:23–38/18–31; Allen Ep. 1944:5–7, 2636:3–9.

[61] Cf. e.g. with regard to the sack of Rome (1527) Allen Epp. 2044:4–6, 2046:24–8 on the one hand; 2423:49–54 on the other.

[62] New and happy epoch: cf. CWE Epp. 1146:5–6/Allen 3–4, 1223:19–20/16, 1237:17–8/14–5, 1238:94/86, 1469:265–7/246–7 (with the remark on women); Allen Epp. 1746:13–4, 2037:177–9, 2046:383–6, 2419:6–10, 2584:26–9. Princes and nobles: cf. *Apologia adversus Sutorem* LB IX 788A, *Spongia* ASD IX-1 200:850–2; CWE Epp. 964:120–4/Allen 110–4, 966:18–23/15–20 (literature is moving from the monasteries to the courts), 1233:106–11/96–102, 1237:15–7/12–4, 1341A:1285–6/Allen I 33:13–4; Allen Epp. 1927:15–20, 2200:17–21, 2299:108–10, 2383:7–19.

[63] Cf. CWE Ep. 1332:8–21/Allen 6–19, dismissing a work of Dionysius the Carthusian, perhaps *De vita et regimine praesulum*: "in these days hardly anything is saleable unless it also breathes all the perfume of the Muses"; dismissing an unknown author: "many things which he repeats from the revelations of St. Bridget as though they could be taken seriously will raise a smile nowadays, I am sure, with every educated reader".

even feigned surprise at still finding readers for his own imperfect writings.[64] Also geographically humanism continued to be triumphant, finally establishing itself in Erasmus' homeland and spreading to countries like Poland, Spain, and Portugal.[65] In the field of good letters, then, the golden age Erasmus had been expecting had materialised. Most notably the Latinity of the age had reached the highest possible standard, so that, in 1530 or 1531, Erasmus could advise the Collegium Trilingue at Louvain to suppress the chair of Latin, which in his view had become superfluous. Like the Collège de France, the Collegium should concentrate on Greek and Hebrew only.[66]

. The blossoming of good letters notwithstanding, Erasmus did think that the Reformation had marred the intellectual climate of his day. Luther had aroused the passions of the last enemies of humane studies, the "monks and theologians." Blaming the Reformation on the rebirth of literary culture (and thus on Erasmus), they now had the opportunity to combat humanism in the name of orthodoxy.[67] In addition, Erasmus increasingly blamed the Protestants for personally disregarding the humanities, even at their own universities. They were only interested in women and pleasure; where Protestantism held sway, literature died out.[68] These grotesque accusations probably issued in part from Erasmus' wish to dissociate humanism from Protestantism so as to escape the charge of having fostered the Reformation. But he may also have been driven to his indictment by his unwillingness to question the axiom that a flowering of good letters would result in peaceful behaviour. Seeing that in the case of

---

[64] Cf. CWE Ep. 1341A:62–3/Allen I 3:11–2.

[65] Low Countries: cf. *Apologia ad Stunicam* ASD IX-2 178:273–81; CWE Epp. 1104:30–6/Allen 28–34, 1237:13–22/10–20, 1238:15–9/11–5, 1411:17–9/15–6, 1467:11/8, 1481:64–5/53–5, 1564:10–3/9–11. Poland: CWE Ep. 1393:22–6/Allen 18–21, Allen Ep. 2584:55–9. Spain: *Apologia ad Caranzam* LB IX 432C; Allen Epp. 1701:1–13, 1875:174–88, 1876:13–5, 1885:28–39 (highlighting Erasmus' own role), 1805:371–4. Portugal: Allen Ep. 3043:94–5. See also *Ciceronianus* CWE 28 428–9/ASD I-2 689–92.

[66] Allen Ep. 2456:14–8. Erasmus proposed not to hire a new Latinist after the retirement of the present one (Conrad Goclenius) but to divide the latter's salary between the professors of Greek and Hebrew. On the continuing progress of Greek studies cf. *De recta pronuntiatione* CWE 26 388/ASD I-4 32:592–4, *Spongia* ASD IX-1 198:800–2, Allen Ep. 2446:137–8.

[67] For this development see Rummel, *The Humanist-Scholastic Debate*, esp. 126–52.

[68] Cf. e.g. *Epistola ad fratres Inferioris Germaniae* ASD IX-1 344:396–7, 396:478–9; CWE Epp. 1514:5–7/Allen 3–5, 1558:316–7/295–6; Allen Epp. 1887:20–1, 1901:14–21, 1973:12–5, 1977:40–3, 2446:72–5, 2615:427–9.

the Lutherans humane studies did not have the expected effect of
"taming the mind"[69] of their adepts, Erasmus may have preferred
to deny that the Lutherans were interested in learning at all rather
than to revise his fundamental views on the civilising effect of a liberal education.

For Erasmus, however, the real trouble caused by the Protestants
was not that they endangered the flowering of humane studies, but
that they made the ensuing restoration of religion and piety more
difficult precisely at the moment that the glory of Christ was "just
beginning to blossom again".[70] Although the "monks and theologians" whose fierce resistance they had provoked could not stem the
recovery of literature any more,[71] they could try to impede humanism from a joyous entry into the faculties of theology, the one discipline it had not been able yet to bring under its control. The
Reformation thus frustrated the completion of Erasmus' project of
reform. The renascence of humane studies was kept from serving
the end for which Erasmus had destined it: the reform of theology
and hence the moral and spiritual revival of Christian society at
large. Through Luther's fault, Christian humanism could only boast
a half success. It had triumphed in the field of letters but was still
wanting in the field of religion. If only this age, Erasmus moaned,
would show as much progress in piety as in eloquence![72] Instead,
the "flourishing state of the ancient tongues and humane studies in
general in every land all the world over" coincided with a climate
of dissension and revolt.[73]

None the less, Erasmus remained firmly convinced that Christian
humanism would eventually triumph. First, he continued to observe

---

[69] For this idea cf. *Antibarbári* CWE 23 64, 76, 81/ASD I-1 87:6–9, 98:13–4,
102:17–8; Allen Ep. 2584:3–8.

[70] *Acta contra Lutherum* CWE 71 101/Ferguson 317.

[71] Cf. CWE Epp. 961:18–9/Allen 14–5, 967:187–8/171–2, 1104:35–6/32–3 (at
Louvain the scholastics "will eventually be overwhelmed by the tide of humane
studies that rises day after day"), 1134:15–7/12–4, 1218:42–3/38–9, 1237:20–2/16–8
(many students at Louvain make progress in literary studies "while the devotees of
ancient ignorance protest in vain"), 1334:960–1/919; Allen Epp. 1909:2–7, 2466:78–81
("nunc sic eluxit linguarum fulgor vt magis operae pretium sit flagrantis iam et
inflammatae iuuentutis studia prouehere quam cum rabulis male feriatis rixari").
But cf. the warnings at Allen Epp. 2136:254–68, 2379:438–42 that barbarism is
not defeated yet.

[72] Allen Epp. 2088:20–1, 2880:21–2.

[73] Cf. CWE Epp. 1465:19–27/Allen 17–23 (cited are lines 20–2/18–9), 1504:
20–3/17–9.

signs of progress in the domain of academic theology after 1520.
Most universities at least tolerated humane studies, with the result
that scholastic theology had lost much of its credit. Erasmus' very
enemies had no choice any more but to consult Scripture and the
fathers,[74] while their style was improving and the knowledge of Greek
was losing its suspicious reputation. One could therefore hope that
"some day there will be a great concord between theology and good
letters".[75] Along with sacred study, piety already showed some amelioration,[76] although Erasmus recognised as late as 1534 that Christian
humanism still had a long way to go:

> If only I could drive the whole church on to where I have tried to
> get it, so that, having shed superstition, hypocrisy, a love for earthly
> things, and frivolous little questions, we could all serve God with sin-
> cere minds, everyone in his own vocation![77]

There was no reason for despair, however. The improvements in
education which Erasmus had witnessed in the course of his own
life, such as the rise of Greek studies in Northern Europe, kindled
his optimism. "Changes like this give me hope", he stated in *De recta
pronuntiatione* (1528). "It may be that every branch of learning can
purge itself of the elements in it which are there for profit or show
rather than for true erudition, and by so doing confine itself to teaching the things which are worth knowing".[78] Resistance in the faculties of theology came mainly from old men who, vainly resisting the
tide of progress, stuck to the outdated forms of learning with which
they had been brought up (ironically Erasmus kept repeating this
charge when he had become an old man himself). But time would
surely outrun them, since all the young and an increasing number

---

[74] Erasmus had some reason to believe this. John Mair (see above p. 80 n. 77)
acknowledged in 1523 that the coming of Protestantism had forced theologians to
get to work on Scripture, which they had neglected before. See James K. Farge,
Orthodoxy and Reform in Early Reformation France: The Faculty of Theology of Paris, 1500–1543
(Leiden 1985), 179–80.

[75] Allen Epp. 1805:51–63 (cited are lines 62–3), cf. 209–13; cf. also *Divinationes ad
notata Bedae* LB IX 477B, *Supputatio* LB IX 520B ("Videmus nunc in Academiis efflo-
rescere aliud Theologorum genus, quibus utrumque doctrinae genus amplexis, multo
certius graviusque iudicium est"), *Apologia adversus rhapsodias Pii* LB IX 1167C–E.

[76] Cf. CWE Ep. 1248:36–8/Allen 30–2 ("it is my joy to see the doctrine of the
Gospels flowering again and as it were kindling into flame. If only I could put as
much strength behind that movement as I wish!"); Allen Epp. 2583:12–4 , 2584:26–9.

[77] Allen Ep. 2899:27–30.

[78] *De recta pronuntiatione* CWE 26 388/ASD I-4 32:594–7.

of elders were won over to humanism.[79] To his satisfaction Erasmus observed the rise of "a new generation of men . . . who are able to defend and promote the cause of literature and religion".[80] As Erasmus knew, as the twig is bent so the tree will grow:

> This new crop will one day spring up and will overwhelm even without a struggle these men who are not merely untaught but unteachable. If we bring up children on the right lines and produce the writings of the Ancients in the light of day, we shall see a gradual fading away of a religion and education in which is neither piety nor culture.[81]

This line of reasoning supported Erasmus' conviction that Christian humanism would create a better world. Success was just a matter of time; one had to await the effects of attrition. Eventually the rebirth of the humanities would lead to a restoration of the *simplicitas studiorum* and hence to a revival of piety.[82] Accordingly, Erasmus continued until his last days to welcome any propitious phenomenon as a sign of the forthcoming recovery of true Christendom. One had good reason to hope for a better future, he wrote in 1529, in view of the advent of several bishops with much piety, sacred learning, and prudent moderation.[83] And although evil was widespread, as he pointed out to Pope Paul III in 1535, one should not despair of a happy solution (*tamen non est desperandus successus*); most human beings, especially those who excelled in learning and dignity, had kept their integrity, and many of those who had been infected by the spirit of strife now felt remorse.[84] Once he even stated that the very hatred against humane studies in his own country was in fact

---

[79] Cf. *Antibarbari* CWE 23 45/ASD I-1 70:29–71:1, *Responsio ad annotationes Lei* LB IX 277F, CWE Ep. 1581:497/Allen 441–2; Allen Epp. 1664:69–70, 1716:34–8; 1828:25–32, 41–3 ("Sed intra paucos annos videbis scenam rerum humanarum inuersam", and the theologians will become as modest as Erasmus); 2037:177–9, 2299:110–3. For the humanists' belief that they were fighting against an older generation, especially at the universities, cf. Rummel, *The Humanist-Scholastic Debate*, 63–72. See also above pp. 65–6.

[80] CWE Ep. 1627:9–11/Allen 5–7, similarly Allen Ep. 2789:17–9.

[81] CWE Ep. 1234:21–5/Allen 18–21.

[82] Cf. *Apologia adversus Sutorem* LB IX 788A ("in omni professione disciplinarum habebimus, et exactius eruditos, et moribus commodioribus"), *Declarationes ad censuras Lutetiae* LB IX 919D–F (defining "simplicitas studiorum" as drawing from the sources and the absence of subtleties).

[83] Allen Ep. 2164:35–8.

[84] Allen Ep. 2988:86–91. Cf. *De recta pronuntiatione* CWE 26 389/ASD I-4 32:603–4: "One must never despair, especially in view of the great change of scene we have already witnessed".

a good omen, since beautiful and lasting achievements had always
been acquired at the cost of much resistance.[85]

True, Erasmus was not always optimistic. One can point to passages in several letters which reflect his doubt about whether the evil
forces in society could ever be defeated and announce his wish to
retire from the world, commending himself to Christ. Leaving humanity to its devices and keeping his own conscience clear, these letters
suggest, Erasmus could only hope for a well-deserved rest in heaven
after his many labours for the benefit of Christian civilisation.[86] But
such moments of apparent resignation never lasted very long. Fundamentally, Erasmus was unable to detach himself from this world.
Being devoted with heart and soul to the restoration of true culture,
he knew (and stated in so many words) that he would never abandon his work but continue to fight for the betterment of the lot of
Christendom until his last breath.[87] Comparing himself to Simeon,
who did not pronounce the phrase *nunc dimittis* until he had seen
Christ (Luke 2:29), Erasmus revealed in one of his last letters that
he would depart from this world in calm "if after so many tempests
in human affairs and so many turmoils of dissent I see tranquillity
restored to the church by divine intervention".[88] Erasmus never really
intended to leave the vale of tears in all its desolation like a true
Christian pilgrim. In a sense, he was the altruist he pretended to
be: he did not work merely for his own salvation, but indeed spent
his energy "for the public prosperity of our time",[89] "for the benefit
of our generation and indeed of posterity".[90] If he deserved a heavenly abode, it was, in his estimation, because of his endeavours to
construct a palace for all Christians on earth. Despite his complaints
about the century in which his old age had been cast,[91] his first concern always remained with the *saeculum*.

---

[85] Allen Ep. 2449:1–4.

[86] Cf. CWE Epp. 1134:35–8/Allen 31–4, 1139:125–31/115–21, 1166:11–7/11–7,
1248:43–5/37–9, 1314:1–5/1–4, 1347:341–6/317–22, 1581:107–13/97–104,
1645:17–22/14–7; Allen Epp. 2260:48–62, 2789:24–6.

[87] Cf. e.g. CWE Ep. 1522:50–3/Allen 45–7: "I do not cease to pursue the same
aim I have always had, that true religion and sound learning might flourish together,
and I lose no opportunity here, if only I might be allowed some success"; Allen
Ep. 1980:18–20: "bonas litteras et pietatem pro mea virili prouehere conabor vsque
ad extremum halitum".

[88] Allen Ep. 2988:5–7; similarly Allen Epp. 1747:1–11, 1819:24–6.

[89] CWE Ep. 686:22–4/Allen 20–2.

[90] CWE Ep. 703:33–4/Allen 29–30.

[91] Cf. e.g. CWE Epp. 1342:786–9/Allen 714–7, 1365:79–80/68–9, 1472:10–2/7–9.

Erasmus' concern with earthly history does not imply, of course, that he regarded history as a purely secular process. Ultimately, all history, and thus all progress as well, was the work of God. In the last decade of his life, Erasmus put his trust increasingly in Providence, repeating what he had only occasionally asserted before, that "one day Christ will grant us better times".[92] The apparent ruin of the church was no reason for despair, Erasmus emphasised, for God would never desert the elect; he only taxed their patience by his apparent absence.[93] Taking recourse to the idea of theodicy, Erasmus insisted that God, as the supreme choreographer of life, brought all events to a happy end, using also the stupidity and evil intentions of human beings for the benefit and the salvation of his people.[94] Thus the tragedy caused by Luther and his followers was perhaps willed by God as a necessary evil in order to arouse the world from its slumber. Did Luther's name in German not sound like "purifier" (*Läuterer*, Dutch *louteraar*)?[95] One might well regard him as God's instrument, sent as a cruel physician to heal the ills of the age. The tumult involved was inevitable; without a drastic medicine, the body would not recover.[96] Eventually the Lutheran trouble might lead to a restoration of ecclesiastical unity and religious truth.[97] Frequently Erasmus called the Wittenberg reformer a scourge of God and compared the troubles in the church (and likewise the wars which struck Christianity, and even the sweating disease which affected Europe in 1529) to the plagues sent by God to the Egyptians or, more generally, as a divine warning to the Christians to mend their ways and not to blame the cause of the disasters of their century on others than themselves.[98] Erasmus' orientation to the *saeculum* is apparent

---

[92] CWE Ep. 1157:14–5/Allen 12; likewise Allen Epp. 1672:143–6, 2361:53–60, 2375:113–4, 2383:7–19. Cf. also Erasmus' view (expressed e.g. at Allen Ep. 2583:15–8) that the deaths of Zwingli and Oecolampadius, shortly after each other, seemed to reveal God's intention to put an end to the troubles of the time.

[93] Cf. Allen Epp. 2136:30–42, 2315:92–5.

[94] Cf. Allen Ep. 2459:10–2 (choreographer, happy end); 1828:67–70, 2443:421–4 (using evil).

[95] Cf. Allen Epp. 1672:30–2, 44ff. (with the observation on Luther's name); 1804:118–20. Cf. also Allen Epp. 1968:48–50, 2868:29–30: at least Luther had taken down the monks a peg or two.

[96] Cf. CWE Epp. 1495:8–12/Allen 7–11, 1515:62–6/57–61, 1522:15/13, 1523:145–9/137–41, 1526:139–45, 200–3/133–9, 190–2; Allen Epp. 1672:94–111, 1805:213–7, 2136:136–43. Cf. also Allen Ep. 2588:7–9: "Mirum est humani ingenii fastidium. Obdormiscit, nisi subinde vel voluptate vel nouitate excitetur".

[97] Cf. *Epistola contra pseudevangelicos* ASD IX-1 302:533–303:593.

[98] Comparison to Egypt: Allen Epp. 1805:223–5, 1925:26–9, 1967:240–4, 2029:40–6,

from these passages as well. From his perspective, the trials of life
on earth were not to be patiently endured by the faithful in expectation of a reward in the hereafter, but should impel them to improve
themselves here and now and to build a better future within the
bonds of earthly history.

Occasionally Erasmus expressed confidence in the historical process
as such, without invoking divine guidance. Time itself would heal
the seemingly incurable afflictions from which Christendom suffered,
he asserted in a letter from 1529;[99] one year later he wrote in the
same vein that time would mitigate, simply by its own progress,
the hatred of the monks against good letters.[100] We have seen in the
previous chapters that Erasmus appears to have regarded the degeneration of learning and piety in the past as a nearly inescapable
development; similarly, he seems to have conceived the future recovery of civilisation as a feature imbedded, as it were, in the plan of
history. In order to sustain his trustful outlook, Erasmus frequently
referred to earlier situations in history when Christianity had been
able to overcome difficulties similar to those which ravaged his times.
The ever decreasing number of true Christians in the present century was not necessarily catastrophic, as he pointed out in one of
his Psalm commentaries (1525). Christians had started as a tiny lot
which grew into a multitude in spite of continuous persecutions;
moreover, one could never know how many true believers were lurking in the dark.[101] Erasmus' favourite historical parallel for his own
times, however, was the age of the emperors Arcadius and Theodosius,
around AD 400. In this age, the church had gone through troubles
which Erasmus sometimes classified as equal to the afflictions of his
own century but more often as worse than these. Not only had a
bewildering number of heretical sects torn apart the Christian world,
affecting many bishops and even the imperial court, but forceful con-

---

2037:324–9, 2134:222–7, 2136:127–30, 2209:187, 2253A:51–9, 2285:11ff.; scourge,
divine warning: *Epistola ad fratres Inferioris Germaniae* ASD IX-1 336:175–6, *Apologia
adversus rhapsodias Pii* LB IX 1128B–C; Allen Epp. 1976:93–5, 1983:42–6, 2030:45–6,
2032:16–20, 2043:25–7, 2134:65–73, 2136:30–8, 2149:42–50, 2164:17–34, 2177:66–7,
2205:34–70; sweating disease: Allen Epp. 2209:184ff., 2223:11–30.

[99] Allen Ep. 2366:53: "Ipsum tempus interdum affert remedium immedicabilibus
malis".

[100] Allen Ep. 2449:7: "hec inuidia paulatim ipso temporis progressu mitiganda".
Cf. CWE Ep. 974:10–1/Allen 7–8: "with the passage of time truth will win the day".

[101] *In psalmum IV concio* CWE 63 268–9/ASD V-2 270:488–9.

tingents of pagan tribes had threatened the faith from outside. Nevertheless the church had triumphed. One should therefore not lose one's hope that the present church would find a way out of its misfortunes as well.[102]

Two basic assumptions concerning the nature of history underlay Erasmus' indestructible optimism. First, he believed that history would continue for a long while. Second, he believed that history could not but develop according to his wishes, progressively realising the project of Christian humanism and eventually bringing its total success. It follows from both assumptions that Erasmus was exempt from the fear of an imminent apocalypse which haunted so many of his contemporaries.[103] Most notably, the Lutherans believed themselves living in the final phase of history. Not until the seventeenth century did they conceive of Luther's recovery of the gospel as the beginning of the modern era. For Luther himself, the Reformation did not usher in a new phase of human history but preluded God's real and definitive Reformation at the end of times.[104] Erasmus, on the other hand, who thought that history would go on and heal the wrongs of the present at some day in the future, expected such a new phase—a "Renaissance era" (naturally he did not employ the term) free from the ills of the medieval past. There is no reason, then, to assume that Erasmus considered human history as a plane without a structural pattern, and sacred history as a superior plane of timeless, unhistorical continuity.[105] In his view, human and sacred history not only coincided but advanced together toward the goal which Christ had set for his followers. It is this conviction which enabled Erasmus to have patience with the evils of his century. He did not have to prepare the world for the Last Judgement, but for an era of general welfare and happiness in which the tares would

---

[102] Cf. *Epistola ad fratres Inferioris Germaniae* ASD IX-1 423:117–425:134; Allen Epp. 2366:39–52, 2383:42–8. Cf. also Allen Epp. 2643:29–33, 95–108 (on the troubles of the church in Basil's time, "non ita multum abhorrentem ab horum temporum statu"); 2651:41–3 (the times of Jerome engendered "similes improborum tumultus" and survived them). See also above p. 28.

[103] Cf. O'Malley, "Introduction", CWE 66 xxiv: "In [Erasmus'] eschatology . . . we read nothing about the cosmic terrors of the 'last day,' the *dies irae*".

[104] Cf. Heiko A. Oberman, *Luther: Mensch zwischen Gott und Teufel* (Berlin 1981), 279–85 esp. 281: "Reformation ist für Luther nicht Wende zur Neuzeit, sondern Anfang der Endzeit"; Mertens, "Mittelalterbilder in der frühen Neuzeit", 41–2, 45ff.; Neddermeyer, *Das Mittelalter in der deutschen Historioraphie*, 36–7.

[105] This is the view of Bietenholz, *History and Biography*, 38.

give way to the wheat in a natural process. History developed toward felicity, provided the good forces in human society took their responsibilities seriously and made every effort to realise an age of gold.

In fact, Erasmus' view of future historical development comes close to the modern idea of progress. The concept of progress is not alien, of course, to Christian thought. But in the traditional Christian view, history is advancing to its dissolution, to be followed in the hereafter by the contemplation of God by the community of the saints. In Erasmus' view, however, history is heading toward perfection on earth. It is not only the medium through which God directs his people toward heaven, but it is itself directed to an almost heavenly end, a universal reign of peace, charity, and true culture. The City of God, though incapable of realising itself on earth, could and would be foreshadowed as closely as possible by the ultimate triumph of Christian humanism. Even in the moments when he longed for heaven himself, Erasmus remained confident of his eventual and lasting worldly success. It was this perspective which for him gave history its sense; without it, earthly existence would be a meaningless chaos.

CHAPTER FIVE

THE NEW TESTAMENT RENEWED

Throughout his life Erasmus kept insisting that the flowering of civilisation which he had inaugurated and which future reformers would complete meant nothing other than a restoration of ancient forms of culture and piety. He emphatically rejected charges that humanism was striving for something new (and thus suspect). In reality, he affirmed, humanist studies were very ancient. They only sought to reclaim the position they had occupied of old. The slanderous accusation of favouring new things applied rather to the medieval-minded accusers themselves. It was the scholastics who had introduced countless novelties in learning and religion; the aim of Erasmus was precisely to recover what they had buried under their newfangled additions[1]—"unless, maybe, 'new' means coming from the century of Origen, and 'old' means what started up three hundred years ago and has gone from bad to worse ever since", as he stated in his *Adagia*.[2] The accusation that he was promising a new theology was unfounded: "I am trying, to the best of my ability, to restore an old theology which until now has been far too widely neglected",[3] as he said in a tract against his critic Jacobus Latomus (1518). Likewise, Erasmus' philological activities represented nothing new but aimed at the restoration of old, respectable products of civilisation by purging

---

[1] *Capita argumentorum* LB VI ***1v, Allen Ep. 1805:54–8; likewise Reeve 219 on John 1:1 "Erat verbum", 270 on John 21:22 "Sic eum volo manere"; *Supputatio* LB IX 527D–E, CWE Ep. 1062:60–1/Allen 55–6, Allen Ep. 1664:59–68. The colloquy *Senatulus* contains an ironic variant of the argument: the women claiming independence from men emphasise that they are not introducing a novelty but restoring a situation of over 1300 years ago, when emperor Heliogabalus installed a women's senate (CWE 40 906–7/ASD I-3 630:20–35). For denunciations of scholastic learning as "new" or "modern" cf. also Reeve 54 on Matt. 11:30 "Iugum meum suave", *Vita Hieronymi* CWE 61 52/Ferguson 178; CWE Epp. 23:98–101, 105–6/Allen 92–6, 99–100; 337:420–1/400–1, 843:645/587, 856:52–3/48–9; Allen Epp. 1679:33–5, 2771:20. For the charge of novelty against humanism, especially in relation to biblical scholarship, cf. Rummel, *The Humanist-Scholastic Debate*, 98–9.

[2] *Adagia* IV v 1 ASD II-7 241:204–6 (cited after Phillips, *The "Adages" of Erasmus*, 378).

[3] *Apologia contra Latomi dialogum* CWE 71 80/LB IX 104A.

them from the blemishes of a later age.[4] Actually the Herculean labour of emending ancient texts "which have been corrupted in various ways through fault of the times and copyists but above all because of the rashness of half-learned and foolhardy men",[5] was more beneficial than producing modern works.[6]

Furthermore, Erasmus maintained that "old" and "new" were only relative terms. In his *Colloquia* he countered the view of a conservative theologian that everything new was to be shunned by not only suggesting that this would imply that one should eat rotten eggs, drink sour wine, and never change shoes or underwear, but also by arguing that "if everything old is good and everything new is bad, whatever's good now was bad once upon a time and what's now bad will some day be good".[7] The work of Thomas Aquinas had also been new in its time, he affirmed in a tract against Pierre Cousturier (1525), as were all things which were now considered old.[8] Sometimes one gets the impression that with Erasmus the term "new" applied to all of his adversaries, not only the scholastics but also the Protestants (he used *nova dogmata* as a synonym for Lutheranism)[9] and the "new sect" of Ciceronians,[10] whereas he employed the adjective "old" to denote anything which fitted the cause of

---

[4] Cf. e.g., with regard to the edition of Jerome, CWE Epp. 541:100–02/Allen 90–1 (some criticise Erasmus "as though I altered what was written by Jerome and did not rather restore what he wrote"), 843:620–1/564–5 ("am I inventing a new Jerome, and not rather restoring the ancient one?").

[5] CWE Ep. 1334:10–2/Allen 4–7; Herculean labour: cf. e.g. *Adagia* II i 1 CWE 33 10/LB II 402F, III i 1 CWE 34 170–82/ASD II-5 23–41; CWE Ep. 396:282–6/Allen 261–6; Allen Epp. 2157:458, 2466:58–74, 2468:45–8.

[6] CWE Ep. 919:24–6/Allen 23–4.

[7] CWE 39 247/ASD I-3 267:19–21. Cf. also below p. 167.

[8] *Apologia adversus Sutorem* LB IX 800E.

[9] Cf. e.g. *Detectio praestigiarum* ASD IX-1 258:598; *Epistola ad fratres Inferioris Germaniae* ASD IX-1 332:80, 340:283, 364:772, 402:584–5, 414:861ff.; *Adversus epistolam non sobriam* ASD IX-1 449:188, CWE Ep. 1385:15–6/Allen 12; Allen Epp. 2134:143, 2410:69–70; 2443:142, 145; 2465:477; 2615:329, 414; 2750:126, 137–8, 150; 2874:119–20, 3122:12. For the designation of the Lutherans as "new gospellers" see *Epistola contra pseudevangelicos* ASD IX-1 291:225, *Epistola ad fratres Inferioris Germaniae* ASD IX-1 394:424, CWE Ep. 1514:5/Allen 4. Cf. also *Paraphrasis ad Galatas* LB VII 943–4 (argumentum) ("novos cultus, & prodigiose insignes"), CWE Ep. 1341A: 1176–7/Allen I 30:32–3 ("the new wine of this modern teaching"); Allen Epp. 2196:128, 2911:8 ("res nouae"). Sometimes he called his Lutheran adversary Gerard Geldenhouwer not Noviomagus ("of Nijmegen") but Novimagus ("magician of new things"), see Allen Epp. 2329:88; 2371:26, 31; 2587:29; 2615:159, 305. At Allen Ep. 2615:129, to Martin Bucer, he calls Catholicism "veterem religionem".

[10] E.g. Allen Epp. 1706:37, 1948:25, cf. 3127:47–50.

humanism, even if it dated from the later Middle Ages. Thus he described the stipulation from canon law promulgated after the Council of Vienne in 1314 and demanding (as Erasmus understood it) university instruction in biblical languages as "a very ancient decree" which unfortunately had been forgotten by posterity.[11]

Many of Erasmus' statements betray, however, that he was aware of the novel character of his ideas of intellectual and religious reform. He sometimes contrasted scholasticism with humanism as the old and new learning respectively,[12] and once referred to his enemies as men "who are so far soaked in the old vinegar that they cannot take my new wine".[13] Those who introduced new but useful things always provoked resistance, Erasmus asserted, just like those who restored what was old.[14] But new ideas *per se* should not cause alarm. After all, universities had been founded for the purpose of coming ever closer to the truth. If certain unknown insights had been revealed to men of fairly recent date like John Duns Scotus, William of Ockham, or Jean Gerson, what would impede the Spirit from disclosing more hidden truths in the present?[15]

The ambivalence of Erasmus' statements as to whether his project of reform implied restoration or renewal is particularly striking with regard to his edition of the New Testament (1516). On the one hand, Erasmus showed great irritation when his adversaries branded him an innovator. Against Nicolaas Baechem, who had attacked him "as though I had produced a modern Gospel, and not rather given the old one new life and light", he retorted in his usual manner, putting the ball back in his opponent's court: "In reality, to him what is new counts as old, and the old is new. All I do is restore the old; I put forward nothing new".[16] Men like Baechem feared losing

---

[11] CWE Ep. 337:733–5/Allen 697–8, cf. above p. 72 with n. 44. See also *Responsio ad annotationes Lei* LB IX 261E: according to Sandeus Felinus (1444–1503) "aliique Jureconsulti veteres", confession was commanded by human law.

[12] Cf. *Responsio ad annotationes Lei* LB IX 279F ("novum hoc studiorum genus" versus "veteris inscitiae"), *Apologia ad Stunicam* ASD IX-2 178:280, CWE Ep. 1238: 45–8/Allen 40–2. Cf. also CWE Epp. 1062:64/Allen 58, 1167:15–9/13–6, opposing the humanists as new guests to the ancient denizens (the scholastics) of the field of theology.

[13] CWE Ep. 1098:16–7/Allen 13–4.

[14] Allen Ep. 1885:66–8.

[15] *Apologia adversus Sutorem* LB IX 759C; CWE Ep. 1581:618–24, cf. 693–6/Allen 557–61, 624–6; see also *Supputatio* LB IX 523F–524A. See also above p. 22.

[16] CWE Ep. 1153:92–3, 208–9/Allen 82–3, 185–6.

their authority "if we read the Scriptures in a corrected text and seek our understanding of them from the fountain-head"; they therefore preferred "widespread ignorance, widespread error in the reading and citation of Holy Writ".[17] On the other hand, Erasmus recognised that his edition had earned ill will by its novelty,[18] and sometimes contrasted his "new" translation with the "old" Vulgate.[19] If it is novelty that offends, he argued in his prefatory material, one should remember that the old (Vulgate) translation had once been new, and that his new translation would become old in the future.[20] His playful qualification of the second edition of 1519 as "the New Testament renewed"[21] may have sounded like self-incrimination to some of his contemporaries.

The question of the novel character of Erasmus' New Testament edition requires more detailed analysis. After all, his engagement with the New Testament, the principal and only absolutely reliable source of *philosophia Christi*,[22] represents the central project of Christian humanism. Did Erasmus really attempt the reconstruction of the original text by undoing its medieval distortions, thus putting forward only a seemingly novel product, or did he aim at innovation?

---

[17] CWE Ep. 967:64–8/Allen 58–61.

[18] Cf. *Capita argumentorum* LB VI **3v ("veriti, ne tantam novitatem non ferrent quidam", but cf. ibid. ***3v: "si quid tumultus fuit, non isthuc peperit novitas, sed quorundam intempestivi clamores apud imperitam multitudinem"); CWE Epp. 373:44–6/Allen 39–42 (preface to the first edition), 407:12–4/10–2, 456:283–5/354–5, 649:10–2/9–10, 996:5–6/3, 1007:19–21/17–9.

[19] Reeve 220 on John 1:1 "Erat verbum", CWE Ep. 1010:9–10/Allen 6–7. It should be noted that Erasmus consistently contradicted Jerome's authorship of the Vulgate translation. Modern scholars believe that Jerome at least translated the gospels. However, Erasmus had good reason to believe that the Vulgate text as it circulated in his day was not Jerome's work, as the text had been corrupted on a large scale. Cf. Bruce M. Metzger, *The Text of the New Testament: Its Transmission, Corruption, and Restoration*, 3d ed. (Oxford 1992), 76.

[20] *Apologia in Novum Testamentum* Holborn 168/LB VI **2v, *Capita argumentorum* LB VI ***1v (adding that it is most stupid to judge something by its age instead of by its intrinsic value: if things should be evaluated according to their age, drunkenness, which dates from antiquity, must be good).

[21] Cf. CWE Epp. 757:26–7/Allen 22 ("the renewal of my New Testament") 758:11–2/9 ("to restore to its novelty the New Testament"), 793:34/33 ("My New Testament has been made new a second time"), 950:43/38–9 ("The New Testament has come out again in its new form"); letter to Hutten, ed. Paul Oskar Kristeller, "Una lettera inedita di Erasmo a Hutten conservata a Firenze", *Tradizione classica e letteratura umanistica*, ed. Roberto Cardini et al. 2 vols. (Rome 1985), 629–41 638:16–7 ("Novum Testamentum prorsus innovatum").

[22] Cf. *In psalmum XXII enarratio triplex* ASD V-2 346:587.

In examining Erasmus' edition of the New Testament we have primarily his Latin translation in view (the priority of Erasmus himself and his contemporaries), not the Greek text facing it. Contrary to what has often been asserted, it was not Erasmus' main intention to edit the Greek text, even though his 1516 edition actually contains the *editio princeps* of the Greek New Testament.[23] Recent scholarship has demonstrated that Erasmus' principal aim was to bring out a revised Latin translation, sustained by a Greek text and annotations.[24] Rejecting the Vulgate, in the form current in his time, as a product of medieval incompetence which obscured the Word of God,[25] Erasmus wished to provide the world with a more suitable Latin version which would bring the faithful back to Christ.[26] To be sure,

---

[23] In fact, the New Testament volume of the so-called Complutensian Polyglot (a Bible edition in several languages, including Greek, prepared at Alcalá) was printed in 1514 already, but only by 1522 was the Polyglot released for publication. See Metzger, *The Text of the New Testament*, 96–8.

[24] See most notably Henk Jan de Jonge, "Novum Testamentum a nobis versum: The Essence of Erasmus' Edition of the New Testament", *Journal of Theological Studies* 35 (1984), 394–413. Rummel, *Erasmus' Annotations*, 20–6 notes that Erasmus originally started his work on the New Testament with the idea of publishing only annotations; later he decided to include a Greek text, and still later he chose to add a Latin translation as well. Still, the final result centred around the Latin translation. Jerry H. Bentley, *Humanists and Holy Writ* (Princeton 1983), 114n.9 objects that Erasmus did not publish a new translation until the second edition of 1519; in 1516 he would have printed a revised Vulgate text. However, the difference is only a matter of degree. Even in the second to fifth editions Erasmus' translation bears the character of a revised Vulgate text, cf. Henk Jan de Jonge, "The Character of Erasmus' Translation of the New Testament as Reflected in His Translation of Hebrews 9", *Journal of Medieval and Renaissance Studies* 14 (1984), 81–7 esp. 82: in his fifth edition (1535) Erasmus retained 60% of the Vulgate text at Heb. 9, in some cases even inadvertently following the Vulgate when his Greek would require a different translation.

[25] Erasmus' controversy with Agostino Steuco (1531) is illuminating of his bias. Steuco had demonstrated that the current Vulgate text offered a more reliable translation of the Hebrew Old Testament than the Greek Septuagint. Although Steuco's conclusions were based on solid philological investigations and a thorough knowledge of Hebrew and Aramaic, Erasmus, who did not have Hebrew, contradicted Steuco as much as he could—obviously unwilling to recognise the superiority of the Vulgate over ancient Greek sources, since in his New Testament edition he had criticised the Vulgate against Greek evidence. See Ronald K. Delph, "Properly Positioning the Polemic: The Steuco/Erasmus Debate" (unpublished paper read at the Sixteenth Century Society Conference, Atlanta, October 1997; cited by kind permission of the author).

[26] Cf. CWE Ep. 384:44–56/Allen 42–53 (preface to the first edition): "our chiefest hope for the restoration and rebuilding of the Christian religion . . . is that all those who profess the Christian philosophy the whole world over should above all absorb the principles laid down by their Founder from the writings of the evangelists and

he based his translation on the Vulgate text:[27] a completely new
translation might have resulted in a text at even greater variance
with the Vulgate. But such a translation would have been different
from the Vulgate without being necessarily better. It is precisely because Erasmus' translation was based on the Vulgate that the deviations from it strike the reader (and were presented by Erasmus) as
corrections. Erasmus' New Testament edition may thus be considered his major attempt to undo what he saw as the harmful influence
of the Middle Ages on the Christian civilisation of his day.

Restoration or Renewal?

In Erasmus' writings, his intention of restoring the original New
Testament figures as the chief legitimation of his enterprise. "We
have merely restored what had been corrupted through the fault of
the times or the copiers", he insisted in the *Apologia* preceding his
edition; "do not condemn what is new, but accept what is more correct".[28] It was certainly not his intention to improve the Bible itself,
as some critics alleged: on the contrary, he sought to restore the
New Testament to its original splendour.[29] He did not find fault with
Matthew or Luke, but "with those whose ignorance or carelessness
has corrupted what those writers set down correctly".[30] His dealings
were only with the flaws of the text, introduced in later times by
translators, scribes, and other irresponsible persons who, apart from
being ignorant, inane, and bold, had been too numerous to be able
to preserve the original wording.[31] "We restore the true reading",
he affirmed in a preliminary piece added to his second edition.[32]
Uncovering "the true, authentic reading" was the purpose of his
philological efforts.[33] The charge of innovation did not apply: "he
who teaches what is right instead of an ingrained error does not

---

apostles . . . And so I have revised the whole New Testament (as they call it) against
the standard of the Greek original".

[27] See above n. 24.

[28] Holborn 170/LB VI **2v.

[29] CWE Ep. 745:34/Allen 31.

[30] CWE Ep. 541:97–99/Allen 87–8.

[31] Cf. e.g. *Apologia in Novum Testamentum* Holborn 166/LB VI **2, *Capita argumentorum* LB VI **4.

[32] *Capita argumentorum* LB VI ***1.

[33] *Apologia contra Latomi dialogum* CWE 71 52/LB IX 88D, cf. Allen Ep. 2807:48–50.

introduce new things but restores the old".[34] Erasmus would do no more than restore to its pristine integrity what had been tainted through human faults. Also, apparent novelties like the reading *sermo* instead of *verbum* at John 1:1 corresponded to the accepted text of the early church and were confirmed by patristic and even medieval tradition.[35]

In the preamble of his annotations on the New Testament Erasmus proudly announced that he had not only purged the text from the stains of ages past but safeguarded it against future corruption:

> What had been depraved is emended, what was obscure is explained, what was ambiguous and confusing is made understandable, what was hideous through an intolerable solecism is restored. And this is done in such a way that the reading is not only purified but cannot be easily depraved by posterity.[36]

Although this passage suggests that Erasmus regarded his text as definitive, he kept revising and correcting his Latin translation, as the five subsequent editions of his New Testament prove, and often referred to his work as a proposal which should stimulate learned discussions and help the future establishment of a standard text on ecclesiastical authority.[37] Yet he also expressed the belief that his translation, by virtue of its restorative character, represented a great leap forward. One should take with a grain of salt his assurance that, for his part, the schools and churches were free to retain the Vulgate, which was merely improved upon rather than pulled up by the roots or weakened by his work.[38] Erasmus did not offer his "recommendations" without engagement; his contemporaries were free

---

[34] Reeve 270 on John 21:22 "Sic eum volo manere".

[35] *Apologia de "In principio erat sermo"* LB IX 121D ("ita verterim ut olim publice legit Ecclesia"). For an evaluation of this translation see Marjorie O'Rourke Boyle, *Erasmus on Language and Method in Theology* (Toronto 1977), esp. 3–31. At 15–8 Boyle discusses Erasmus' use of patristic and medieval authorities; she seems unaware of the confusion between Anselm of Laon and Anselm of Canterbury (cf. above p. 44).

[36] Reeve 1. The preamble appeared in all five editions, but the phrase "what was hideous..." was added in 1519. For similar remarks on the preservation of the work in the future cf. CWE Epp. 373:52–4/Allen 47–9 (preface to the first edition), 860:55–6/51–2. See also Rummel, *Erasmus' Annotations*, 31.

[37] Cf. *Apologia in Novum Testamentum* Holborn 168/LB VI **2v, *Capita argumentorum* LB VI ***1; *Responsio ad annotationes Lei* LB IX 133D, 137C; *Apologia de "In principio erat sermo"* LB IX 112E–F, *Apologia ad Stunicam* ASD IX-2 78:363–5, *Apologia adversus Sutorem* LB IX 752A–C. See also Rummel, *Erasmus' Annotations*, 26–31.

[38] Cf. previous note and Reeve 220 on John 1:1 "Erat verbum"; CWE Epp.

to follow the Vulgate in the sense that they were free to remain blockheads. As he wrote to Pierre Cousturier:

> Those who do not know Latin and are ridiculed in *Epistolae obscurorum virorum* have the New Testament in impure translation . . . Those who take pleasure in a purer form of speech read my version in private.[39]

The same kind of self-assurance occasionally appears in Erasmus' *Annotationes in Novum Testamentum*:

> To be sure, I am not instigating an erasure [of the Vulgate flaw in question] or promoting another version to be read in the churches; I merely indicate the genuine reading on the basis of evidence gathered from texts in both languages and from the interpretations of the most approved doctors of the church. Whoever does not believe the demonstrated truth, then, could perhaps be called obstinate; whoever protests, shameless; whoever disregards the man adducing the proofs, thankless; and whoever does not follow such manifest things, dull.[40]

In sum, the choice between the Vulgate and Erasmus' translation amounted to a choice between ignorance and reason—or between chewing acorns and eating corn, as Erasmus once put it himself.[41] The traditional status of the Vulgate carried little weight with him, as it had slipped into circulation without having ever been officially approved.[42]

Are we to believe, then, that the principles underlying Erasmus' New Testament edition were indeed "entirely restorative and conservative?"[43]

From a modern point of view, Erasmus' claim to have restored

373:199–200/Allen 183 (preface to the first edition), 446:65–71/59–65, 456:86–92/77–82, 860:49–53/44–9; Allen Ep. 2807:27–38. At CWE Ep. 1010:9–10/Allen 6–7 Erasmus even denies "that my new version offered any criticism or correction of the old".

[39] *Apologia adversus Sutorem* LB IX 783D. *Epistolae obscurorum virorum* refers to a collection of forged letters in abominable Latin, composed 1515–7 by the humanist defenders of Johann Reuchlin and purportedly written by Reuchlin's medieval-minded adversaries; on this affair see Heinz Scheible's notice on Reuchlin in *Contemporaries of Erasmus: A Biographical Register of the Renaissance and Reformation*, ed. Peter G. Bietenholz and Thomas B. Deutscher 3 vols. (Toronto 1985–7) III 145–50.

[40] Reeve 270 on John 21:22 "Sic eum volo manere", similarly 4 on Matt. 1:16 "Qui vocatur Christus".

[41] *Capita argumentorum* LB VI ***1v.

[42] Cf. ibid. LB VI **4v; CWE Epp. 337:806–28/Allen 768–89, 456:48–53/40–5. But cf. Allen Ep. 2807:32–8: Erasmus does not criticise the "veterem ac tot seculis receptam versionem" of the New Testament but its corruption in later periods.

[43] Richard Waswo, *Language and Meaning in the Renaissance* (Princeton 1987), 214.

the original New Testament as closely as he could is untenable. Henk Jan de Jonge has pointed out that the Greek manuscripts of the Byzantine church, which Erasmus chose as his criterion in criticising the Vulgate, represent "a relatively late and inferior stage of transmission" in the textual tradition. As a consequence, "one must admit that the Vulgate contained a more reliable text of the New Testament than Erasmus' Greek manuscripts, let alone his new Latin translation". De Jonge hastens to add that, since the relation between Byzantine manuscripts and the Vulgate was unknown in Erasmus' time, one cannot blame Erasmus for his preference of his Greek texts.[44] However, the fact that the aforesaid relation was unknown is something which Erasmus could have taken into consideration. He might have been aware that he could not know the value of his Greek manuscripts, but his typically humanist bias for Greek "sources" over Latin "derivatives" made him act as if he knew everything. In fact, he trusted his Greek manuscripts for the very reason that they departed from the Vulgate. As a rule he assumed that their alternative readings stemmed from an earlier stage of textual transmission while theoretically it was equally probable that he was dealing with deformations of a later age. To justify his preference for deviant Greek readings, he once contended that it was more difficult to corrupt Greek script than Latin.[45] But his most important argument was the assumption, dismissed as a wild tale in modern scholarship, that numerous Greek manuscripts had been emended according to the Vulgate after the council of Ferrara and Florence (1438–9) in order to foster the reunion of the Greek and Roman churches.[46] Consequently, Greek texts

---

[44] Introduction to *Apologia ad Stunicam* ASD IX-2 19–20. See also id., "Novum Testamentum a nobis versum", 408–10; id., "The Character of Erasmus' Translation", 86–7: "Erasmus' translation is a monstrous mixture of [Vulgate] and Byzantine elements . . . Both from an exegetical and a text-critical viewpoint Erasmus' version is a failure. Only linguistically, by the standards of humanistic Latin, is it an improvement". Metzger, *The Text of the New Testament* likewise qualifies Erasmus' principal Greek manuscripts as "rather inferior" (99) and his Greek edition as "inferior in critical value to the Complutensian" and a "debased form of the Greek Testament" which gained "an undeserved pre-eminence" in scholarly tradition (103). But cf. Bentley, *Humanists and Holy Writ*, 173: "There can be no doubt that his [Latin] version reflected the original Greek text more truly than the Vulgate". None the less Bentley concedes in his examination of Erasmus' use of Greek manuscripts (ibid. 125–39) that Erasmus preferred inferior codices.

[45] CWE Ep. 337:803–5/Allen 765–7.

[46] Cf. *Capita argumentorum* LB VI ***1, ***2; Reeve 187 on Luke 10:1 "Et alios septuaginta duos", 527 on 2 Cor. 2:3 "Tristitiam super tristitiam", 531 on 2 Cor. 3:31 "In faciem", 738 on James 1:22 "Et non auditores tantum"; *Apologia ad Stunicam*

which sustained the Vulgate were suspect in Erasmus' eyes, while
he regarded the deviations in other texts as arguments for their reli-
ability. "I would rather put my trust in a Greek manuscript that
does not agree in everything with ours", he wrote to his critic Zúñiga;
correcting the Greek on the basis of the Latin would be turning
matters upside down.[47] It would seem, then, that Erasmus was deceived
not so much by an excusable ignorance with regard to the Greek
manuscript tradition as by his eagerness to accept and present as
authentic all textual evidence which permitted him to formulate a
translation different from the Vulgate.[48]

The same eagerness characterises Erasmus' treatment of the Latin
textual tradition. He continually stressed that the Latin manuscripts
which corroborated his deviations from the Vulgate reading were
"old", "very old", or "extremely old", but never gave precise indi-

---

ASD IX-2 192:503–5 with n., 258:542–4; *Apologia adversus monachos hispanos* LB IX
1049C–D (dismissing the actually superior codex now at Basel, University Library
A.N. IV.2, which dates from the 12th c., cf. Bentley, *Humanists and Holy Writ*, 130).
At Allen Ep. 2905:39–45 Erasmus maintains that a *bulla aurea* proved his assumption; at 40–1n. Allen identifies this as a (mistaken) reference to *Aurea bulla domini
imperatoris graecorum lecta in sessione publica et congregatione generali*, dated November 1435,
cf. *Conciliorum quatuor generalium . . . tomus primus; Tomus secundus aliorum aliquot conciliorum generalium* 2 vols. (Cologne 1530) II fol. 168r–v. Sepúlveda, the recipient of Ep.
2905, informed Erasmus at Allen Ep. 2938:99–100 that no golden bull mentioned
the subject. In his reply, Allen Ep. 2951:49–57, Erasmus admitted not having read
the bull; Cuthbert Tunstall told him about the emendations in question. See also
Bentley, *Humanists and Holy Writ*, 135.

[47] *Apologia ad Stunicam* ASD IX-2 192:506–7, 166:51–3. Erasmus' words invalidate his claim at *Responsio ad annotationes Lei* LB IX 246D that he only puts trust
in Greek manuscripts if they are supported by the facts, Latin manuscripts, or
exegetical writings in both languages.

[48] Cf. De Jonge, "Novum Testamentum a nobis versum", 410: "For his purpose
a not too scrupulously prepared Greek text was adequate. The quality of the edition of the Greek made little difference, as long as it could serve to justify the
choice of wording and phraseology of the Latin translation". But the justification
would only work if the Greek text was presented as authentic. Cf. Erasmus' comment on the preparation of his first edition at CWE Ep. 348:13–4/Allen 10–2: "In
the press is also the New Testament in Greek, *as it was written by the apostles*, and
in Latin, as translated by me" (my italics). De Jonge, "The Character of Erasmus'
Translation", 85–6 notes that sometimes Erasmus consciously replaced probably
superior Vulgate readings with alternatives based on his Greek manuscripts, since
he had undertaken to translate whatever his Greek codices might give. Yet he sometimes adapted his Greek text to suit his Latin translation, not only in one notori-
ous case (in 1516 he added the last six verses of Apoc., which were missing in his
Greek manuscripts, to his Greek text in his own translation from Latin) but also
in other passages, sometimes introducing novel readings which became part of the
so-called Textus Receptus in the West, see Metzger, *The Text of the New Testament*,
99–100.

[handwritten marginalia: Vulgate readings, acc to Metzger]

[handwritten annotation:) in Rev, acc. to Metzger, and elsewhere (e.g. Acts 9:6)]

cations as to their dating. In the final version (1535) of his annotations on Matthew, for example, the adjective he used most frequently to designate his codices is *vetusti*; besides, one finds the qualifications *vetustiores*, *pervestusti*, and *vetustissimi*. Likewise, *antiqui* occurs along with *antiquissimi*. But nowhere does Erasmus explain what criteria a codex has to meet in order to earn one of these epithets or what his comparatives and superlatives stand for. The same thing holds for his recurrent use of the qualifications *emendatus* and *emendatior*. Strikingly, Erasmus employed the adjective *vetus* not only for manuscripts but also for a printed text in his possession which on no account can have originated before the middle of the fifteenth century, whereas his aim was to retrieve textual errors which had crept in during the last thirteen hundred years![49] Only once in his annotations on Matthew did Erasmus give more specific information: his four manuscripts from St. Donatian's chapter at Bruges would be over eight hundred years old, as the notes on some of them proved.[50] Since the manuscripts are now lost[51] one cannot verify Erasmus' statement, but considering that in a treatise against Zúñiga he referred to the same codices as being "so old that they could seem to have been written in the time of Jerome",[52] extending their age by three centuries, one must concede that he did not shrink from exaggerations. The fact that Erasmus took the Carolingian minuscule for an invention of antiquity, as we have seen in Chapter One, and likewise considered parchment (the usual writing material of the Middle Ages) typical of ancient books,[53] may also have encouraged him to antedate his materials.

---

[49] His references to a book "vetustae/veteris typographiae" were all inserted in 1527, cf. Reeve 109 on Matt. 27:34+ "Ut impleretur quod", 118 on Mark 2:2 "Nec ad ianuam", 118 on Mark 2:17 "Vocare iustos", 134 on Mark 8:38 "Qui enim me confessus", 156 on Luke 1:45 "Et beata quae credidisti", 205 on Luke 19:30 "In castellum quod contra vos est". The Bible was first printed between 1450 and 1456 at the press of Johann Gutenberg in Mainz, cf. Metzger, *The Text of the New Testament*, 95. Thirteen hundred years: cf. *Capita argumentorum* LB VI ***1 (purging the Bible text "non contigit post annos mille trecentos, nec fortassis unquam continget ad plenum", but Erasmus has done it as thoroughly as possible).

[50] Reeve 22 on Matt. 3:16 "Baptizatus autem Iesus".

[51] Cf. Bentley, *Humanists and Holy Writ*, 136. Also Erasmus' manuscript borrowed from St. Bavo's chapter at Ghent is now lost (ibid.), so that one cannot verify his statement at *Apologia adversus Sutorem* LB IX 766F that it had been used by St. Livinus (who, according to legend, had died in 657).

[52] ASD IX-2 256:510.

[53] *Apologia ad Stunicam* ASD IX-2 232:134, but cf. *De recta pronuntiatione* CWE 26 397/ASD I-4 39:849–52: the ancients wrote on waxed tablets (and on leaves, bark, and cloth); we use paper or parchment.

Thus, whereas Erasmus suggested—and probably believed in earnest—that he was checking the (corrupt) medieval Vulgate text against (pure) ancient versions, what he really did was compare several medieval texts with each other[54] and opt as a rule for those readings which allowed him to depart from the Vulgate. The majority of the Latin texts he consulted might not have been much older than the Vulgate, but his conviction that the latter text was corrupt usually made him accept suitable alternative readings as older and better ones, unless proof to the contrary was adduced (among others by his Catholic critics, who in some instances made him restore the Vulgate reading in his own translation).

Another striking feature of Erasmus' textual criticism is his tendency to regard erasures or additions in his manuscripts which corresponded to the Vulgate as interventions of later times, sprung from deliberate attempts to bring old and good texts in accordance with the corrupt version of the Middle Ages. To be sure, Erasmus was often right. Many, if not the majority of his emendations are accepted today even in the Catholic church.[55] But what is relevant to our argument is his assumption that textual changes in keeping with the Vulgate, which theoretically could result from a revision of the codex in question against more reliable material, were corruptions, unless, again, the opposite case was made evident.

All this is not to deny that Erasmus' edition of the New Testament constituted a major contribution to biblical philology and exegesis. Our present interest is only with the characterisation of his edition

---

[54] This holds also for his Greek text, cf. De Jonge, "Novum Testamentum a nobis versum", 408: "It was based on recent manuscripts . . . which Erasmus nevertheless described as *vetustissimi*". Erasmus' treatment of two Greek manuscripts from the 12th c. lent to him by Johann Reuchlin is most significant. He dismissed one of these manuscripts because of its alleged emendation according to the Vulgate after the Council of Ferrara and Florence (see above n. 46), thus implicitly dating it at the middle of the 15th c. or later. The other manuscript (now Schloß Harburg, Donauwörth, Öttingen-Wallersteinsche Bibliothek I 1 40 1; cf. CWE Ep. 384 headnote) might well date, according to Erasmus, from apostolic times (see Reeve 778 on Apoc. 3:7 "Qui aperit et nemo claudit"). We have therefore some reason to suspect that Erasmus dated his manuscripts as it suited him, situating codices from the same period at the beginning of Christian tradition if they deviated from the Vulgate, and at the end of tradition if they corresponded to it.

[55] The majority of the over 200 emendations attacked by Edward Lee and defended by Erasmus in *Responsio ad annotationes Lei* are accepted in the most recent officially promulgated version of the Vulgate, *Nova vulgata Bibliorum Sacrorum editio* (Vatican City 1979), commonly called *Neovulgata*. See the relevant notes in CWE 72 (forthcoming).

as a restorative enterprise. It would seem that Erasmus' editorial practice, rather than restorative and conservative, was eclectic and innovative. His bias against the Vulgate prevented him from being sufficiently cautious about accepting deviant readings. Scrutinising all textual variants available to him for readings which diverged from the Vulgate, he endeavoured to assemble a version strikingly different from the current translation. What he thus produced was not the authentic text, but a Counter-Vulgate of his own making. Possibly Erasmus' conviction that the Vulgate was corrupt made him assume in good faith that his own version came closer to the original Greek of the apostles. However, some of the arguments he used to justify his enterprise reveal that he was consciously working at the renewal of the New Testament text rather than at its restoration.

To begin with, Erasmus questioned the existence of an original text. He admitted that nobody could know what exactly the apostles had written, since both the Greek and the Latin textual traditions were inconsistent.[56] In every century scribes had introduced flaws when copying the texts, Erasmus observed, so that a modern editor had to make choices according to his own insights.[57] Erasmus' observation was correct, but it weakened his claim to restore the original text. What could restoration mean if in the course of the centuries the original text had vanished in an ocean of variants? Doubts about the true reading could only be solved "through consulting the archetypes", as Erasmus pointed out to his opponent Pierre Cousturier.[58] But what if the archetypes had disappeared? Moreover, Erasmus recognised the possibility that the evangelists, by writing Greek, had transformed the words pronounced by Jesus in Hebrew,[59] which would have hampered the reconstruction of God's message to mankind even if the original gospel texts had been extant.

The argument that different versions of the New Testament had existed from the outset recurs frequently in Erasmus' apologetic writings. He used it notably to refute the charge that by bringing out

---

[56] Cf. *Responsio ad annotationes Lei* LB IX 126B: "Si nobis compertum esset, quid esset scriptum ab Apostolis et Euangelistis, impius profecto foret, qui vel apicem conaretur immutare: nunc cum nec Graecorum codices, nec Latini satis inter se consentiant, cum quotidie depraventur a Librariis, velimus nolimus aliquid est immutandum nonnunquam".

[57] Cf. *Apologia in Novum Testamentum* Holborn 166–7/LB VI **2v. See also previous note.

[58] *Apologia adversus Sutorem* LB IX 773A.

[59] Cf. *Responsio ad annotationes Lei* LB IX 245A.

a new version of the text he was undermining the authority of the
Bible or opening the door to heterodox interpretations. From the
times of the earliest fathers to the present, Erasmus insisted, Greek
and Latin texts had diverged from each other. Not a single extant
codex was flawless, and yet this had never resulted in religious discord. In flagrant contradiction to his assertions (advanced in the very
same writings in order to stress the utility of his edition) that the
difference between orthodoxy and heresy could depend on a comma
and that the flaws of the Vulgate endangered the Catholic truth,[60]
Erasmus maintained that "nowhere is the degree of variation great
enough to imperil the orthodox faith".[61] Errors, heresies, and schisms
had not emerged from different scriptural texts, but from different
interpretations of the same text. Consequently his new translation
did not present any danger to the church. As he asserted in the
Apologia prefacing his edition:

> In what way has the Christian religion been affected by the fact that
> for so many centuries Jerome has read one thing, Cyprian another,
> Hilary still another, Ambrose a fourth thing, Augustine a fifth? With
> those authors you will not only discern divergent readings but conflicting
> ones, although they agreed on the main points of the Christian faith . . .
> What will you do, considering that not even the edition used in these
> times is in all respects internally consistent? . . . And yet during all
> those centuries the authority of Scripture has stood firm.[62]

---

[60] *Apologia in Novum Testamentum* Holborn 172/LB VI **3: "Quid minutius
hypostygma? At tantula res haereticum gignit sensum"; *Responsio ad annotationes Lei*
LB IX 244E: "At Leus negat esse crimen, si interpres vitiata lectione deceptus,
secus interpretetur quam oportet, modo citra damnum ullum veritatis catholicae.
Verum si id passim ignoscemus interpreti, an existimamus nullum esse damnum
veritatis catholicae?"

[61] CWE Ep. 860:68–9/Allen 63–4. Erasmus likewise trivialises the significance of
textual flaws at Reeve 14 on Matt. 2:6 "Et tu Bethlehem", *Apologia adversus Sutorem*
LB IX 773Eff., CWE Ep. 337:860–3/Allen 820–3 ("Nor can there be any danger
that everybody will forthwith abandon Christ if the news happens to get out that
some passage has been found in Scripture which an ignorant or sleepy scribe has
miscopied or some unknown translator has rendered inadequately").

[62] *Apologia in Novum Testamentum* Holborn 166–7/LB VI **2r–v, likewise *Capita
argumentorum* LB VI ***1 ("Si varietas abrogat fidem libris, jam olim variabant codices
aetate Origenis, aetate Hieronymi, aetate Bedae, aetate Thomae, denique nostris
etiam temporibus hodieque variant, et tamen adhuc sacris Libris sua constat auctoritas"), *Apologia invectivis Lei* Ferguson 272–3 ("Aliter legit Augustinus, aliter Ambrosius,
aliter Cyprianus. Ipse Hieronymus non semper eadem legit. Quid hinc ortum est
discriminis religioni Christianae?", cf. ibid. 274), *Responsio ad annotationes Lei* LB IX
127B ("aetate Origenis variabant Graecorum Exemplaria, temporibus Ambrosii et
Augustini variabant Exemplaria, variant et hodie non paucis in locis, nec vacillat
tamen auctoritas divinae Scripturae").

He voiced the same thought in several controversies with Catholic critics:

> We have various translations of the Psalter. What sort of evil has resulted from it? As for the Epistles of Paul, we have Ambrose's translation which is different from our Vulgate. Where are those schisms? . . . Surely no more danger has originated from the multitude of translations than from the multitude of commentaries.[63]

Erasmus did not seem to notice that his often repeated argument not only implied a recognition of the novel character of his edition, as it reflected his own selection among a wide diversity of possible readings, but also reduced the usefulness of his work. If the proliferation and unremitting corruption of Bible texts did not do any serious harm to its contents, what was the point of correcting the New Testament, even supposing that the archetypes were accessible? True, Erasmus insisted that many fathers and medieval commentators had made mistakes on the basis of textual corruptions.[64] But at the same time he asserted that the church would not perish on account of flaws in the New Testament text, not even in case of deformations introduced on purpose by malign heretics.[65] One might infer from these words that apparently religion could get along very well without the aid of languages and literary studies—an inference which would undermine the very idea of Christian humanism.

In one of his Psalm commentaries Erasmus even went so far as to state that the corruption of Bible texts was not only harmless to piety but could strengthen it. God allowed the development of deviant readings in the course of history

> so that these extra difficulties would rouse us from our torpor. Salvation is not imperilled by a slight departure from the original sense of Scripture, so long as the new reading conforms to piety and truth; even if our interpretation does not entirely fit into its original context, our labours will have been worthwhile if our reading contributes to moral improvement, and fits in with other scriptural texts.[66]

---

[63] *Apologia adversus Sutorem* LB IX 777A–B, likewise 799B–C; cf. *Responsio ad annotationes Lei* LB IX 247E: "Sed unde existerunt Graecorum haereses? An ex lectionis varietate. Nequaquam, sed ex diversa interpretatione".

[64] Cf. e.g. *Apologia in Novum Testamentum* Holborn 171/LB VI **3, *Capita argumentorum* LB VI ***2; see also *Soloecismi* LB VI *5r–v, *Loca obscura* LB VI *6r–v, and *Loca manifeste deprauata* LB VI *6v–*7r which list the most striking mistakes discussed in *Annotationes in Novum Testamentum*.

[65] Cf. *Apologia invectivis Lei* Ferguson 278.

[66] *In psalmum IV concio* CWE 70 239–40/ASD V-2 246:723–7.

In the *Apologia* to his New Testament Erasmus asserted, moreover, that the apostles themselves had scarcely been interested in textual purity. "Unconcerned with letters and accents", they had quoted from the Septuagint, Hebrew sources, and their own memories in the form which had seemed fit to them, not being so superstitious as to consider accuracy in citations from Scripture absolutely necessary.[67] Erasmus said this in order to justify his editorial decisions, but the same argument would, ironically, invalidate his own philological diligence. Moreover, the evangelists, according to Erasmus, had been human beings liable to error. He attributed a number of flaws and inconsistencies in their Old Testament quotations to their defective memories, assuming that by some unfathomable strategy God had permitted them to make mistakes which were unessential to faith but would eventually strengthen it. Only Christ had been utterly infallible.[68] But did Erasmus' smooth and thoughtful translation not run the risk, then, of departing from apostolic discourse rather than to get closer to it?

Still more remarkable are Erasmus' observations on apostolic style. In his opinion, Christ as well as his apostles had used corrupt language. Christ had spoken to the people in their own Hebrew dialect, contaminated by Syriac and Chaldean.[69] Likewise, the apostles had expressed themselves in popular, flawed, and awkward Greek, affected by other languages because of its wide diffusion. Among the evangelists, Luke had shown the best command of Greek, but even he had written in a poor style, tainted by Hebrew.[70] Moreover, the

---

[67] Holborn 169/LB VI **2v.

[68] Cf. Reeve 13–4 on Matt. 2:6 "Et tu Bethlehem", 107 on Matt. 27:8+ "Ager ille Acheldemach", 114 on Mark 1:2 "In Esaia propheta", 298 on Acts 10:38 "Quomodo unxit eum"; CWE Ep. 844:36–54/Allen 29–47. Cf. *Enarratio psalmi XXXIII* ASD V-3 108:486–96: inconsistencies in the Bible text which are not the result of scribal errors are signs of hidden mysteries, for the understanding of which we must pray. See also Rummel, *Erasmus' Annotations*, 136–42.

[69] Cf. Reeve 28 on Matt. 5:22 "Qui dixerit fratri suo racha", 125 on Mark 5:14 "Puella tibi dico", 299 on Acts 10:38 "Quomodo unxit eum"; *Responsio ad collationes gerontodidascali* LB IX 967A, Allen Ep. 2206:42–4.

[70] Cf. Reeve 148 on Luke 1:1 "Quoniamquidem", 298–300 on Acts 10:38 "Quomodo unxit eum"; *Responsio ad annotationes Lei* LB IX 208B–D, *Responsio ad collationes gerontodidascali* LB IX 966F–967A, Allen Ep. 2206:35–42. But at Reeve 588 on Gal. 6:1 "Considerans teipsum", 602 on Eph. 3:13 "Quae est gloria" Erasmus defends Paul against Jerome's charge of displaying a bad command of Greek; see also Rummel, *Erasmus' Annotations*, 99–100; id., "God and Solecism: Erasmus as a Literary Critic of the Bible", *Erasmus of Rotterdam Society Yearbook* 7 (1987), 54–72:65–6.

apostles, like all speakers of Greek, had distorted Latin loan words.[71] Erasmus emphasised, however, that their use of popular and corrupt speech had been appropriate in their time. Originally the New Testament was not addressed to the learned, Erasmus explained, but to cobblers, sailors, wagoners, weavers, pimps, and brothel keepers.[72] In order to be expedient, then, the language of the apostles had to be "not only unpolished and uncouth, but even faulty, freakish, and sometimes plainly ungrammatical". In addition, God willed that the people were won over to Christendom without the aid of human eloquence. The speech of the apostles had to be just as simple and uncultivated as their way of life, so that they would gain authority only by their spirit, not by rhetorical tricks, lest converts be attracted for improper reasons.[73]

also an argument of Paul

The idea of expedient language provided Erasmus with an important argument in favour of his own translation. Every epoch, Erasmus reasoned, had its own requirements of style. Just as the apostles had written in accordance with their times and their audience, so had Erasmus. It was his responsibility as a translator, he affirmed in a prefatory treatise included from the second edition, to use such language as would make his readers receptive to the word of God:

> For those times perhaps it was useful that the discourse of the apostles was rather unrefined; now it may be profitable to change it (*nunc expediat mutari*) ... In those days it was fitting that the apostles used the kind of speech that was most widely divulged and understood by the literate and the illiterate alike ... Thus, as formerly the apostles made use of the language which they found to be most familiar to the people, so it would now be appropriate to translate Holy Scripture into the idiom familiar to all learned Latin speakers.[74]

In a published letter of 1518 he put it thus:

> That countrified and simple style in which the New Testament was left to us by the apostles suited those early days; nowadays perhaps it

---

[71] Reeve 142 on Mark 14:3 "Nardi spicati", cf. 299 on Acts 10:38 "Quomodo unxit eum".

[72] Cf. *Apologia adversus Stunicam* LB IX 399D–E, *Responsio ad collationes gerontodidascali* LB IX 966F, CWE Ep. 1304:158–61/Allen 140–2.

[73] Reeve 298–9 on Acts 10:38 "Quomodo unxit eum", likewise *Antibarbari* CWE 23 113/ASD I-1 130:11–4, Allen Ep. 2315:65–8; cf. also *Supputatio* LB IX 530C.

[74] *Capita argumentorum* LB VI **4. Cf. *Supputatio* LB IX 658C: "Sic pro illo tempore decebat Apostolum scribere, me Paraphrasten decet aliter scribere, praesertim hisce temporibus".

is fitting that we should have it in neater dress, provided it be simple still.[75]

The same idea occurs in the preface, addressed to Pope Adrian VI, of Erasmus' edition of Arnobius (1522):

In those days it was advisable to write like that, because one was writing for the common people; and in the same way it is folly now to parade one's blunders, which are no help to those who are not educated and a stumbling-block to those who are, and which obscure the meaning and reduce the influence the writer can exert.[76]

The common people, Erasmus argued, did not read Latin or Greek any more and would have more profit from translations into the vernacular. The Latin translation should be adapted to the standards of the audience which was left for it, that is, the learned, who had recently become used again to classical eloquence. A popular, awkward translation no longer served anybody: "what we need is a simple, yet pure and spotless Latin, to do justice to the reputation of the Gospel and the propagation of its teaching".[77]

The argument of expediency was compelling, although one could ask why it was no longer appropriate to win people over to Christ's teaching solely by a truly religious spirit. The translations of the gospel into French and German proved, after all, that "a good law can be written in a barbarous language".[78] But more important for our present concern is that Erasmus' argument implies a renunciation of the claim that his translation restored the original text of the New Testament. Erasmus' objective was to *change* the original text, as the passages quoted above make clear, tackling not only the supposed errors of the translator and medieval scribes but apostolic idiom itself, which had become unendurable in his times.[79] Rather

---

[75] CWE Ep. 843:259–61/Allen 231–3.

[76] CWE Ep. 1304:165–9/Allen 146–9.

[77] *Apologia ad Stunicam* ASD IX-2 76:314–7. For Erasmus' argument that in his day an aesthetic appeal could serve a pious purpose cf. also Erika Rummel, *Erasmus as a Translator of the Classics* (Toronto 1985), 92–3; id., "God and Solecism", esp. 67–8.

[78] *Apologia contra Latomi dialogum* CWE 71 45/LB IX 84D.

[79] Cf. CWE Ep. 843:29–40/Allen 26–36: although Erasmus leaves the Vulgate "intact and untouched", he has been "correcting anything corrupt, explaining ambiguities, elucidating obscurities, and changing anything that is notably barbarous in expression, because I understand that very many people are so disgusted by the prodigious errors (which however are nearly always the translator's work and not

than restore the text to its pristine ineptitude, Erasmus intended to depart from the rustic speech of the apostles and to elevate his translation to the standards of Latinity of his own day—standards which had risen, in his perception, thanks to his own efforts. Implicitly he admitted that it was actually the Vulgate translator who had been more faithful to the character of the original text, rendering the speech of the apostles in a simple Latin which like their Greek was corrupted by its wide diffusion and fit for preaching to the populace but not to the learned:

> The language of the apostles, we may be sure, was the kind of thing in which they have given us the New Testament in writing. That was how wagoners and sailors talked then. Such was the language in which the books of the New Testament were first translated into Latin; and if there are blunders in them which nowadays offend an educated ear, they should be ascribed to the customary practice of those distant days rather than to the translator's lack of skill.[80]

The practice of Erasmus' own day, however, asked for a different method:

> The translator rendered the text in this way as a concession to the inexperienced people at a time when the gospel was read by all laymen, when it was recited by farmers at the plough, by cobblers in the shop, and by women at the loom, because Latin was the common language of all . . . Today life is different and requires a different approach.[81]

---

the author's) that they cannot bring themselves to read the Scriptures. Nor for that matter have all mortals such an iron digestion that they can endure the style of it. But if we simplify our language for the benefit of ignorant and simple folk, should we not help educated readers too by purifying the language?" True enough, Erasmus blames first of all the translator, but cf. next note.

[80] CWE Ep. 1304:158–65/Allen 140–6. Cf. also *Responsio ad collationes gerontodidascali* LB IX 966F–967B: "Quod si tum Lingua Graecorum tam fuisset corrupta, quam est hodie . . . opinor [Apostolos] ea lingua fuisse usuros . . . Sic et Interpres Latina, quem arbitror fuisse primum, ea Lingua vertit, quae viris, pueris, mulierculis, et infimae plebi tum erat communis"; *Capita argumentorum* LB VI **4: "Tametsi videtur hic Interpres magis incogitantia peccasse, quam imperitia, multaque tribuisse vulgo idiotarum, quibus ista tum scribebantur"; *Annotationes in Novum Testamentum* CWE 56 82–3/Reeve 355 on Rom. 2:15 "Cogitationum accusantium": "In my opinion the best excuse we can make for the Translator is to say that in his day the common people were accustomed to speak thus in imitation of the Greeks; and it was they rather than the educated whom he endeavoured to serve". The point was also made by Erasmus' adversaries, e.g. Frans Titelmans, cf. Erika Rummel, *Erasmus and His Catholic Critics* 2 vols. (Nieuwkoop 1989) II 17.

[81] *Responsio ad annotationes Lei* LB IX 137C–D.

In the age of humanism the flawed Greek of the apostles was to be rendered in good Latin, Erasmus believed. His translation seems indeed to measure up to this idea. Erika Rummel confirms that Erasmus, being clearly uncomfortable with non-classical speech, not only expunged unidiomatic expressions but introduced changes in the New Testament text for the sake of improving its literary quality.[82] One cannot therefore agree with Erasmus' often repeated contention that he did not add any rhetorical flourishes to his translation but rather preserved the simplicity of apostolic speech, merely purging it of solecisms and coming to the aid of the reader in case of awkward wording (formulas which still reveal his intention of modernising the text).[83] This characterisation would perhaps hold, if at all, for his first edition, which offered a comparatively moderate revision of the Vulgate text, but not for the subsequent editions which presented a thoroughly redressed translation. More to the point would seem his later remark: "I have tried to add rhetorical splendour to the New Testament".[84] Still, Erasmus condoned certain stylistic peculiarities in the gospels, and in his later editions of the New Testament, especially when he thought the wording too entrenched to be changed without causing a stir.[85] Probably his indulgence stemmed not so much from his heart as from his wish to anticipate attacks by his Catholic critics who invariably insisted on maintaining the peculiar idiom of Scripture.[86]

A passage from Erasmus' commentary on the first Psalm (1515) indicates that in his dealings with sacred texts he believed in steering a middle course:

> I have not said this because I want my Doctor of the church to frolic among the flowers of rhetoric. I am not asking him to use extrava-

---

[82] Rummel, *Erasmus' Annotations*, 97–105.

[83] Cf. e.g. *Apologia ad annotationes Lei* LB IX 181A, 182D, 208C; CWE Epp. 446:65–71/Allen 59–65, 860:35–46/32–42, 1010:14–7/10–2; Allen Ep. 1891:100–02. Cf. also *Apologia in Novum Testamentum* Holborn 173/LB VI **3, *Capita argumentorum* LB VI **3v for the statement that God (having changed his mind, apparently, since the first days of Christendom) was not pleased with solecisms.

[84] *Apologia adversus Sutorem* LB IX 783F.

[85] Cf. *Capita argumentorum* LB VI **3v; Reeve 50 on Matt. 10:41 "In nomine prophetae", 155 on Luke 1:28 "Benedicta tu", 262 on John 16:23–4 "In nomine meo". See also Rummel, *Erasmus as a Translator*, 91; id., *Erasmus' Annotations*, 31. But cf. Rummel, *Erasmus as a Translator*, 100: Erasmus was "an uncompromising biblical translator. Rarely did regard for audience reaction lead him to diverge from his principles".

[86] See Rummel, *Erasmus and His Catholic Critics*, passim.

gant embellishment, but on the other hand I cannot abide shoddy language. I would not want Christ's teaching to be corrupted by meretricious eloquence, but equally I would not want it to be disfigured by tawdry words and images.[87]

The passage reveals that, his qualifications notwithstanding, Erasmus insisted on eloquence, in obvious contrast to the apostles themselves.

It seems safe to conclude that it was Erasmus' aesthetic fastidiousness rather than a concern for the original text which drove him to compose a new-fashioned translation of the New Testament—new-fashioned in the sense that it departed on purpose from the rustic original. Measured by Erasmus' own standards, his translation was an innovation which not only did not stem from the apostolic age but would not even have been appropriate to it on account of its very neatness. His "restoration to new lustre"[88] of the New Testament resulted in a translation in accordance with apostolic speech not as it had been, but as it should have been had the apostles addressed themselves to an audience which, thanks to an Erasmian education, had developed an exquisite literary taste.

What is more, the nature of Erasmus' edition challenges the basic assumptions of Christian humanism. In the case of the New Testament it appears not to be true that the rebirth of letters would bring the Christian world closer to the sources of faith and hence to genuine piety. Instead, the sources of faith themselves had to be adapted in

---

[87] *Enarratio in primum psalmum* CWE 63 47/ASD V-2 67:41–5. Erasmus refers to theological writings in general (pointing to the scholastics as those who diffuse filthy speech), but his words would also apply to the translation of Bible texts. See also CWE Ep. 1304:153–5/Allen 135–7: "even now a neat and simple style is not to be despised in a Christian author, provided the absence of rhetoric and claptrap is matched by an absence, on the other side, of meanness". For Erasmus' middle course as a translator cf. Bentley, *Humanists and Holy Writ*, 164 and the assessments of Rummel, *Erasmus as a Translator*, 89–102; id., *Erasmus' Annotations*, 89–121. Rummel believes that in translating the Greek classics Erasmus had little difficulty with altering form as well as content for stylistic reasons, often imposing his own taste on the original; in dealing with the New Testament he showed more restraint. Nevertheless his concern for correct idiom and clarity of expression outweighed his ideal of fidelity and made him depart occasionally from the Greek text (as he had reconstructed it).

[88] I have borrowed this phrase from Engelina B.F. Pey, *Herstel in nieuwe luister. Ideeën en praktijk van overheid, kerk en architecten bij de restauratie van het middeleeuwse katholieke kerkgebouw in Zuid-Nederland (1796–1940)* (Nijmegen 1993). There exists indeed a striking parallel between Erasmus' work on the New Testament and the treatment of Gothic churches by Viollet-le-Duc and his followers: removing all historical elements which disturbed the idealised picture of the original, both men produced artefacts which in fact had never existed before.

order to meet the new literary standards lest learned Christians be deterred from the gospel. Without the rebirth of letters the Vulgate could just as well have remained the standard text. But as a result of the literary revolution which Erasmus, in his own opinion, inaugurated, not only the Vulgate but the very speech of the apostles had become indigestible, so that a new translation was necessary.[89] The revival of literary culture did not lead to a restoration of the old text, but to the production of a new one because the old text had lost its attraction. A veritable restoration of the old text would actually have made more sense in the Middle Ages, before literary culture had been elevated beyond apostolic grasp.

Remaking History

Our examination of Erasmus' New Testament edition puts the historical legitimation of his Christian humanism into perspective. It seems that Erasmus was indeed the innovator his adversaries took him to be. His prime intention in bringing out his Latin translation of the New Testament was not so much to restore the original text as to propose an alternative to the Vulgate. Antiquity did not provide him with an archetypical New Testament which he merely purged from later distortions. With reference to a Greek text designed for the purpose of defending his work he composed a new translation, knowingly breaking not only with intervening tradition as epitomised in the Vulgate but with the very character of apostolic speech. He led his readers not from muddy pools to the crystal springs of Christendom, to use his own favourite metaphor, but to a canal dug and dredged by his personal efforts. True enough, his edition was based on all textual material available to him. But his material allowed many different readings. Erasmus' decisions were primarily dictated by his bias against the Vulgate. He may have seriously believed that his emendations brought the New Testament closer to its authentic state, although he admitted that the original text had dissolved in the fog of its reception, and although he knew that the apostles themselves had cared little about correct and consistent writing. As

---

[89] Erasmus' contemporary critic Frans Titelmans already blamed humanism for the fact that some had become dissatisfied with the Vulgate, cf. Rummel, *Erasmus and His Catholic Critics* II 17.

for style, however, Erasmus' preferences have certainly less to do with a search for the original than with a wish to improve the literary quality of Scripture. It is probably his understandable fear of being stigmatised as a revolutionary which made him claim to be a mere restorer of old texts.

To be sure, Erasmus' approach does not imply that he disregarded or misunderstood the historical character of Bible translation. It was precisely his belief that translations should adapt to historical circumstances in order to be effective (as the rhetorical idea of *accomodatio* required) which made him compose a version suitable, in his perception, to the new times introduced by humanism. The problem with the Vulgate was not so much its infidelity to the original Greek (it actually reflected the apostolic idiom more faithfully than his own version, as Erasmus implicitly acknowledged) as its anachronistic character with respect to Erasmus' age. By rendering the New Testament in neater dress Erasmus undertook the historical task of Christians, as outlined in *Antibarbari*, to combine God's gifts to mankind, most notably pagan learning and Christian Revelation. Erasmus' edition blended God's Word with classical Latin, and in this respect at least it was successful.[90] If Erasmus was not the first "to give literary studies a Christian voice",[91] he may well have been among the first to give a literary voice to Christ.

None the less, Erasmus' project contradicts his ideas on the historical development of Christian society. The prime intention of his New Testament edition was to produce a Latin text in accordance with the taste of his times—or, specifically, to his own taste, to which he believed his times should defer. At the same time he acknowledged, speaking of the transmission of the Bible text through the ages, that faulty speech and textual corruption did not affect the Christian truth. Christians had always used flawed texts, in ancient as well as medieval times, without putting the church in peril. It would seem, then, that literary culture and religion could do without each other, so that a renewal of the New Testament was unlikely to lead to a restoration of Christian piety. But such a conclusion would have destroyed the image Erasmus had been cultivating of himself as the

---

[90] See above n. 44 (De Jonge); Metzger, *The Text of the New Testament*, 100: Erasmus produced an "elegant Latin translation, differing in many respects from the wording of Jerome's Vulgate".

[91] As he claimed at CWE Ep. 1581:124–6/Allen 115–7, see above p. 109.

man who, thanks to his contributions to scholarship, would save
Christendom from spiritual ruin. Admitting that he replaced the
hideous products of medieval literature and scholarship by more
attractive ones for mere aesthetic reasons would have implied that
he was no better than the Italian humanists whom he had adored
in his youth but later condemned as frivolous and irreligious men.

Thus Erasmus remained a Christian humanist almost against his
better judgement. The past informed him that learning and religion
had declined independently of each other, while the present displayed a flowering of learning without significant moral or spiritual
improvement. Still, Erasmus maintained the ideal of a joint revival
of literature, scholarship, and religion—not through the mere revival
of ancient forms, but through the novel combination of classical form
and Christian content. The real historical reference underpinning his
programme of reform was not so much antiquity, whether pagan or
Christian, as the scholastic period in which learning and religion had
reached rock bottom. Erasmus' aspiration was to build a future at
maximum variance with that period. Rather than to restore ancient
culture, he worked to create a new age embodying all elements from
the classical and the Christian past which offered, in some way or
another, suitable alternatives to late medieval barbarism. The new
age he envisaged would be better and more beautiful than anything
humanity had seen thus far, precisely because it would integrate all
the valuable contributions of the past.

CHAPTER SIX

BACK TO THE FUTURE

Erasmus' expectation of a new and happy epoch went hand in hand with his acknowledgement of a debt to the past. His picture of an ideal future included all elements from Western history to which he attached particular value. But his reverence for the past amounted to more than just exalting the good and dismissing the bad. Especially his later writings display a willingness to pay regard even to medieval traditions which stood in the way of his dreams.

To a certain extent, his indulgence was a matter of strategy. An all too rigid condemnation of ideas or habits which had enjoyed wide popularity for several centuries might have provoked more resentment than Erasmus was willing or able to cope with, and might thus have harmed the cause of Christian humanism. This is one reason why he was generally more tolerant of defective religious usage than of faulty literary conventions. The Renaissance of letters had become firmly established in the first decades of the sixteenth century, so that Erasmus could afford to be exigent in the domain of language and literature. The renewal of Christian religion was a much more difficult and controversial affair, which demanded circumspection.

However, allowing for the imperfections of medieval tradition gradually developed into an attitude of principle with Erasmus. He fiercely repudiated the two "new sects" of his times which rejected the Middle Ages altogether—Ciceronianism in the field of literature, Lutheranism in the field of religion—for the very reason that they refused to take history sufficiently into account. In the final analysis, Erasmus recognised that the way to build a new future was not to engage in wholesale rejection of the past, not even of the medieval period. One must rather embrace the entire history of Western Christendom, in full awareness of all its shortcomings, in order to steer the future in a more desirable direction.

The Tyranny of Tradition

Erasmus repeatedly stated in his writings that the antiquity of firmly entrenched wrongs did not make these wrongs worthy of respect. Bad habits or opinions did not become less objectionable because people were used to them,[1] although their acceptance did make reform more difficult—for "everybody knows how strong a custom is once it is accepted".[2] Not even habits dating from antiquity always found forgiveness in his sight.[3] Several times in his *Colloquia* Erasmus depicted custom (*consuetudo, mos, usus*) as a fierce tyrant who made many unjust demands and was chiefly responsible for the evil in society.[4]

In the sphere of language and literature, many of Erasmus' own demands seem no less tyrannical, intended as they were to extirpate all deviations from classical use. His youthful wish to crush literary barbarism relentlessly, formulated with brio in writings like *Antibarbari* and *Conflictus Thaliae et Barbariei*, never quite died out, notwithstanding his insistence on rhetorical *accomodatio* (which, in Erasmus' conception, encouraged the use of various classical models but barely allowed post-classical speech). Successful educational works of his like *De conscribendis epistolis* (1499/1522), *De copia* (1512), *Parabolae* (1514), and *De recta pronuntiatione* (1528) invariably aimed at the re-establishment of classical norms and the suppression of nearly all developments from a later age, not only in vocabulary and style but even in matters like pronunciation and script. For Erasmus, such later developments were nothing but facets of decline. "[A]ny figure of speech that departs from the practice of the ancients" counted with him as a fault which Latin teachers ought to correct in the same way as plain grammatical errors.[5] Concessions to those who found it difficult to accustom themselves to classical idiom were out of the question

---

[1] Cf. *De recta pronuntiatione* CWE 26 471/ASD I-4 99:880–1, *Colloquia* CWE 40 917/ASD I-3 638:26, *Apologia contra Latomi dialogum* CWE 71 45/LB IX 84B.

[2] Reeve 473 on 1 Cor. 7:39 "Liberata est a lege".

[3] Cf. e.g. *Apologia pro declamatione matrimonii* CWE 71 90/LB IX 107C: the procedure for obtaining a doctorate—"a tradition, it appears, that was passed on to us from ancient pagan rites"—constitutes "a custom that is more traditional than worthy of respect"; *Adagia* IV iv 29 ASD II-7 198:312–5, Allen Ep. 3032:417–9: the bull-fights surviving from antiquity are rejectable instances of cruelty.

[4] Cf. CWE 39 141 with 158n.58, 481, 503, 593; CWE 40 835/ASD I-3 204:2577–9, 2580–1; 400:393, 406:96, 455:75, 587:69.

[5] *De conscribendis epistolis* CWE 25 39/ASD I-2 255:1.

(unless perhaps in order not to upset uneducated but powerful readers and listeners). Erasmus' purpose was to correct the use of language, not "to accommodate speech to the ears and sentiments of the foolish":[6]

> Or do you think it right that the learned should allow the Roman tongue, to which so many excellent branches of learning and the Christian religion itself have been entrusted, to die out in order not to give offence to the ignorant conceit of these individuals?[7]

And again:

> Do you think it just that out of deference to you men should speak barbarously and contrary to the practice of the ancients?[8]

Reacting to Jacobus Latomus' reproof that the humanists would rather not be understood than deviate from classical Latin, Erasmus stated (in fact confirming the view of his opponent) that it was not up to Latin speakers to adapt themselves to the ignorant: "It should be the other way round. The other side should learn to speak Latin correctly, and get rid of their barbarous expressions".[9] Post-classical habits like the use of the *vos* form of address, which constituted a tradition of almost thousand years, were utterly despicable in his eyes. Conversely, linguistic customs were to be spared if they accorded with humanist predilections. Replacing Greek terms by Latin ones in the sciences, for example, was not recommendable in Erasmus' view because the scientists might not be prepared, at an advanced age, to learn new expressions; moreover, differences of meaning could arise. It should be noted that with Erasmus these arguments seldom counted if applied to the substitution of classical for medieval Latin, even if sheer anachronisms were the result.[10]

In much the same way that he concealed his uncompromising attitude as a Bible translator by his emphatic maintenance of some apostolic peculiarities of style, Erasmus presented the few exceptions to classical practice which he allowed as proofs of his magnanimity as a Latin instructor. Commenting on his approval of certain medieval conventions like the use of last names and of spaces between words,

---

[6] Ibid. 54/285:7.
[7] Ibid. 17/219:19–21.
[8] Ibid. 45/268:7–8.
[9] *Apologia contra Latomi dialogum* CWE 71 82/LB IX 104F.
[10] Ibid. 46/85A–B, cf. above p. 13.

he asserted: "we are not so ungracious, surely, as to refuse to accept modern innovations when they are improvements".[11] Some other deviations from ancient idiom were allowed if circumstances required it, "as long as the imperfections are not too obtrusive".[12] In the case of deeply rooted flaws, a gradual cure might be more effective than an immediate attack.[13] In *De recta pronuntiatione* he even admitted that a uniform and universally accepted standard of correctness had never existed,[14] while in his *Copia* he blamed Valla for reducing Latin to rigid rules.[15] But normally Erasmus proceeded as if a standard of correctness did exist in the form of classical Latin, and demanded that current practice adapt to it. "What once existed can be re-established", he formulated his motto.[16] Unwilling to recognise medieval Latin as a system in its own right, he rejected any feature which did not represent an obvious amelioration as a symptom of decline. In principle literary habits had to disappear—either straightaway or in the long run in case of ingrained custom—if Erasmus could demonstrate that they were "wrong", that is, divergent from classical use.

The intellectual climate of the early sixteenth century obviously permitted Erasmus to retain the demanding attitude which he had adopted in his juvenile works. Especially the success of humanism in secondary education (a success which, by 1520, had become fairly complete) gave Erasmus hope "that the error introduced by the corruption of morals and ignorance [can] be uprooted by the authority and practice of good and learned men".[17] The historical developments of his own time thus supported his basically anti-historical ideal of eloquence. Erasmus' essential aim was to purge Latin of historical corrosion. Processes of change are inherent to every living language, but for Erasmus nearly all post-classical modifications of Latin were corruptions which he sought to expunge. Although he explicitly rejected archaism or antiquarianism,[18] his writings tend to

---

[11] *De recta pronuntiatione* CWE 26 396/ASD I-4 38:811–2, cf. ibid. 471/99:889–90.
[12] *De conscribendis epistolis* CWE 25 55/ASD I-2 285:21, cf. *De recta pronuntiatione* CWE 26 472/ASD I-4 100:905–7.
[13] Cf. *De conscribendis epistolis* CWE 25 39/ASD I-2 255:9–16, *De recta pronuntiatione* CWE 26 472/ASD I-4 100:907–13.
[14] CWE 26 471/ASD I-4 896–7.
[15] CWE 24 616/ASD I-6 240:61–5.
[16] *De recta pronuntiatione* CWE 26 422/ASD I-4 61:560–1.
[17] *De conscribendis epistolis* CWE 25 54/ASD I-2 285:9–11, cf. *De recta pronuntiatione* CWE 26 388/ASD I-4 32:594–7.
[18] Cf. *De recta pronuntiatione* CWE 26 393, 471/ASD I-4 36:730–4.

fix the Latin language in a classical model, slightly protracted by the inclusion of some minor improvements of later date. Erasmus' remedy against the corruption of literary culture, then, was to mummify it.

The latter metaphor might seem fantastic were it not Erasmus' own. In the preface to his edition of Jerome, first published in 1516, he set forth a passionate defence of the humanist endeavour to restore ancient texts. The heathen rulers of antiquity, Erasmus asserted, were greatly concerned that the memory of their best authors "should never succumb to the attacks of time that effaces all things".[19] Not only did they furnish their libraries with images and statues of the authors or carve their maxims in bronze, but "they bought their works at vast expense and had them faithfully and almost religiously copied, enclosed them in chests of cedar wood and rubbed them with cedar oil, then laid them up in their temples"; some of them even "laid up their books like some incomparable treasure in store-houses deep under the ground, intending by these precautions to protect them from destruction by fire or by storms of war".[20] The obvious parallel with the treatment of the deceased is worked out by Erasmus himself. The heathens would have perceived "that it was barbarous for the corpses of the dead to be so carefully embalmed sometimes . . . to preserve them from decay . . . and to take no such care to preserve the relics of the mind".[21] Through the preservation of their works, great men were enabled to "live on for the world at large even after death"; what is more, "they then most truly come alive for us when they themselves have ceased to live".[22] A mummified author, then, was preferable to a living one. Great authors could reach immortal status if duly protected against the effects of history. The worst fate which could befall their work was to be treated as

---

[19] CWE Ep. 396:19–20/Allen 13–4.

[20] Ibid. 23–6, 32–5/17–9, 24–7.

[21] Ibid. 38–43/29–33.

[22] Ibid. 44–5, 49–50/35, 38–9. Cf. CWE Ep. 396:351–2/Allen 322: the edition of Jerome amounts to his "restoration to life in the world"; for the "rebirth" of Jerome cf. also CWE Epp. 333:67–70, 87–8/Allen 64–6, 80–1; 334:104–6, 140–1, 162/99–100, 134–5, 155; 335:308, 312, 331, 343–5/292, 297, 316, 328–30; 421:122–3/113, 446:82/76–7. Indeed, Christ was almost more fully present in the gospel than he had been in real life, cf. *Paraclesis* Holborn 146/LB V 142E, VI *4: "in his litteris praecipue praestat, in quibus nobis etiamnum vivit, spirat, loquitur, paene dixerim efficacius, quam cum inter homines versaretur"; 149/V 144D, VI *4v: "hae [paginae] tibi . . . Christum . . . totum ita praesentem reddunt, ut minus visurus sis, si coram oculis conspicias".

a living object, as happened in the Middle Ages to Jerome who was, in Erasmus' rhetoric, adulterated by ignorant scribes and sacrilegious men who mixed in their own scribbles.[23] Ironically, the growth and change (and thus the life) of ancient writings was for Erasmus tantamount to their death.[24] Only if carefully embalmed could authors live on forever in a dead poets' society.[25]

To observe all this is not to degrade Erasmus' merits as a Latinist or a textual critic. It goes without saying that his editions of Jerome and numerous other ancient authors were great achievements and that as a philologist he indeed "paved the way" for later generations, including our own. But our present interest is with Erasmus' historical consciousness. The point is that his ideas about the purification of the Latin language and of ancient texts were not unhistorical (as his concerns sprang from the awareness of the influence of history on literary culture) but anti-historical (as he judged the influence of history pernicious and tried to efface it). As in the case of the New Testament, his philological endeavours aimed at the establishment of artefacts purged from the stains of the past and resistant against future corruption.[26] Ancient texts had to live on perpetually, not as alterable products of their reception history but in their immutable ideal form—petrified so as not to putrefy. A manifest difference with his work on the New Testament is that in his dealings with ancient Latin literature Erasmus' principles were indeed restorative. In his view, he was not improving on the original text (as was sometimes the case with his New Testament edition), but merely restoring it to what it once had been.

In the domain of religious thought and practice Erasmus showed more lenience, not because he considered religious degeneration less

---

[23] CWE Ep. 396:154–69/Allen 142–56, similarly e.g. Allen Ep. 2157:387–94, 564–70 (preface to his Augustine edition).

[24] Cf. Allen Epp. 2091:184–7 ("Attamen illud debemus Christianorum studio, quod quum tot clarissimi scriptores interciderint, Seneca nobis magna ex parte superest; si tamen hoc est superesse"), 2569:11–4 ("ex [veteris autoribus] qui extabant aliquot non minus perierant quam qui maxime videbantur intercidisse. Liber enim prodigiosis mendis vndique scatens crux est verius quam liber").

[25] Correspondingly, Erasmus desired a mummified state for his own work, cf. Allen Ep. 1659:36–45, 61–71 (preface to the 1526 edition of *Adagia*): after his death, nothing should be corrected or added; books have to be treated with religious respect; to change and corrupt them is a crime.

[26] Cf. CWE Ep. 396:313–4/Allen 292–3: Erasmus added annotations to his Jerome edition "[so] that it may not be so easy in the future for anyone to corrupt what other men have restored".

harmful than literary decay—rather to the contrary—but first of all because his contemporaries had more difficulties in accepting reform. In accordance with his dictum that a wise man should not do battle against his own century,[27] he took a patient attitude to certain ingrained vices in Christian society, in particular to popular forms of superstition like the excessive veneration of saints and the addiction to pilgrimages. Notably in his works composed after 1520 Erasmus pleaded tolerance of such practices if they were not too harmful and did not result in impiety, arguing that common believers who were inclined to superstition mostly acted out of ignorance, not out of bad intentions.[28] The Reformation prompted Erasmus to adopt this moderate posture. In his earlier years he had showed little tolerance for popular ceremonialism; only after 1520 did he expressly advocate the moderation rather than the abolition of religious customs which inclined to superstition, depicting himself as a temperate figure standing between a Catholic faction unwilling to accept changes and a Protestant one wishing nothing to remain.[29] Especially in his writings to prominent reformers he called for the toleration of relatively innocent traditions, in particular with regard to the cult of saints, and for the gradual and wary correction of those unacceptable wrongs to which Christians had grown accustomed through long familiarity.[30] A lack of prudence would result in grave turmoil, as he warned the town council of Basel in an advice on religious reform (1525):

> For what is most likely to cause sedition is a sudden and unexpected attack upon some established practice or deeply held belief. Any innovation which seems more likely to stir up trouble than to promote piety should be particularly avoided. In this category I would place all discussion of images, the tonsure of priests and their vestments, the rite of the mass, sacred music, and other practices which are good, or

---

[27] Reeve 33 on Matt. 6:7 "Nolite multum loqui", cf. CWE Ep. 1257:10–1/Allen 8: "The only wise man is he who can match his wisdom to the times we live in".

[28] Cf. *Modus orandi Deum* CWE 70 197–9/ASD V-1 154:126–156:221; *Enarratio psalmi XXXIII* ASD V-3 118:888–98, *De ecclesiae concordia* ASD V-3 305:668–306:713; *Interpretatio in psalmum LXXXV* ASD V-3 334:91–6, 358:782ff.; *Ecclesiastes* ASD V-4 226:733ff.

[29] Cf. e.g. *Apologia ad blasphemias Stunicae* LB IX 368B–369B, *De ecclesiae concordia* ASD V-3 303:581–4, Allen Ep. 2443:196–234.

[30] Cf. e.g. *Spongia* ASD IX-1 174:197–214 (to Ulrich von Hutten), CWE Ep. 1523:49–55/Allen 46–50 (to Philipp Melanchthon); Allen Ep. 2615:465–8, 495–9 (to Martin Bucer). For an elaborate, balanced discussion of Erasmus' attitude toward the cult of saints see Pabel, *Conversing with God*, 69–108.

at least tolerable, if properly used; for it is less painful to put up with
these things than to apply the remedy ... Men are wrong to put too
much trust in human ordinances; but it is equally dangerous to despise
utterly all regulation and tradition, for without these the peace of the
state cannot be preserved.[31]

There is a parallel between these statements and Erasmus' appeal
to Catholic authorities for a circumspect approach to Lutheranism.
Reminding them of ancient and medieval examples (Arius, Tertullian,
Wyclif, the Templars), he pointed out that grim repression often
stimulated rather than extinguished dissension.[32] None the less, even
after the spread of the Reformation Erasmus remained attached to
the ideal of a church purged of the abusive customs which had been
introduced after the patristic period. Not only did he continue to
express his abhorrence of novelties such as popular church music,[33]
but his tactics aimed at disentangling the church from superstitious
beliefs and practices[34] even if reform had to proceed slowly, carefully, and variously "to suit the changing character of the age".[35]
This is not, of course, to assent to the view that Erasmus favoured
a purely spiritual religion devoid of all tangible manifestations of
sanctity and grace, even including the sacraments.[36] Erasmus never
rejected the sacraments and only attacked devotional practice in as
far as he believed it had degenerated into superstition, expressly dis-

---

[31] CWE Ep. 1539:84–100/Allen 80–96.

[32] Cf. CWE Ep. 1352:169ff./Allen 148ff.; Allen Epp. 1721:68–70, 2136:147–84,
2780:53–4. See also Hilmar M. Pabel, "The Peaceful People of Christ: The Irenic
Ecclesiology of Erasmus of Rotterdam", *Erasmus' Vision of the Church*, ed. Hilmar M.
Pabel (Kirksville 1995), 57–93:73–7.

[33] Cf. e.g. *Institutio christiani matrimonii* CWE 69 426–7/LB V 718A–C, *De ecclesiae
concordia* ASD V-3 308:760ff., Reeve 507–8 on 1 Cor. 14:19 "Quam decem milia",
Apologia adversus rhapsodias Pii LB IX 1155B. For an incisive analysis of Erasmus'
rejection of contemporary music see Jean-Claude Margolin, *Erasme et la musique* (Paris
1965).

[34] Cf. CWE Ep. 1341A:1132–9/Allen I 29:29–36: "has anyone been a more
active opponent in print [than I] of putting one's trust in ceremonies; of superstition concerning food and liturgy and prayer; of those who give more weight to
human inventions than to Holy Scripture, who value the decrees of man more than
the commandments of God, who put more trust in the saints than in Christ himself; of academic theology, corrupted as it is by philosophic and scholastic quibbling; of the rash practice of laying down rules for every mortal thing; of the
topsy-turvy judgments of the multitude?"

[35] CWE Ep. 1620:66–7/Allen 57, cf. *Ecclesiastes* ASD V-5 376:276–9.

[36] For this view see esp. Augustin Renaudet, *Etudes érasmiennes (1521–1529)* (Paris
1939) passim; Chomarat, *Grammaire et rhétorique*, 654–65. For critiques see O'Malley,
"Introduction", CWE 66 xvii–xviii; Pabel, *Conversing with God*, esp. 4–6, 31.

regarding the basic traditions of Catholic worship. It was actually in order not to imperil these traditions that he called for cautious reform, preferring to bear some superstition for the time being rather than to dissolve the bonds of religious life altogether.

The development of Erasmus' attitude to scholastic theology bears a close resemblance to his shifting position on religious practice. Although his dislike of scholasticism remained as strong after 1520 as it was before, he came to present himself as a champion of moderation, advocating a middle course between two radical parties: one that clung tooth and nail to things as they were, the other breaking in with undue violence. In order to reassure potential critics, Erasmus often stressed that the humanities were not brought in to dispel theology but merely to purify it by abolishing "barbarism", "frivolous quibbles", and "logic-chopping". What he proposed was a mixture of polite literature and religious studies.[37] However, his alleged moderation did not imply any substantial change in the programme of Christian humanism. Significantly, Erasmus did not propose a conjunction of humanism and scholasticism, but of humanism and theology, which had been his aim ever since the beginning of the century. The humanist purification of theology was precisely intended to deprive the discipline of its scholastic character. The only new element in Erasmus' attitude was his appeal to courtesy. Only after the beginning of the Reformation did he insist that in religious studies humanists should behave as guests, gradually installing themselves side by side with the representatives of traditional learning. Like the deeply rooted forms of superstition, scholastic theology had to be gradually removed and could even be tolerated until a better approach was forthcoming.[38] But there can be little doubt that in Erasmus' view theology should eventually discard the scholastic tradition altogether.

In the field of religious doctrine, however, Erasmus seems to have positively valued tradition. Not that he regarded all received opinions as sacrosanct. Being convinced that, with the exception of the articles of the faith, all ecclesiastical regulations had originated as pragmatic solutions for temporary situations, he believed that they

---

[37] Cf. e.g. CWE Epp. 950:20–2/Allen 16–8, 1062:50ff./45ff., 1111:14–27/11–22, 1124:14–8/12–6, 1125:43–50/37–43, 1127:10–3/6–9, 1136, 1167:15–26/13–22, 1427:61–77/55–69, 1581:121–33/113–24; Allen Epp. 1856:37–8, 2466:67–81. See also Allen Ep. 2157:569–620: the Spanish universities and John Fisher's colleges at Cambridge prove that a "medium" between literary and religious studies does exist.

[38] Cf. CWE Epp. 1002:11–20/Allen 8–16, 1127:16–20/12–6.

could and should be modified if changing historical circumstances required it. In Erasmus' perception not even the precepts from apostolic or patristic times should be considered unalterable, as we have seen in Chapter One. Accordingly, in his longest single annotation on a New Testament verse (1 Cor. 7:39) Erasmus explicitly set out to examine the expedience of divorce in his own times, in spite of his recognition that the nearly absolute interdiction of divorce had the apparent support of many patristic authors, papal decrees, and the consensus of scholastic theologians and canon lawyers. In his ensuing exposition, however, Erasmus took great pains to demonstrate that neither the fathers nor the popes or the scholars of more recent date had unanimously pronounced against divorce, thus revealing his reluctance to set himself against traditions which had been universally accepted for over a millennium.[39] As several commentators have observed, the perpetual consensus of Christendom constituted for Erasmus the prime authority of the church in disputable questions of religious doctrine. In the end he always bowed to this authority, even though his historical reason made him point to the lack of scriptural basis of some doctrines as well as to variations in the tradition of their understanding, and even though he allowed for modifications in current definitions of doctrines as well as their practical application.[40]

There exists only a seeming incongruity between Erasmus' claim to free enquiry, which in some instances he expressly linked to scepticism, and his deference to consensus. It was precisely because Erasmus considered the ascertainable essentials of the faith to be very few that he chose common agreement through the ages as his criterion of acceptability for most religious tenets.[41] Obviously, "through

---

[39] Reeve 467–81 on 1 Cor. 7:39 "Liberata est a lege". Cf. also 78 on Matt. 19:3 "Quacunque ex causa": if the church never departed from patristic opinion, it should not do so now either; but if it did, it should also allow for the possibility of divorce.

[40] James K. McConica, "Erasmus and the Grammar of Consent", *Scrinium erasmianum* II 77–99 esp. 96–7; John B. Payne, *Erasmus: His Theology of the Sacraments* (Richmond 1970), esp. 18–34; cf. also Pabel, "The Peaceful People of Christ", 77–81. Erasmus likewise maintained that the traditional status of many ancient adages spoke in favour of their truthfulness, cf. *Adagia* CWE 31 17/ASD II-1 64:360–2 (prolegomena): "What is more likely to be true than what has been approved by the consensus, the unanimous vote as it were, of so many epochs and so many peoples?"

[41] McConica, "Erasmus and the Grammar of Consent", esp. 97; cf. Richard H.

the ages" would mean principally: from patristic times on. In Erasmus' opinion the medieval continuation of ancient tenets corroborated their respectability, but with traditions which had originated in the Middle Ages he was generally less impressed, even if he subscribed to some predominantly medieval views like the sacramental nature of marriage[42] or the perpetual virginity of Mary.[43] It is especially with respect to doctrines which had first been established in the Middle Ages that Erasmus permitted sceptical discussions before accepting the definitions in question—thus following the same path as the church itself, which had, in Erasmus' view, passed through a stage of scepticism by suspending its judgement for many centuries before finally decreeing the truth.[44]

To conclude that Erasmus respected most literary and religious traditions which dated from antiquity but had more difficulty with traditions from the Middle Ages would seem to be stating the obvious. Ancient forms of civilisation were intrinsically respectable in Erasmus' eyes, even if they did not constitute an unbroken tradition but had vanished "through the fault of times"; likewise, he considered medieval culture intrinsically inferior, whether it could boast of lasting traditions or not. In the Reformation era, however, Erasmus

---

Popkin, *The History of Scepticism from Erasmus to Spinoza* (Berkeley 1979), 5–8; Boyle, *Rhetoric and Reform*, 132ff.

[42] See Payne, *Erasmus: His Theology of the Sacraments*, 109–25. In order to sustain his view that the sacramental status of matrimony (which seemed to prohibit divorce) was a late medieval invention, Erasmus frequently adduced proof from the writings of Peter Lombard and Durand of St. Pourçain. Payne's assessment corrects the view of Telle, *Erasme de Rotterdam et le septième sacrement*, esp. 257–92 that Erasmus denied the sacramental nature of marriage.

[43] Cf. *Modus orandi Deum* CWE 70 187/ASD V-1 146:886ff. with 147:886–7n.

[44] Erasmus professed to exclude from sceptical discussion what had been recorded in Scripture or transmitted by the authority of the church, but to permit a sceptical approach to tenets on which the church itself had suspended judgement (and thus had been a sceptic) for many centuries; with regard to these tenets, Erasmus followed consensus. See esp. Boyle, *Rhetoric and Reform*, 21–3. Accepting Erasmus' distinction, Boyle rejects "the opinion that Erasmus' willingness to accept the decisions of the Church was a result of his Skepticism" (171n.83); his yielding to the consensus of the church in contentious issues, however, would count as a proof of a sceptical attitude (132ff., 156). But the consensus of the church would normally involve authoritative decisions and definitions, so that the difference between the "consensus" and the "decisions" of the church seems invalid. The essential distinction is rather between tenets of ancient and of medieval date. Erasmus seems to have refrained from a sceptical approach to tenets on which not even the (orthodox) fathers had permitted difference of opinion. But he permitted a sceptical discussion of questions first settled in the Middle Ages.

adopted a more circumspect attitude to long-standing imperfections of medieval origin, especially in the field of popular religious practice and academic theology. Yet his alleged moderation does not represent a substantial change of outlook. It remained his purpose to purge the church of superstitious custom and scholastic learning. The only difference is that he came to recommend gradual improvement in an attempt not to stir up conservative theologians and common believers.

Erasmus' attachment to tradition in the field of dogmatics is a different matter. In the absence of clear precepts from Christ himself, Erasmus could not but resort to the views sustained by universal consensus throughout Christian history. From this perspective, traditions from ancient times also had much more weight than medieval ones. Yet it is important to note that for Erasmus the Middle Ages had at least a certain value in that they had incorporated and prolonged many traditions from antiquity. By handing down the essentials of the faith from generation to generation, the Middle Ages had added to the lustre of the Christian truth (Erasmus' appraisal of early medieval scholars who had tried to preserve the truth as well as they could becomes understandable in this context). Discarding the Middle Ages, then, would imply a loss of truth. This latter idea provided Erasmus with an important argument against those two movements which, in his perception, acted as if the Middle Ages could be completely ignored: Ciceronianism and Lutheranism.

Saving History: The Conflict with the Ciceronians

Erasmus' *Ciceronianus* (1528) can be considered his definitive declaration of independence from Italian humanism. The prime object of Erasmus' satire is not so much Ciceronianism in itself—the literary current, particularly strong in Rome and some other Italian cities, which accepted Cicero as the sole model of good Latin—as the aspiration of authors from Northern Europe, in particular from Erasmus' own country, to be recognised as veritable Ciceronians by the Italian literary set instead of devoting themselves to the programme of Christian humanism. Erasmus' famous accusation of paganism, cast into the teeth of the Italian Ciceronians, has its function in this context. Although the danger of paganism was negligible in reality, for Erasmus the accusation served to vindicate Christian humanism, which he claimed to be his brainchild, as morally superior to Italian humanism, which he had denounced many times before as a frivolous and irreligious movement.[45] For our present concerns a related charge against Ciceronianism is of primary interest, namely, that it was an anachronism.

The charge was not new in 1528. For many years before the composition of his dialogue, Erasmus had been railing at the Ciceronians, stating, among other things, that they had history against them. In his biography of Jerome (1516) he observed:

> The religion is different, the manner of life is different, the authors are not the same, everything is changed. And will you deny eloquence to me unless I speak just as if I were living in the age of Cicero, even though aptness in the use of language is a special merit?[46]

One of the reasons why one could not maintain a pure Ciceronian speech, Erasmus continued, was that sometimes one was compelled to cite authors who lacked elegance of style, such as Bonaventure, Thomas, and Scotus.[47] The unrealistic negation of history by the Ciceronians thus included an unacceptable disregard of the medieval past, little appealing though the Middle Ages had been in themselves.

In his *Ciceronianus* Erasmus repeated his charge in an elaborate way. In the course of the dialogue, Bulephorus, the character who (it is generally agreed) voices Erasmus' ideas, adopts a historical point of view. He argues that Cicero spoke in the best possible way in the age he lived in. His style would not have been suitable, however, in another age of Roman history, let alone in the present. Like clothing, painting, and sculpture, language is modified through the ages. One can only speak appropriately if what one says suits present persons and circumstances. Now who could fail to see that the world in its actual state has hardly anything in common with Cicero's times? "Everything has been completely altered—religion, empire, government, constitution, law, customs, pursuits, even men's physical appearance".[48] Speaking in a totally Ciceronian manner would only

---

[45] See my "Erasmus versus Italy", esp. 133–8.
[46] CWE 61 56/Ferguson 183–4, similarly Allen Ep. 1706:41–3 (1525): "Quid autem ineptius quam toto seculo nouato, religione, imperiis, magistratibus, locorum vocabulis, aedificiis, cultu, moribus, non aliter audere loqui quam locutus est Cicero?"
[47] CWE 61 57/Ferguson 184.
[48] CWE 28 383/ASD I-2 636:23–5.

make sense if the world of ancient Rome were completely restored, which for Erasmus was naturally as impossible as it was undesirable. For Christian speakers and writers living in the Christian world of 1528, a pure Ciceronian idiom was of no avail:

> Wherever I turn I see everything changed, I stand on a different stage, I see a different theatre, a different world. What am I to do? I am a Christian and I must talk of the Christian religion before Christians. If I am going to do so in a manner befitting my subject, surely I am not to imagine that I am living in the age of Cicero . . . and scrounge a few poor words, figures and rhythms from speeches which Cicero delivered in the senate?[49]

Not only religion but also history proper separated Erasmus' contemporaries from the age of Cicero—also in the sense that a large proportion of Cicero's works had disappeared through the fault of times, while his extant works were so much distorted by ignorant scribes and falsifiers that those who set out to reproduce Cicero blindly would risk imitating medieval solecisms as if they were Ciceronian felicities.[50] As in the case of the New Testament, the archetypes had disappeared during the fifteen centuries of their reception. History, then, made it impossible to copy Cicero in his entirety, and even if it had been possible, history made the effort inexpedient as well.

Erasmus' historical reasoning in *Ciceronianus* has been subjected by G.W. Pigman to a double criticism. First, the necessity of accommodating one's style to the standards of the times would not only plead against Ciceronianism but against the use of Latin in general. In Erasmus' day Latin was no longer a living language; the future would belong to the vernacular. Second, Erasmus' insistence on the radical difference between the present and the ancient past would subvert the exemplarity of antiquity to which he otherwise adhered.[51]

Pigman's first argument hardly seems convincing. True enough, Erasmus recognised in his dialogue that the opportunities for using Latin had greatly diminished since antiquity. Political business was carried out in the vernacular, and the general public did not under-

---

[49] Ibid. 383/637:3–8; cf. also 407/656:6–9.
[50] Ibid. 363–4/622:2–18.
[51] G.W. Pigman, "Imitation and the Renaissance Sense of the Past: The Reception of Erasmus" *Ciceronianus*', *Journal of Medieval and Renaissance Studies* 9 (1979), 155–77.

stand Latin any more.[52] But this does not imply that an audience for Latin speakers no longer existed. Erasmus' own success offers sufficient proof to the contrary. Not despite but thanks to his refined Latin style he became Europe's most widely read author, whose books attained sales figures of which most modern scholars, notwithstanding the general spread of education, wealth, and leisure, can only dream. As a scholarly language Latin was still hardly challenged in Erasmus' day and would live on for about three more centuries.

Pigman's second argument has greater validity. The idea that everything has changed since antiquity does indeed call the relevance of ancient culture to the age of humanism into question and hence undermine Erasmus' own position. Like the Ciceronians, Erasmus moulded his style on ancient authors, albeit on a variety of authors instead of a single one and on Christian authors as well as pagans. If of necessity style had to change with the times, how could the Latin of antiquity offer a standard of correct speech, and on what grounds could medieval Latin still be dismissed? After all, the idea that one set of words is polished, the other ugly, is rejected in *Ciceronianus* as a matter of prejudice.[53] Echoing one of Erasmus' arguments in favour of his New Testament edition, Bulephorus asserts that "[i]f whatever is new and [has] recently come into the world is considered barbarous, every word must have been at one time barbarous", adding thereupon a list of neologisms introduced by Cicero himself.[54] The object of his reasoning is to render the Christian vocabulary acceptable, but one could employ the same argument in favour of medieval Latin. Erasmus might have countered that times had changed since the Middle Ages as well. But it was Erasmus himself who, in his own view, ushered in that change through his insistence on ancient standards of speech and behaviour.

However, Erasmus did make some allowance for medieval Latin in his Ciceronian dialogue. Twice Bulephorus admits that the language of the scholastics, though not exemplary, had relative merits. In contrast to the Ciceronians, the scholastics had been able to avoid the fault of stylistic inertia:

---

[52] CWE 28 405/ASD I-2 654:17–33; cf. the commentary similar to Pigman's argument at ASD I-2 654:18n.

[53] CWE 28 393–4/ASD I-2 645:20–3.

[54] Ibid. 390/642:29–30.

> It's wonderful how [the Ciceronians] turn up their noses in disgust at
> the barbaric language of Thomas, Scotus, Durandus, and their fellows;
> yet if the matter is called into strict account, they, who made no pro-
> fession of being either eloquent or Ciceronian, are more Ciceronian
> than these creatures who expect to be considered not just Ciceronian
> but veritable Ciceros.[55]

Nosoponus, the character who strives after the title of Ciceronian,
rejects this statement as monstrous and asks somewhat later incred-
ulously if the style of Thomas and Scotus would present a suitable
alternative to Ciceronianism. Bulephorus replies:

> If the better speaker is the one who speaks more appropriately to the
> subject, then to speak as they did on sacred subjects was certainly
> preferable to copying Cicero in such a context—though there is some-
> thing in between the extremes of Scotuses and Cicero's apes.[56]

Thus for all his abhorrence of scholasticism, Erasmus' historical sense
enticed him into giving qualified praise of the schoolmen who had
at least tried to write in accordance with their times. Moreover, by
locating his ideal of eloquence between medieval academic jargon
on the one hand and radical Ciceronianism on the other, he could
again parade as a moderate, in spite of his own exclusive devotion
to the Latinity of ancient times.

It seems ironic that Erasmus, who ceaselessly pretended to introduce nothing new but merely to restore the old, rejected Ciceronianism
because it stuck to an ancient model and refused all novelties. But
apart from its refusal to take historical change into account, he also
held against Ciceronianism its apparent unwillingness to accept even
the uninterrupted traditions of Christendom. Forgetting that he had
corrected numerous apostolic solecisms against classical standards in
his New Testament edition, he declared that one should not reject
the words handed on by the apostles or patristic authors "received
up to this very day by the consensus of all the intervening centuries".[57] The language used by Latin authors for the past fifteen
hundred years had every right to be considered just as Roman as
classical idiom, Erasmus insisted a few years after the publication of
his dialogue.[58] It is, of course, ancient, not medieval custom for which

---

[55] Ibid. 387/640:2–6.
[56] Ibid. 390/642:13–5.
[57] Ibid. 391/643:26–7.
[58] Allen Ep. 2493:114–7. Cf. also the invective at CWE Ep. 1504:27–8/Allen

Erasmus stepped into the breach. But again we see him implicitly recognising the value of the medieval period as an indispensable link in the chain of Christian tradition. Though adding nothing valuable and often distorting the inheritance from antiquity, the Middle Ages had tried, with reasonable success, to preserve the ancient treasures of Christendom. For this reason the Middle Ages could not be ignored. As a conduit between antiquity and modernity, the period was conducive to the glory of Christ. Even if the future created by Christian humanism was to have a completely different outlook, the Middle Ages had too many merits to be erased from memory.

Another apologetic statement of Erasmus in favour of medieval Christendom seems worth mentioning here because it likewise originated in a dispute with Italian humanism, though not with Ciceronianism. In 1531 Erasmus wrote a long and angry letter to the Italian Augustinian canon Agostino Steuco, who in Erasmus' opinion had unduly laid the charge of Lutheranism at the door of the German nation. In his response Erasmus pointed out that, however thrown into confusion Germany might be at the moment, it had never yielded in true religion to Italy during the last eight centuries[59]— that is, since the conversion of the German world to Christendom by Willibrord and Boniface. Erasmus' remark smacks of what John D'Amico has called "a humanist renaissance of the Middle Ages" in Germany. Unable to subscribe fully to the historical conception of the Italian humanists, in which their ancestors were made responsible for thousand years of cultural decline, the German humanists took pride in medieval German history to vindicate their greatness. The Lutherans in particular eagerly studied and edited medieval texts in order to add historical support to their anti-papal and anti-Italian views, according to which papal interference, despite the counterweight provided by the emperor, had caused all Germany's problems.[60] Normally Erasmus took little pride in German greatness and

---

23–4 against arrogant writers who after having learnt a few words of Latin and Greek turn up their noses against authors "hallowed by the unanimous verdict of so many centuries".

[59] Allen Ep. 2465:491–6. Cf. CWE Ep. 1236:118–9, 172–3/Allen 104–5, 155–6 (to Paolo Bombace): "No part of the world upholds the papal dignity more strongly than this land of ours", even if "[s]ome people are trying to persuade the public that the Lutheran plague started in this part of the world" on Erasmus' instigation.

[60] John F. D'Amico, "Ulrich von Hutten and Beatus Rhenanus as Medieval Historians and Religious Propagandists in the Early Reformation", *Roman and German Humanism, 1450–1550*, ed. Paul F. Grendler (Aldershot 1993) [XII] esp. 2–5. On

he was certainly no keen supporter of imperial rule, in spite of his occasional anti-Italian sentiments. With the exception of his remark to Steuco we do not find with him instances of devotion to the Northern Middle Ages comparable to the enthusiasm of the Lutherans. But we do find, remarkably enough, many passages in his writings which blame the Lutherans for their disregard of history, in particular of the unbroken traditions of the church.

Saving History: The Conflict with the Lutherans

The indispensability of the Middle Ages in the framework of Christian history, a secondary argument in Erasmus' *Ciceronianus*, gained major importance in his dealings with the Lutherans, who in Erasmus' opinion likewise attempted to dissolve all ties with the medieval past. The argument is put forward most notably in Erasmus' tracts written against Martin Luther himself on the subject of free will. Occasionally his indignation at Luther's supposed break with the ancient opinions of the church makes an even more vehement impression than his defence of the doctrine as such.

In *De libero arbitrio* (1524) Erasmus limited his investigation of the doctrine of free will chiefly to a study of relevant Bible passages, paralleling Luther's wilful disregard of all human authorities from Christian history. But he could not refrain from adding that if this Scriptural disquisition did not convince the reader, then tradition, the Middle Ages included, should tip the scale in his favour:

> None the less I would remind readers that, if Luther and I seem to be evenly matched on the basis of scriptural testimonies and sound arguments, they should then take into consideration the long list of highly learned men approved by the consensus of very many centuries, all the way up to our own day, most of them commended by their exemplary life as well as by their admirable learning in the Scriptures. Some even gave their testimony in blood to the teaching of Christ which they had defended in their writings. Such are, among the Greeks, Origen, Basil, John Chrysostom, Cyril, John Damascene, and Theophylact; and amongst the Latins Tertullian, Cyprian, Arnobius, Hilary,

---

the difficulties of German humanists with the historical conception of their Italian colleagues see also Ferguson, *The Renaissance in Historical Thought*, 32–9; Mertens, "Mittelalterbilder in der frühen Neuzeit", 34ff.; Neddermeyer, *Das Mittelalter in der deutschen Historiographie*, esp. 20–6; Ridé, "Les humanistes allemands et le moyen âge".

Ambrose, Jerome, and Augustine. I say nothing of those such as Thomas, Scotus, Durandus, Capreolus, Gabriel, Giles, Gregory, or Alexander (*ne recenseam interim Thomas, Scotos, Durandos, Capreolos, Gabrieles, Aegidios, Gregorios, Alexandros*), whose force and adroitness in argument I feel no one should entirely disdain; not to mention the authority of the many universities, councils, and popes. From the apostles' times to this day, there has not been a single writer who has completely denied the power of free will, excepting only Manichaeus and John Wyclif [and Lorenzo Valla].[61]

In spite of the typical use (unfortunately lost in translation) of denigrating plural forms in the list of scholastic theologians and the qualification relating to their intellectual capacities, the passage makes clear that for Erasmus the persistence of the ancient view of free will during the Middle Ages was of singular importance. Luther's alleged departure from a vast continuity of Christian thought, to which no more than two manifest heretics and one scholar had made exception, sustained Erasmus' idea that the Reformation was a novel and revolutionary movement and not, as the Lutherans maintained, a current which sought to recover evangelical truth (with Erasmus one finds the phrase *evangelia renascens* only used ironically). The Lutherans acted, in Erasmus' opinion, "as though there had been no gospel in the world these thirteen hundred years". But who could believe in earnest that Christ would suffer his followers to stick to errors during such a long period, not thinking even a single saint worthy to receive the truth which, according to Luther, was essential to evangelical doctrine?[62] In the conclusion of his treatise Erasmus adduced the argument that if he was mistaken about the Christian conception of human will, he would share his misunderstanding with the whole community of believers during thirteen centuries,[63] which would obviously be too monstrous to be true.

In Erasmus' next tract on the subject of free will, *Hyperaspistes I* (1526), we find the same line of reasoning. Erasmus identified his

---

[61] CWE 76 15/LB IX 1218D–F.

[62] Ibid. 19–20/1220B–D. For Erasmus' appeal to history against Luther cf. also Charles Trinkaus, "Erasmus, Augustine, and the Nominalists", *Archiv für Reformationsgeschichte* 67 (1976), 5–32:10, also in *The Scope of Renaissance Humanism* (Ann Arbor 1983), 274–301:278

[63] CWE 76 88/LB IX 1248D. Likewise Erasmus blamed Jacques Lefèvre d'Etaples for departing from the interpretation of Heb. 2:7 which during many centuries had been approved by the church, "quae ut labi possit alicubi, certe sensum haereticum non amplecteretur tot aetatibus", see Reeve 707, 710 (citation) on Heb. 2:7 "Minuisti eum paulominus ab angelis" = ASD IX-3 226:29, 232:215–7.

appeal to the perpetual consensus of the church as the core of his argument.[64] In several instances he extended the tradition of Christian thought and belief which Luther allegedly rejected to fifteen hundred years, suggesting that the Reformation was breaking with opinions established at the very outset of Christendom:

> [Y]ou should have considered the role you have undertaken to play, namely that of a person who professes to bring back into the light the gospel, which had been buried under mounds of earth for more than fifteen hundred years, one who abrogated all the authority of popes, bishops, councils, and universities, and promised the whole world a certain and true road to salvation hitherto unknown on earth.[65]

In *De servo arbitrio* (1525) Luther had tried to use a similar argument against Erasmus: only the humanist from Holland failed to see the manifest truth in the biblical passages concerning grace and human will, in contrast to all theologians, ecclesiastical authorities, and councils of ancient as well as modern times. This Erasmus denied forcefully, retorting that it was Luther who was asserting new and unheard-of ideas.[66] In Erasmus' view, Luther's historical isolation sufficiently proved him to be in the wrong:

> And you want us to go right ahead and believe that for so many centuries the gospel has been shrouded by Satan, that it is now unveiled by you, and that there is no pure interpretation of Scripture anywhere but in Wittenberg[?][67]

To oppose oneself as a Christian to the unbroken traditions of the church amounted to impiety, as Erasmus pointed out in another anti-Protestant tract of 1526.[68]

---

[64] CWE 76 213/LB X 1298C, cf. 252–4/1315D–1316B.

[65] Ibid. 99/1250B; similarly 108/1254D, 139/1267C ("Christian people have held this doctrine for fifteen hundred years"), 250/1314E ("free choice . . . held in good faith by the Catholic church for more than thirteen hundred years"), 259/1318C–D (Luther's charge of blasphemy falls "on all the most approved Doctors of the church almost from the time of the apostles to this very day"). Cf. also *De ecclesiae concordia* ASD V-3 312:893–4: why would the baptism which was good enough for the church for over 1400 years not satisfy the anabaptists?

[66] CWE 76 243–5/LB X 1312A–F. For the discussion on the clarity of Scripture cf. Cornelis Augustijn, "*Hyperaspistes I*: la doctrine d'Erasme et de Luther sur la 'claritas scripturae'", *Colloquia Erasmiana Turonensia*, 737–48; Boyle, *Rhetoric and Reform*, 50ff.

[67] CWE 76 254/LB X 1316B.

[68] *Detectio* ASD IX-1 244:267–8: "Impugnare quod tot seculis ecclesiae consensu receptum est, impietas est".

Thus almost in spite of himself Erasmus came to respect the intellectual heritage of the Middle Ages, not for its own sake but as a
necessary medium which had handed down the essentials of Christendom from the first centuries to the present. From his point of
view, the Lutherans committed the same fault as the Ciceronians:
they acted as if history could be ignored. Erasmus considered his
own hopes for a better future to be in accordance with the nature
of history, as we have seen in Chapter Four. His conviction that
time itself would realise his dreams enabled him to content himself
with a process of gradual improvement in his own lifetime. The
Lutherans, by contrast, would aspire to the immediate creation of a
"new world",[69] thus opposing themselves to history. Detesting "everything that has been a part of our human existence in the past",[70]
they intended to change everything, with as sole results confusion
and upheaval, and a deterioration of the climate in which real and
durable improvements could be introduced. Significantly, Erasmus
ignored the claim of the Lutherans that they had not broken with
history but continued the true, invisible church which had never
ceased to exist, not even in the Middle Ages, despite its oppression
by the visible, papist church.[71] In fact, both Erasmus and the Lutherans
considered themselves representatives of uninterrupted ecclesiastical
traditions. But only Erasmus adhered to a tradition of universal
dimensions, including the medieval authorities with whom he had
hardly more affinity than his Protestant adversaries.

The alleged pretension of the Lutherans to disclose the Christian
truth after many centuries of concealment continued to annoy Erasmus
and provoked recurrent misgivings in his polemical writings. In his
Epistola ad pseudevangelicos (1530), directed against his former friend
Gerard Geldenhouwer, he noted sarcastically that the Lutherans had
set themselves a more difficult task than the apostles. The latter had
combated the conspicuously absurd beliefs of Jews and pagans; the
Lutherans, by contrast, were fighting against "what the progeny of
the church during so many centuries taught, venerated, accepted,
and still accept with great consensus as divine oracles".[72] But what

---

[69] *Hyperaspistes II* LB X 1483C; Allen Epp. 1901:96–8, 1976:21.
[70] CWE Ep. 1558:315–6/Allen 294–5.
[71] See Mertens, "Mittelalterbilder in der frühen Neuzeit", 44–5; Neddermeyer,
Das Mittelalter in der deutschen Historiographie, 32–60.
[72] ASD IX-1 291:211–3.

prophet had announced that the world would forget Christ and that
the successors of the apostles would be struck with blindness, so that
the new gospellers should lead the church back to the truth?[73] Why
was it at all necessary to give up what Christians had become accustomed to?[74] Christianity, corroborated by miracles, martyrs, and the
modesty of the apostles, had needed several centuries for its diffusion,
but the Lutherans expected the world to give up at once what had
been conferred upon it thousand years ago. In their opinion Christ
had been absent for fourteen centuries marked by the cult of idols,
exegetical blindness, and false miracles.[75]

Reacting against Erasmus' invectives, the Strasbourg reformers, to
whom Geldenhouwer belonged at the time, denied that they sought
to unearth a truth which had lain buried for thousand years, as
Erasmus had put it.[76] But Erasmus refused to take their defence seriously. The absence of revolutionary intentions must be a Strasbourg
peculiarity, he jeered in his *Epistola ad fratres Inferioris Germaniae* (1530),
since Luther himself rejected the Christian tradition in its entirety.
For Erasmus the traditional beliefs of the church were sacrosanct
precisely because they were traditional: "for me, the consensus of so
many fathers, so many councils, and the whole Christian world is
as good as an oracle".[77] The Lutheran dissimulation of their novelty
was amiss:

> They deny . . . that they set forth new dogmas; instead, they restore
> the old. As if those things are not old which the church has taught
> and preserved from fourteen hundred years ago up to the present day,
> with the great consensus of the world, or as if it were evident to them
> what the apostles handed down to their churches.[78]

The last charge would also seem to apply to Erasmus himself, who
claimed to defend a tradition which had existed since apostolic times.[79]
But it is interesting to see that the Lutherans, in Erasmus' view,

---

[73] Ibid. 291:221–6.

[74] Ibid. 292:241–2.

[75] Ibid. 300:466–72.

[76] Cf. ibid. 291:208–9, *Epistola ad fratres Inferioris Germaniae* ASD IX-1 338:240–1.

[77] ASD IX-1 338:250–1.

[78] Ibid. 414:861–5, similarly 418:968–70, 979–82 ("An non nouum adferunt euan-
gelion, qui secus interpretantur quam hactenus interpretata est ecclesia? . . . Nec
potest subsistere nouum nisi subuerso vetere").

[79] Cf. ibid. 364:771: "nos, qui quod a mille quingentis annis tradidit ecclesia tene-
mus"; see also above p. 172.

showed a lack of historical sense not only by throwing into confusion everything which had been established in the past, but also by their unhistorical assumptions about apostolic practice from which they derived their standards of ecclesiastical reform. As in the case of the New Testament, Erasmus considered the archetypical situation irretrievable. Alleging, however, that neither the apostles nor the fathers had ever disagreed upon dogma, he adduced the mutual discordance among the Protestants as a proof that they were inventing new doctrines.[80]

In a third sense, too, the Lutherans displayed an inadequate understanding of history. They did not distinguish between the essential and the accidental in historical development. Instead of restoring the original piety of the church, they were rather concerned with its pristine ritual. Rituals, however, were no more than outward practices which in Erasmus' opinion could be changed in accordance with the times, as would often have happened since the days of the apostles.[81] The Lutherans, then, had a mistaken sense of what changing historical circumstances required.

Erasmus' growing insistence on the value of the Christian tradition, including its medieval phase, does not mean that he came to appreciate the Middle Ages for their own sake. We have seen that, for a variety of reasons, his attitude to medieval civilisation became slightly more conciliatory after 1520, but this is not to say that the Reformation prompted Erasmus to recognise the intrinsic value of the medieval past. He shared most of the Lutherans' criticism of medieval life and thought, but dealt differently with it, obliging himself to moderate reform and urging the Lutherans to do the same thing. From his first letter to Luther (1519) it is already obvious that he did not want the reform of religion and morality to end in a rupture with the church and its traditions:

> It is more expedient to protest against those who misuse the authority of the bishops than against the bishops themselves; and I think one should do the same with kings. The universities are not so much to be despised as recalled to more serious studies. Things which are of

---

[80] Ibid. 364:798ff. Of course the fathers had disagreed upon dogma, but those who had lost the case were excluded from orthodox tradition. And even within orthodox tradition controversies had existed, as Erasmus knew very well, see above pp. 29–30.

[81] Ibid. 338:255–7, 339:264–6.

such wide acceptance that they cannot be torn out of men's minds all
at once should be met with argument, close-reasoned forcible argument, rather than bare assertion . . . Everywhere we must take pains
to do and say nothing out of arrogance or faction; for I think the
spirit of Christ would have it so.[82]

The warning that the reform of social and ecclesiastical institutions
should not lead to their abolition but limit itself to a correction of
what had grown wrong became standard in Erasmus' writings during the Reformation era. In many cases he emphasised, moreover,
that even this modest kind of reform required a prudent implementation and forbearance of lesser evils. "Hair by hair gets the tail
off the mare", he held out to Luther.[83] Ten centuries of steady degeneration could not be removed at once, as was believed by

> those who pour oil on the flames and are in a great hurry to remove
> by violent drugs a disease which has by now grown chronic over a
> thousand years, to the very great peril of the whole body. The apos-
> tles showed toleration to the Jews . . . and the same, I believe, they
> would rightly show to these men who for so many centuries have
> accepted the authority of all those councils and popes and distinguished
> teachers, and find some difficulty in swallowing the new wine of this
> modern teaching.[84]

Erasmus' moderation seems initially to have been dictated by a concern for peace.[85] Not wishing to disturb the social order or to play
into the hands of reactionary forces, he aimed at achieving the best
possible results in the given circumstances rather than at a radical
change of the circumstances themselves. As we have seen, his confidence
that time itself would bring betterment allowed him to adopt a relaxed
attitude toward the imperfections of human society. But from the
mid-1520s Erasmus came to insist that imperfection was intrinsic to
the human condition as such. Not only was an ideal church or society not to be created at once, but it would not come into existence
within historical time at all. "Whatever changes heaven may bring
about in the state of the world", Erasmus cautioned Melanchthon,

---

[82] CWE Ep. 980:47–56/Allen 41–9, likewise CWE Ep. 967A:112–8/Allen Ep.
985:102–7.
[83] CWE Ep. 1127A:56/Allen 55, referring to the reform of academic studies. For
the saying cf. *Adagia* I viii 95 CWE 32 175–6/ASD II-2 316–7.
[84] CWE Ep. 1341A:1169–77/Allen I 30:26–33.
[85] Cf. Pabel, "The Peaceful People of Christ".

"there will never be any shortage of things to complain about. Our problems can be mitigated, but not removed completely".[86] Harsh measures of religious reform would overshoot the mark, he warned the town council of Basel, for "however radically it changes, the world will never reach so happy a state that it will not have to overlook many faults".[87] Evil had existed in all ages past and would exist in all ages to come. Not only from a pacifist but from a historical perspective, a tolerant attitude was the only reasonable option. In *Detectio praestigiarum* (1526), written in order to dissociate himself from the views of the Eucharist set forth by the Swiss reformers, Erasmus stated:

> Finally, the Christian world has never been so happily organised in any century that we have not noticed the existence of many and great complaints . . . It has always been and will always be the case that those who live piously and spiritually complain and suffer.[88]

One year later he made the same point against Luther himself in *Hyperaspistes II*:

> Never have human affairs been so suitably dealt with, nor will they ever be during earthly history, that many things are not susceptible to correction. Actually it is better to turn a blind eye to certain things, while other things should be overlooked on behalf of the emotions of simple folk. What cannot be endured should either be tolerated if the applicable cure would seem to present a greater danger than the disease itself, or be corrected with skill and reason, so that present wrongs would not seem to be uprooted but developed into better things.[89]

Erasmus propounded similar views in his polemics against the Strasbourg reformers in the 1530s. The rule that throughout history there had been imperfections to put up with would apply in particular to the church, which from the outset, despite the enthusiasm of apostolic times, had seen bad Christians outnumber the good ones. Should one wonder, then, that the church exhibited some deficiencies now that it had spread across the whole world?[90] Surely the new

---

[86] CWE Ep. 1523:58–61/Allen 54–6.

[87] CWE Ep. 1539:92–4/Allen 88–90.

[88] ASD IX-1 260:660–5, likewise Allen Ep. 2134:233–6: "nunquam tam bene cum rebus humanis actum fuit, nec agetur, vt non iustissima querela futura sit de plurimorum moribus. Mutare rerum statum procliue est, mutare in melius dificillimum".

[89] LB X 1483C–D.

[90] *Epistola contra pseudevangelicos* ASD IX-1 302:530–3, 303:594–304:597, 304:606–9.

church of the Lutherans would not be any better protected against corruption than the old one:

> As long as the net of the church is trailed through the course of earthly history and has not yet reached the shore, one should tolerate the mixture of good and evil. It has always been and will always be the case for the human condition that it yields more bitterness than honey.[91]

Complaints about the morality of Christians had always existed. Different faults had prevailed in different epochs, but never had they not occurred at all. If one was not to allow for any wrongs whatsoever, one should rather abolish life itself.[92]

In *De recta pronuntiatione* (1528) Erasmus affirmed that it was the idea of the imperfection of the world which had always deterred him "from joining the extremists who are so appalled by the failures of human society that they want to abolish every existing institution" like monasteries, schools, and colleges:

> They are dissatisfied with the working of some, so all must go, as if whatever replaced them was bound to be free of all fault and possible deterioration. When an institution has been well founded in the first place it is much better to repair it, even if it means turning a blind eye to certain failings in the mean time. This will be all the easier to do if we remember the inevitable conditions of human life. Even at the best, nothing is perfect. There is always something missing, something to be repaired, something to be renewed.[93]

Unable to move the course of history in a more beneficial direction, the Protestants would merely replace existing evils by new ones,

---

[91] Ibid. 304:615–8. The phrase "more bitterness . . ." echoes Juvenal, *Satirae* 6:181. Cf. also *Lingua* CWE 29 263/ASD IV-1A 26:65: "where there's honey there's gall, where there's good soil, there are weeds" (after Apuleius, *Florida* 18).

[92] *Epistola ad fratres Inferioris Germaniae* ASD IX-1 340:291–5, 422:101–4; cf. Allen Ep. 2615:461–5 (to Bucer): "Querela de ratione studiorum, de moribus eorum qui gubernaculis assident ecclesiae, iam vetus est, tametsi nunquam fortassis antehac quam hoc seculo iustior. Sed nunquam tam feliciter agetur cum rebus humanis vt non multa futura sint de multis querimonia".

[93] CWE 26 379–80/ASD I-4 24:348–54. The phrase "Even at the best . . ." echoes Horace, *Carmina* 2.16:27–8, cf. *Adagia* III 1 87 CWE 34 215–7/ASD II-5 88–92 "Nihil est ab omni parte beatum" cited at *Apologia contra Latomi dialogum* CWE 71 59/LB IX 93A. For a similar statement cf. *Exomologesis* LB V 146B: "fere nihil est in rebus humanis tam sanctum, tam pium, tam, ut ita dicam, coeleste, quod hominum corruptissimi mores non vertant in perniciem. Mihi vero vehementer displicent isti quidam, qui rem per se bonam tollere moliuntur, ob hominum vitia, quum his medicina magis fuerit adhibenda".

changing nothing but the labels.[94] But evils to which one was accustomed represented a lesser burden. As Erasmus asserted against Luther:

> I know that in the church which you call papistical there are many with whom I am not pleased, but I see such persons also in your church. But it is easier to put up with evils to which you are accustomed. Therefore I will put up with this church until I see a better one . . . a person does not sail infelicitously if he holds a middle course between two evils.[95]

Thus tradition not only adorned the Christian truth but attenuated the effects of what was undesirable. As a consequence, Erasmus could put the Lutherans in the wrong whenever they proposed or enforced a break with the past. Even the tyranny of monks and superstitious custom seemed more bearable to him than a total and no less tyrannical revolution.[96] Moreover, his "middle course" enabled him once more to claim his favourite position as a moderate in the storms of the century.

Only rarely did Erasmus go so far as to counter the Lutheran desire for change by presenting medieval developments which he otherwise repudiated as examples of historical progress. Some instances do however spring to mind. Attacking in his *Purgatio adversus epistolam Lutheri* (1534) Luther's insistence on the clarity of Scripture, Erasmus alleged that in patristic times a variety of interpretations and many doubts had existed concerning exegetical and doctrinal issues which were now settled by clear definitions. Would this not indicate, Erasmus asked rhetorically, that in the course of times biblical scholars had managed to penetrate to deeper layers of meaning, disclosing truths which had remained hidden to earlier generations?[97] Erasmus' statement contradicts his frequent claim that the doubts of the fathers in questions of dogma had been healthy, largely preferable to the scholastic urge to define everything. More

---

[94] Cf. *Epistola contra pseudevangelicos* ASD IX-1 293:284–7.

[95] *Hyperaspistes I* CWE 76 117/LB X 1257F–1258A, cf. *Adagia* II ix 85 CWE 34 123–4/ASD II-4 268–70 ("An evil thing known is best"), *Detectio* ASD IX-1 260:686–7 ("mala commodius feruntur quam ignota"). See also my "*Tolerantia*: A Medieval Concept", 381–2 for the argument that the most cogent examples of Erasmian tolerance stem from his concern to preserve Catholicism.

[96] Cf. *Epistola de esu carnium* ASD IX-1 38:562–4, CWE Ep. 1495:30–3/Allen 25–9.

[97] ASD IX-1 459:474–460:493. Cf. also above pp. 22, 131.

than once he had suggested that resorting to definitions, which the struggle against various heresies in late patristic times had necessitated, marked the transition from a rhetorical to a logical approach to religious truth and thus inaugurated the corruption of theology. As his New Testament scholarship abundantly demonstrates, medieval exegesis did not represent for Erasmus a deepening or a refinement of understanding but a degeneration from patristic standards. It is quite remarkable that the Lutheran challenge drove him to adopt, even if only once in a polemical context, such a different point of view. His identification of the very symptoms of decline he had always refused to acknowledge as historical improvements actually echoes the arguments used by his Catholic adversaries against his own criticism of medieval scholarship.[98]

Erasmus' most elaborate defence of medieval history can be found in his *Epistola contra pseudevangelicos*. In it, he expressly imputed a lack of historical sense to the Lutherans. To begin with, they failed to understand the irreversible character of historical development. Like all other human institutions, Erasmus asserted, the church had passed through a primordial stage, a period of growth, and full maturity (significantly he kept silent about its old age, which he had evoked in earlier writings).[99] To reduce the church to its first origins was therefore no less absurd than to put an adult back into the cradle. Time and historical circumstances dragged many things down and changed many other things for the better, but left nothing intact.[100] To these general observations Erasmus added a lengthy enumeration of the vicissitudes of the history of the church since its early days. According to Erasmus, the loose private gatherings of believers had been replaced by orderly worship in church buildings. The Eucharist was now received on an empty stomach rather than during sumptuous meals; moreover, it was not possible any longer to take it home and subject it to magic ritual. Mass, once a chaotic performance, had been tightly organised. Nightly vigils and processions which led to disorder had been suppressed. Bishops were not

---

[98] Cf. e.g. Jacobus Latomus, *Dialogus de trium linguarum et studii theologici ratione* (1519): "in the old times many matters were uncertain and unresolved, which were later determined by the Church ... the old theologians speak of these matters in a rather careless and simplistic fashion" (cited in Rummel, *The Humanist-Scholastic Debate*, 81). Latomus' dialogue prompted Erasmus to write his *Apologia contra Latomi dialogum*.

[99] Cf. Allen Ep. 1844:30–1, see also above p. 33.

[100] ASD IX-1 304:623–6.

designated any more in turbulent and whimsical public elections. In
addition, everyone now listened to them in silence and awe, whereas
in patristic times the bishops had been obliged to play the buffoon
in order to attract the attention of their flocks.[101] Formerly every
attendant at mass had participated in singing psalms and hymns,
with confusing noise as a result; now singing was reserved to the
choir. Formerly divine services were not adorned by instrumental
music; later a restricted use had been admitted which, as human
institutions invariably tended to decline (an old idea of Erasmus),[102]
had degenerated into an infernal racket, but still moderation was
preferable to abolition. Likewise, the early church had abhorred
paintings and images, doubtless in order to break with the idolatry
of Jews and pagans; now churches were overwhelmed with images
offensive to good taste, but as decent representations were beautiful
and instructive, one should strive for a correction of abuse rather
than a complete removal. Formerly no schools existed and only the
bishops provided theological instruction; later schools had been established to the great benefit of Christendom, and although scholasticism had put some stains on public education, the schools should
be summoned to sobriety rather than dissolved. In the early church
the religious, unchecked by any ordinance, diffused in large num-
bers among the world and perpetrated ignominies under the cloak
of religion, which had led to the imposition of wholesome rules in
a later period. Heretics, originally combated with the spiritual sword
only, provoked bloody conflicts endangering the whole of society, so
that later the worldly sword was used as well. Finally, the habits of
savage nations had forced the clergy, living in the days of old from
the gifts of the people, to procure and safeguard some riches in the
course of time. "What more do you want?", Erasmus concluded. "If
Paul were alive today, he would not, in my opinion, disapprove of

---

[101] Cf. Allen Ep. 1800:211–22, repeated at *Vita Chrysostomi* LB III 1345B–D: "Tum
enim paganitatis reliquiae, gladiatorum paria, concursus equorum, athletae, pugiles,
aliaque theatri certamina, plebem auocabant a concione sacra, nec episcopis ullum
alius ius erat quam linguae. Ad haec in ipsis concionibus cogebantur quiddam e
theatro pati, sibilos, applausus, acclamationes, gesticulationes frequenter indecoras,
quibus vel corrumpi vel interpellari poterat dicentis impetus . . . Nunc sublata sunt
auocamenta publica. Populus humilis et quietus magna religione praebet aures, nihil
obstrepens".
[102] ASD IX-1 306:661–2; cf. 300:491–3, 304:596–7, adducing as examples the
mendicant orders and the early church respectively. See also above pp. 60–1.

the present state of the church, but bemoan the vices of human beings".[103]

In his historical survey Erasmus, cautious not to overstate the case beyond credulity, refrained from suggesting that the church had known only progress since the early days of Christendom. In some fields it had; in others it had undergone inevitable decay, controlled however by timely measures (at least some of which were medieval inventions); in still others the innovations of patristic and medieval times, salutary in themselves and therefore worth preserving, suffered from abuse. Yet Erasmus' evaluation permitted only one conclusion. The Lutheran intention to carry the church back to its initial state was not only practically absurd in view of the irreversibility of historical time, but objectionable in principle. A return to the early days would deprive the church of all improvements and healthy regulations thanks to which it had been able to survive during fifteen hundred years in as good a condition as historical circumstances allowed. History had produced not an ideal church, but at least a viable one. A better church was not to be founded, let alone to last. One could only try to ameliorate the existing church by correcting, as far as possible without provoking uproar and bloodshed, the defects of the institutions devised to foster the intellectual and spiritual development of Christendom.

Going Medieval after All

Both by its nature and by its actual course during the Christian era, history, in Erasmus' conception, contradicted those who aimed at the extirpation of the medieval past. By dismissing Christian history, in particular the medieval period, the Ciceronians as well as the Lutherans acted in an unrealistic and irresponsible manner. They merely succeeded in annihilating the healthful products of the past while they retained what was detrimental (corrupted texts in the case of the Ciceronians, corrupted religion in the case of the Lutherans). The history of Latin Christendom was certainly to be improved upon with antiquity as a principal source of inspiration, but attempts to restore ancient civilisation by disregarding or demolishing the cen-

---

[103] Ibid. 308:696–8.

turies which had followed were of no avail. All of Christian history had to be taken into account. Any century was instructive in as much as it presented both features to be emulated and features to be eschewed. A better future would consist in an amalgam of all valuable gifts conferred upon Christianity since the beginning of times, and had to be realised step by step, lest unrest should cause the loss of any good in the process.

At first sight it might seem that Erasmus' apparent conservatism[104] implies a departure from the impassioned struggle of his early years against medieval barbarism and in favour of classical culture. One could be tempted to think that the Lutheran revolution made him feel uneasy about the subversive character of his ideas and impelled him to take a more conservative stance than before. We have seen that the majority of his pleas for moderation and forbearance of medieval wrongs of long standing date from after 1520, when he also came increasingly to defend the relative merits of medieval civilisation. Was it the confrontation with Lutheranism, then, which made Erasmus espouse the traditions of Christendom—or was it rather his attachment to the past which contributed to his choice against Luther, as he asserted in *De recta pronuntiatione*?[105]

The latter possibility deserves serious consideration. The Lutheran revolution may have acted as a catalyst, activating in Erasmus a conservative attitude which had always existed in a more latent form. James McConica affirms indeed that Erasmus' adherence to the tradition and consensus of the Christian community, being at the source of his outlook on theology and the church, explains why he did not move with Luther.[106] John Payne likewise believes that "not only his horror of tumult but also his respect for the value of ecclesiastical traditions, especially ancient and universal, albeit provisional, prevented his leaving the Roman Church".[107] Since, as both scholars agree, the traditions of the church were the only foothold available to Erasmus in discussions on the validity of ecclesiastical doctrine

---

[104] McConica, "Erasmus and the Grammar of Consent", 96–7 characterises Erasmus' adherence to ecclesiastical tradition as both conservative and revolutionary, the latter aspect being related to his idea that the ascertainable essentials of doctrine were very few.

[105] See above p. 178.

[106] "Erasmus and the Grammar of Consent", 96–7.

[107] *Erasmus: His Theology of the Sacraments*, 227.

and practice, a radical break with tradition would in his perception not only have disturbed the social order but upset the mind, depriving it of its necessary paradigms.

In addition, Erasmus' attack on the anti-historical attitude of Ciceronianism and Lutheranism appears to be consistent with the philosophy of history elaborated in *Antibarbari*, the very work which inaugurated the young humanist's rebellion against medieval civilisation. Admittedly, *Antibarbari* was not published until 1520, when Luther became a public enemy of the church, but most of it had been written much earlier, largely antedating the Reformation, and not even in the published version do we find traces of disagreement with Luther. In order to demonstrate the consistency of Erasmus' historical thought we must have recourse to the work in some detail.[108]

We have seen in Chapter One that *Antibarbari* opens with a discussion among Erasmus and four humanist companions on the emergence of medieval barbarism. Three of them propose divergent historical explanations. The physician Joost van Schoonhoven ascribes the decay of learning to the influence of the stars; the burgomaster Willem Colgheenes points to the rise of Christendom; the poet Willem Hermans believes that the world has grown old. These three views involve three different ideas of history. Hermans has a cyclical conception of time. The world, having gone through seasons of youth, full strength, and old age, has completed its movement in the present. The burgomaster's conception of time is linear. He points to unique events which result in irreversible developments. In the physician's view, history is contingent. It does not follow any pattern, whether circular or linear, but represents a "continual flux of change"[109] depending on the constellation of the stars, which may be either favourable or not.

All those philosophies are rejected by Erasmus' mouthpiece, Jacob Batt, who blames the three men for making circumstances responsible for the fault of human beings. The basic principle of his own historical theory is the idea that the world is ordered by divine will. Everything which exists has its own place and its own function, given to it by God. Movement, time, and history also are governed by

---

[108] In the next paragraphs I will make extensive use of my "Overcoming the Middle Ages".
[109] CWE 23 24/ASD I-1 45:32–46:15.

divine rule, nothing excepted. Everything which happens in any age is a meaningful and necessary event in the divine plan of history. More precisely, all events from the beginning of the world, whether benevolent or hostile, are drawn into the service of Christ and contribute to the happiness and glory of his still ongoing age. This theory permits Batt to affirm that classical learning is a divinely disposed source for Christian civilisation.[110]

It is easy to understand why the views of the physician and Hermans offend Batt's theory of history. Both men would agree that historical development is senseless: the physician because history is radically contingent, and Hermans because history, in its circularity, starts with nothing and ends with nothing. Batt believes, on the other hand, that history is ordained meaningfully by God and will culminate in a glorious age, provided that Christians take up their responsibilities.

It is much harder to see why the view of the burgomaster contradicts Batt's ideas. The burgomaster sets forth a linear but not necessitarian conception of history. He explains the decay of ancient civilisation by pointing to conditions created by human beings, namely, the negative attitudes adopted by Christians toward classical learning. Much in line with Batt he seems to suggest that if the Christians would amend their ways, they would be able to combine pagan wisdom and Christian truth and bring about a cultural upheaval in accordance with the divine plan of history.

The essential difference between the two men seems to be that the burgomaster is speaking in the third person, whereas Batt is emphatically using the first. The burgomaster talks about the early Christians and their medieval successors as if they were aliens. It is "they" who are responsible for the harm done to ancient literary culture. The burgomaster dissociates himself from the intellectual tradition which the Christians represent, and thus from Christian history. Without denying human responsibility for history in general, he does deny his personal responsibility for the barbarous past of Christianity. This is the attitude which Batt rejects. In his view, the human responsibility for history implies that Christians are responsible for Christian history, including the deplorable centuries in which ancient literary culture was all but completely destroyed. In spite of his tremendous admiration for antiquity, Batt identifies himself principally as a

---

[110] Ibid. 59–61/82:8–84:18.

Christian, and hence accepts full responsibility for anything in the
course of history which has happened in the name of Christ. In his
view it is "we" who have been unable to add anything valuable to
ancient learning and who have been corrupting the classical heritage
instead. It is therefore also "we" who should hurry to mend our
ways and restore ancient culture to make it serve the Christian truth.
Batt's discourse is, in a way, a crusade against the barbarians in our-
selves. The fact that, in the beginning of the dialogue, Batt accuses
the burgomaster of being the cause of cultural decay[111] means first
of all that the latter should not elevate himself above Christian history but recognise his historical responsibility and act according to
this insight. It is thus not so much the idea of human responsibility
for history in itself which makes Batt spurn the opinions expounded
by the other three men, but his readiness to accept personal responsibility for the wrongs of Christian history, regardless of how these
wrongs came to pass. Assuming responsibility for what went wrong
in the past, notably during the Middle Ages, is the beginning of
future improvement, inspired to a great extent by pagan wisdom but
proceeding within the bounds of Christian history.

Through Batt's insistence that Christians should identify themselves
first and foremost with Christian history, *Antibarbari* makes a sincere
plea for the reform of Christian civilisation. Although antiquity is
hailed as the source of all intellectual culture, the work does not
advocate a return to ancient times. The Christian past, the Middle
Ages included, is no disturbing factor in our historical development
which should be eliminated in order to revive antiquity, but our history proper, which we should accept and improve upon with the
aid of classical learning. We are, in fact, medieval beings rather than
ancients, although the ancient heritage should help us to overcome
our medieval regression. Thanks to his historical reasoning, Batt/
Erasmus is able not only to avoid the rejection of ancient culture in
the name of Christendom, but also the rejection of Christendom in
the name of ancient culture, and to draw up a cultural programme
meeting the needs of "the philosophy of our time, which has joined
together the knowledge of all things human and divine".[112]

The readiness to assume responsibility for the entire Christian past

---

[111] Ibid. 28/50:27–8.
[112] Ibid. 99/119:9–10.

is perhaps the most remarkable feature of Erasmus' mature historical consciousness. His wish to overcome the Middle Ages while acknowledging his complicity with the medieval past distinguishes his position from Italian humanism as well as from the Reformation. As Erasmus saw it, Italian humanists and Protestants tended to deny any responsibility for the medieval decline of intellectual and religious culture, proclaiming themselves the direct heirs of ancient Rome and early Christianity respectively, as if untouched by the intervening centuries. Erasmus' position was not only more historical but also more courageous, in spite of its obvious ambiguity. Giving in to the zest for the restoration of the ancient world, whether pagan or Christian, while dismissing the Middle Ages altogether, would have rendered his position more comfortable perhaps but, in his own esteem, morally inferior. His break with medieval tradition could therefore not be absolute, despite his revulsion against the period as such. As far as his historical consciousness is concerned, Erasmus' was right to see himself as occupying an uneasy position between reactionary and revolutionary forces.

Towards a Historical Balance

If it is true that the principle of divine economy applies to history, as is asserted in *Antibarbari*, then not only must antiquity have a role in the plan of God, but so must the Middle Ages, and also those movements (Ciceronianism and Lutheranism) which denied the medieval past. How should one account, from an Erasmian perspective, for the existence of these negative and mutually contradictory forces in a divinely disposed Christian history?

We have seen that for Erasmus the value of the Middle Ages consisted first of all in its preservation of the ancient religious truth. By prolonging the life of Christendom for ten centuries, albeit in a distorted form, the Middle Ages had added lustre and force to the Word of God. As for the low cultural standards of the period, one might find an answer to our question in *Antibarbari* where Batt illustrates the divine economy of time by stating that "[e]ven winter itself is not idle, but re-establishes things in an interval of quiet".[113] If

---

[113] Ibid. 61/84:1–2.

applied to the Middle Ages, the statement would suggest that culture has been slumbering during the medieval winter, so that it
should arise with all the more power in the spring of humanism.

The overly zealous reaction against the medieval past by both
Ciceronians and Lutherans could likewise be interpreted as a factor
which, though reprehensible in itself, would have a propitious effect
on the renewal of Christian culture. We have seen in Chapter Four
that Erasmus took Luther to be God's instrument, sent to awake the
world by violent means. Naturally this did not alter the evil character of Lutheranism, but as God used even the evil dispositions of
humans for the fulfilment of his plan, history would eventually profit
from the Lutheran challenge.

The existence of Ciceronianism lends itself to a similar explanation. In the famous letter of 1517 in which he cheered the world-
wide successes of humanism, Erasmus pointed already to the possible
rise of paganism under the cover of the reborn classics, adding that
the nature of human affairs did not permit the eradication of one
evil without the introduction of another.[114] In a letter written three
years later Erasmus expanded on this idea. The movement back and
forth between opposed extremes would constitute the irresistible pattern of historical change:

> Whenever I survey the mutability of human affairs . . . I seem to see
> precisely some Euripus or whatever may be more inconstant than that,
> so incessant are the changes as they surge this way and that, up and
> down, and cannot long continue in one stay. They reach a climax
> and swing back to what was left behind, until once more they come
> to such a point that we are obliged to turn our course from some
> excess that has now become intolerable; and what is more, were one
> to try to stand against the sea or bend its course a different way, one
> could never do this without putting all things in serious jeopardy and
> immense upheaval . . . it would be an infinite task to collect in this way
> the many different shapes that things have taken as they rise and fall
> in turn, and flourish and decay, and bloom once more and shoot again
> from time to time in a new shape . . . even sacred studies, which ought
> to be the most consistent thing there is, have their own ebb and flow.[115]

---

[114] CWE Ep. 541:149–62/Allen 133–47. For this letter see above pp. 115–6.

[115] CWE Ep. 1062:4–22/Allen 1–18. See also CWE Ep. 586:76–80/Allen 68–71:
"And then it repays the trouble to watch how human affairs sway up and down
as though in some great Euripus with its tidal ebb and flow, unless this surge is
restrained and disciplined by the solid wisdom and inflexible virtue of princes".
Euripus is the strait between the island of Euboea and the Greek mainland, cf.
Adagia I ix 62 CWE 32 215–6/ASD II-2 382–4.

At first sight, the image of "the regular ebb and flow of history"[116] would seem to contradict Erasmus' idea of human responsibility for history as well as his concept of historical progress under divine guidance, both ardently defended in *Antibarbari*, and imply an ironical view of history in the Kantian sense, presupposing neither progress nor decline but arbitrary, senseless change. But Erasmus' view of history was not quite like that. Rather than an indifferent movement, the alternation of extreme positions in the course of history represented for him a process of trial and error which would finally lead to a betterment of some sort. In *De recta pronuntiatione* he explained, with obvious reference to the purist fancies of Ciceronianism: "Extremes are never corrected except by reversing the swing and as it were curing fault with fault. In my view the imbalance will eventually settle itself".[117] Defects provoked other defects, but in the end history would establish an equilibrium. The extremism of Ciceronianism and Lutheranism, then, did not detract from the divine plan of history. As a counterweight against the forces sticking to the degenerate literary and religious culture of the Middle Ages, it was actually useful. There is no contradiction, then, between Erasmus' notion of historical variability and his idea of progress. History moved toward a state of relative happiness, albeit in a zigzag line rather than straightforwardly.

Thus neither the "monks and theologians" nor the "new sect" of Protestants or the "third sect" of Ciceronians could unsettle Erasmus' prevailing historical optimism. They were agents of progress even against their will or knowing. Between the extremes of medieval civilisation and the irresponsible rejection of it, a better future was already lurking. In order to foster its realisation, some extremism was allowed even on Erasmus' part, namely, an excessive idealism, in accordance with his view that only when making efforts to realise the ideal situation can one hope to bring forth an even modestly better state of affairs. As he insisted in his commentary to the adage "Grasp the summit, and halfway will be yours", to combat evil in all its forms was the sole way to any improvement.[118] Likewise, he explained in the preface to the 1518 edition of his *Enchiridion* that the highest

---

[116] CWE Ep. 1581:684–5/Allen 615–6 ("rerum humanarum omnium vicissitudo": actually, the metaphor of ebb and flow is absent from the Latin).

[117] CWE 26 388–9/ASD I-4 32:600–03. *Ciceronianus* and *De recte pronuntiatione* were first published together in one volume.

[118] *Adagia* II iii 25 CWE 33 142–3/LB II 491F–492B.

goal—Christ and his teaching in all its purity—"must be set before everyone, that at least we may achieve something half way". Granting that his ideal was beyond human grasp, he still affirmed its expedience: in the same way, Plato had rightly put forward in his *Republic* an imaginary state as a model for political life.[119] True enough, Dame Folly considered Plato's utopia a suitable environment for "a new sort of god who never was and never will be in existence anywhere", that is, for a perfectly wise person.[120] But for Erasmus a dash of utopianism was indispensable in order to elevate history to a plane somewhere between the Middle Ages and his undiluted ideals.

---

[119] CWE Ep. 858:346–51, 359–61/Allen 324–9, 336–8.
[120] *Moria* CWE 27 104/ASD IV-3 106:633–4.

CONCLUSION

In a valuable study of Erasmus' view of history Myron Gilmore has advanced the opinion that Erasmus combined two different, fundamentally incompatible conceptions of history, one cyclical, the other linear. His cyclical conception permitted him to draw from history illustrations of timeless truths and apply them to recurrent patterns of situations. From a linear conception he emphasised the lessons offered by a unique historical evolution.[1]

Our study calls for a revision of Gilmore's observation, at least if taken to the letter. Erasmus had little affinity or sympathy with a circular conception of historical time. In his view history proceeded forward, although it did not make progress in every century and although it zigzagged toward its goal instead of advancing in a straight line. History displayed a gradual unfolding of God's gifts to mankind, with classical learning and the Revelation as its principal moments, both situated in antiquity. Although the ancient heritage had suffered major setbacks in the recent (that is, medieval) past, the essentials had been preserved down to the present. The efforts and successes of the humanist generation, headed by Erasmus himself, promised a joyous future which would happily combine all divine attributions for the first time ever.

somewhat contradicts 188-90

The statement that in Erasmus' work anti-historical views coexisted with pro-historical ones would seem to represent his position more accurately. Erasmus did recognise timeless truths and standards of correctness, in religious as well as secular culture. But he believed that humanity entertained a living relationship with the truth, which permitted change of current practice on the one hand while requiring respect for long-standing traditions on the other. His indulgence varied from field to field, being much greater with regard to religion than to literary culture, and it increased slightly in the Reformation

---

[1] Gilmore, "Fides et Eruditio", esp. 108. Bietenholz, *History and Biography*, 29 dismisses Gilmore's view with the curious argument that Erasmus only sparingly employed conventional patterns of successive historical ages. Gilmore's assessment, however, does not bear on Erasmus' formal periodisation of history, but on his conception of its general course and its educational value. *root*

era. As for most religious doctrines, however, Erasmus did not regard
the truth as timeless, the articles of the faith excepted. Here the
truth rather revealed itself through time. The truth of doctrine coincided with the history of its understanding.

The past did not provide Erasmus with epochs which in their
entirety could be taken as models for the present, although notably
the church fathers had set major individual examples of learning and
holiness. But the past did provide him with an anti-model, an epoch
characterised by the nearly complete subversion of his ideals: the
later Middle Ages, dominated by scholasticism and culminating in
the insipid barbarism from which Erasmus claimed to have suffered
as a youth. Erasmus' view of history hinged on the scholastic period.
Taking his point of departure in the negative examples set forth by
it, he forged his image of what the future should be like. Although
he affected to work at the restoration of ancient forms of civilisation, what he envisaged was the creation of a counter-epoch with
regard to the later Middle Ages. His playful confession to Guillaume
Budé that he took his inspiration from medieval ignorance rather
than from the brightness of the classics was actually not far from
the truth.

The problematical relationship between the concepts of restoration and renewal accounts for Erasmus' historical consciousness occasionally appearing ambiguous. He often claimed merely to restore
what was old and to introduce nothing new, accusing the scholastics instead of having introduced countless novelties. But he recognised the novel character of his New Testament translation in so
many words, and fiercely rejected the ambitions of those who, in his
perception, really wished to turn the clock back to ancient times,
notably the Ciceronians and the Lutherans. Erasmus did not want
to return to some point before the Middle Ages in order to start
history anew, but to create a future on the basis of the entire ancient
and medieval past of Christendom, for which, as a Christian, he
took full responsibility. His sense of history thus did play a major
role in his ideas on the reform of civilisation, albeit not as a merely
restorative factor. Restoring antiquity and eradicating the Middle
Ages would have been a regression in his eyes, not an improvement.
Erasmus' departure from medieval civilisation implied a continuation of Christian history along new lines. He actually believed he
was following the path of progress inherent in historical time. A
more open acknowledgement of his position as an innovator might
have rendered his Christian humanism more consistent from a histor-

ical point of view, but would have exposed him to the facile criticism of his adversaries that he was a dangerous revolutionary. Considering that in Erasmus' age innovation was generally regarded with suspicion, it is in fact surprising that we find any instances in his writings where he avows the novel character of his ambitions. In our age, which sets excessive store by originality, scholars often proclaim the novelty of their stale ideas; it should not surprise us that Erasmus generally preferred a strategy of dissimulation. But we should beware of following his rhetoric in our commentaries by presenting Christian humanism as a predominantly restorative movement.

A more fundamental ambiguity in Erasmus' historical conscious-ness pertains to his joint pursuit of cultural and spiritual ideals. The assumption that the rise of literary and intellectual standards would foster piety and virtue was crucial to Christian humanism, but history did not provide Erasmus with convincing evidence of a causal connection. History remained, even in his own presentation, too com-plicated and contradictory a process to justify his outlook on con-temporary society or to corroborate his ideas on reform. From his own writings one can infer that in classical antiquity the flowering of literature coexisted with moral depravity, whereas the first and best Christians had shunned literary culture and were followed in this respect by exemplary saints like Francis of Assisi. In the early Middle Ages, falling literary standards had not led immediately to the degeneration of moral and spiritual life, while the continuous corruption of the biblical text, which had started in the early days of Christendom, had never caused any serious harm in the field of religion. Neither had the indisputable flowering of humane literature and liberal studies in Erasmus' own age made the world a better place to live in. One should therefore not accept without qualification the observation that in Erasmus' view, shared by a large circle of humanists and adopted by the Reformers, classical culture and evan-gelical Christianity had declined together, mainly through the fault of monks and schoolmen, and had later revived together.[2] In Erasmus' perception, letters and religion had declined together only in the scholastic period; moreover, he did not think that evangelical Christianity had revived along with classical culture. Erasmus' account of history since the Incarnation would rather suggest that learning and piety developed independently from each other. To dissolve the

---

[2] See Ferguson, *The Renaissance in Historical Thought*, 46.

ties between letters and religion, however, would have been fatal to
Christian humanism. Thus Erasmus preferred, like many an incurable idealist, to project his optimistic expectations into the future:
the effects of Christian humanism in the field of piety were only
somewhat postponed through the opposition of monks and theologians on the one hand and Protestant troublemakers on the other,
but history would definitely bring improvement on all fronts—partly
as the outcome of a natural process but mainly because God would
have it so and even used his detractors to this end. One day Christian
civilisation would gather in all fruits of history. The idea that God
had implanted the seeds of true culture in the world without granting a full harvest would have struck Erasmus as a monstrosity.

Probably Erasmus' scant formal interest in history explains why
he could accept a view of the past which undermined his ideas on
the reform of Christendom. Being primarily concerned with the present, he may not have cared very much about correct or consistent
representations of the past. He thus never rigorously examined either
his perception of history or the historical assumptions underlying
Christian humanism. Moreover, like most Renaissance humanists, he
neither was nor pretended to be a systematic thinker. His relative
inattention made him, apparently without his realising it, admit views
which, if taken into sufficient account and considered in their consequences (as this study has tried to do), lead to conflicts with his
self-proclaimed larger ideals.

To be sure, scholars have long recognised the numerous ambiguities in Erasmus' thought and character. Perhaps the following anec-
dote may serve to illustrate this point. In 1928 Werner Kaegi wrote
to Johan Huizinga about the excavations recently carried out in
Erasmus' grave in Basel. Two skulls had been found, the better preserved of which had been attributed to Erasmus. Huizinga, who
thought the exhumation of Erasmus an absurdity anyway, answered
Kaegi: "But in examining the skeletal remains, did no one consider
the possibility that Erasmus could have had two heads? That would
certainly explain a great many aspects of his personality".[3]

---

[3] "Hat man in Bezug auf den Knochenbestand nicht an die Möglichkeit gedacht,
dass Erasmus zwei Köpfe gehabt haben könnte? Das würde ja vieles in seiner Person
erklären". Johan Huizinga, *Briefwisseling*, ed. Léon Hanssen, W.E. Krul and Anton
van der Lem, 3 vols. (Utrecht-Antwerp 1989–91) II 232–3.

BIBLIOGRAPHY

Works of Erasmus

Ausgewählte Werke, ed. Hajo and Annemarie Holborn (Munich 1933) [cited: Holborn]

Collected Works of Erasmus (Toronto 1974–) [cited: CWE]

Dilutio eorum quae Iodocus Clichtoueus scripsit aduersus declamationem Des. Erasmi Roterodami suasoriam matrimonii, ed. Emile V. Telle (Paris 1968) [cited: Telle]

Erasmi Opuscula: A Supplement to the Opera omnia, ed. Wallace K. Ferguson (The Hague 1933) [cited: Ferguson]

Erasmus' Annotations on the New Testament, ed. Anne Reeve and M.A. Screech 3 vols. (London 1986; Leiden 1990–3) [cited: Reeve]

Opera omnia (Amsterdam 1969–) [cited: ASD]

Opera omnia, ed. Joannes Clericus 10 vols. (Leiden 1703–6) [cited: LB]

Opus epistolarum, ed. Percy S. Allen et al. 12 vols. (Oxford 1906–58) [cited: Allen]

Works Edited and Annotated by Erasmus

Augustine, *Opera* 10 vols. (Basel 1528–9); Erasmus' scholia are included in *Variorum exercitationes in S. Augustini opera*, PL 47 197–570.

Ps.-Cato, *Disticha moralia* in *Opuscula aliquot Erasmo Roterodamo castigatore et interpraete* (Louvain [1515]).

Irenaeus, *Opus . . . in quinque libros digestum, in quibus mire retegit et confutat haereseon . . . opiniones* (Basel 1526).

Jerome, *Lucubrationes omnes* 9 vols. (Basel 1516).

Lactantius, *De opificio Dei* in *Vidua christiana . . .* (Basel 1529).

Origen, *Opera* 2 vols. (Basel 1536).

Sophronius, *Vitae scriptorum ecclesiasticorum* in Epiphanius, *De prophetarum vita . . .* (Basel 1529).

Other Sources Frequently Cited

Corpus iuris canonici, ed. Aemilius Friedberg 2 vols. (Leipzig 1879–81).

Patrologiae cursus completus . . . series latina, ed. J.-P. Migne 221 vols. (Paris 1844–90) [cited: PL]

Modern Studies Frequently Cited

István P. Bejczy, "Overcoming the Middle Ages: Historical Reasoning in Erasmus' Antibarbarian Writings", *Erasmus of Rotterdam Society Yearbook* 16 (1996), 34–53.

—— "Erasmus Becomes a Netherlander", *Sixteenth Century Journal* 28 (1997), 387–99.

—— "Erasmus versus Italy", *Mediaevalia et Humanistica* 24 (1997), 123–45.

—— "Tolerantia: A Medieval Concept", *Journal of the History of Ideas* 58 (1997), 365–84.

—— "Bede in the Renaissance: The Case of More and Erasmus", *Erasmus of Rotterdam Society Yearbook* 18 (1998), 89–103.

—— "Erasme explore le moyen âge: sa lecture de Bernard de Clairvaux et de Jean Gerson", *Revue d'Histoire Ecclésiastique* 93 (1998), 460–76.

Jerry H. Bentley, *Humanists and Holy Writ* (Princeton 1983).

P.G. Bietenholz, *History and Biography in Erasmus of Rotterdam* (Geneva 1966).

Marjorie O'Rourke Boyle, *Christening Pagan Mysteries: Erasmus in Pursuit of Wisdom* (Toronto 1981).

—— *Rhetoric and Reform: Erasmus' Civil Dispute with Luther* (Cambridge MA 1983).

Jacques Chomarat, *Grammaire et rhétorique chez Erasme* 2 vols. (Paris 1981).

—— "More, Erasme et les historiens latins", *Moreana* 22.86 (1985), 71–107.

—— "La philosophie de l'histoire d'Erasme d'après ses réflexions sur l'histoire romaine", *Miscellanea Moreana* [= *Moreana* 26.100 (1989)], 159–67.

Colloquia Erasmiana Turonensia 2 vols. (Paris-Toronto 1972).

John F. D'Amico, "Beatus Rhenanus, Tertullian and the Reformation: A Humanist's Critique of Scholasticism", *Archiv für Reformationsgeschichte* 71 (1980), 37–62.

Christian Dolfen, *Die Stellung des Erasmus von Rotterdam zur scholastischen Methode* (Osnabrück 1936).

Wallace K. Ferguson, *The Renaissance in Historical Thought: Five Centuries of Interpretation* (Cambridge MA 1948).

Myron P. Gilmore, "Fides et Eruditio: Erasmus and the Study of History", *Humanists and Jurists: Six Studies in the Renaissance* (Cambridge MA 1963), 87–114.

Anthony Grafton and Lisa Jardine, *From Humanism to the Humanities: Education and the Liberal Arts in Fifteenth- and Sixteenth-Century Europe* (London 1986).

Humanismus und Historiographie, ed. August Buck (Weinheim 1991).

J.S. Hirstein, "Erasme, l'Histoire Auguste et l'histoire", *Actes du colloque international Erasme*, ed. Jacques Chomarat et al. (Geneva 1990), 71–95.

Fritz Husner, "Die Bibliothek des Erasmus", *Gedenkschrift zum 400. Todestage des Erasmus von Rotterdam* (Basel 1936), 228–59.

Henk Jan de Jonge, "Erasmus und die *Glossa Ordinaria* zum Neuen Testament", *Nederlands Archief voor Kerkgeschiedenis* 56 (1975), 51–77.

—— "Novum Testamentum a nobis versum: The Essence of Erasmus' Edition of the New Testament", *Journal of Theological Studies* 35 (1984), 394–413.

—— "The Character of Erasmus' Translation of the New Testament as Reflected in His Translation of Hebrews 9", *Journal of Medieval and Renaissance Studies* 14 (1984), 81–7.

Jean-Claude Margolin, "Duns Scot et Erasme", *Erasme: le prix des mots et de l'homme* (London 1968) [III] 89–112.

Jean-Pierre Massaut, "Erasme et Saint Thomas", *Colloquia Erasmiana Turonensia*, 581–611.

James K. McConica, "Erasmus and the Grammar of Consent", *Scrinium erasmianum* II 77–99.

M.L. McLaughlin, "Humanist Concepts of Renaissance and Middle Ages in the Tre- and Quattrocento", *Renaissance Studies* 2 (1988), 131–42.

Dieter Mertens, "Mittelalterbilder in der frühen Neuzeit", *Die Deutschen und ihr Mittelalter. Themen und Funktionen moderner Geschichtsbilder vom Mittelalter*, ed. Gerd Althoff (Darmstadt 1992), 29–54.

Bruce M. Metzger, *The Text of the New Testament: Its Transmission, Corruption, and Restoration* 3d ed. (Oxford 1992).

Uwe Neddermeyer, *Das Mittelalter in der deutschen Historiographie vom 15. bis zum 18. Jahrhundert. Geschichtsgliederung und Epochenverständnis in der frühen Neuzeit* (Cologne 1988).

John O'Malley, "Grammar and Rhetoric in the *pietas* of Erasmus", *Journal of Medieval and Renaissance Studies* 18 (1988), 81–98.

—— "Introduction", CWE 66 ix–li.

Hilmar M. Pabel, "The Peaceful People of Christ. The Irenic Ecclesiology of Erasmus

of Rotterdam", *Erasmus' Vision of the Church*, ed. Hilmar M. Pabel (Kirksville 1995), 57–93.
—— *Conversing with God: Prayer in Erasmus' Pastoral Writings* (Toronto 1997).
John B. Payne, *Erasmus: His Theology of the Sacraments* (Richmond 1970).
Margaret Mann Phillips, *The "Adages" of Erasmus: A Study with Translations* (Cambridge 1964).
R.R. Post, *Scholen en onderwijs in Nederland gedurende de Middeleeuwen* (Utrecht 1954).
—— *The Modern Devotion: Confrontation with Reformation and Humanism* (Leiden 1968).
Albert Rabil, "Desiderius Erasmus", *Renaissance Humanism: Foundations, Forms, and Legacy* II *Humanism Beyond Italy* (Philadelphia 1988), 216–64.
Jacques Ridé, "Les humanistes allemands et le moyen âge", *L'Histoire au temps de la Renaissance*, ed. M.T. Jones-Davies (Paris 1995), 131–45.
Erika Rummel, *Erasmus as a Translator of the Classics* (Toronto 1985).
—— *Erasmus' Annotations on the New Testament: From Philologist to Theologian* (Toronto 1986).
—— "God and Solecism: Erasmus as a Literary Critic of the Bible", *Erasmus of Rotterdam Society Yearbook* 7 (1987), 54–74.
—— *Erasmus and His Catholic Critics* 2 vols. (Nieuwkoop 1989).
—— *The Humanist-Scholastic Debate in the Renaissance and Reformation* (Cambridge MA 1995).
Paul Gerhard Schmidt, "Erasmus und die mittellateinische Literatur", *Erasmus und Europa*, ed. August Buck (Wiesbaden 1988), 129–37.
Scrinium Erasmianum, ed. J. Coppens 2 vols. (Leiden 1969).
Emile V. Telle, *Erasme de Rotterdam et le septième sacrement* (Geneva 1954).

INDEX

The Index does not cover the footnotes.

BRILL'S STUDIES
IN
INTELLECTUAL HISTORY

1. POPKIN, R.H. *Isaac la Peyrère (1596-1676)*. His Life, Work and Influence. 1987. ISBN 90 04 08157 7
2. THOMSON, A. *Barbary and Enlightenment*. European Attitudes towards the Maghreb in the 18th Century. 1987. ISBN 90 04 08273 5
3. DUHEM, P. *Prémices Philosophiques*. With an Introduction in English by S.L. Jaki. 1987. ISBN 90 04 08117 8
4. OUDEMANS, TH.C.W. & A.P.M.H. LARDINOIS. *Tragic Ambiguity*. Anthropology, Philosophy and Sophocles' *Antigone*. 1987. ISBN 90 04 08417 7
5. FRIEDMAN, J.B. (ed.). *John de Foxton's Liber Cosmographiae (1408)*. An Edition and Codicological Study. 1988. ISBN 90 04 08528 9
6. AKKERMAN, F. & A. J. VANDERJAGT (eds.). *Rodolphus Agricola Phrisius, 1444-1485*. Proceedings of the International Conference at the University of Groningen, 28-30 October 1985. 1988. ISBN 90 04 08599 8
7. CRAIG, W.L. *The Problem of Divine Foreknowledge and Future Contingents from Aristotle to Suarez*. 1988. ISBN 90 04 08516 5
8. STROLL, M. *The Jewish Pope*. Ideology and Politics in the Papal Schism of 1130. 1987. ISBN 90 04 08590 4
9. STANESCO, M. *Jeux d'errance du chevalier médiéval*. Aspects ludiques de la fonction guerrière dans la littérature du Moyen Age flamboyant. 1988. ISBN 90 04 08684 6
10. KATZ, D. *Sabbath and Sectarianism in Seventeenth-Century England*. 1988. ISBN 90 04 08754 0
11. LERMOND, L. *The Form of Man*. Human Essence in Spinoza's *Ethic*. 1988. ISBN 90 04 08829 6
12. JONG, M. DE. *In Samuel's Image*. Child Oblation in the Early Medieval West. 1996. ISBN 90 04 10483 6
13. PYENSON, L. *Empire of Reason*. Exact Sciences in Indonesia, 1840-1940. 1989. ISBN 90 04 08984 5
14. CURLEY, E. & P.-F. MOREAU (eds.). *Spinoza. Issues and Directions*. The Proceedings of the Chicago Spinoza Conference. 1990. ISBN 90 04 09334 6
15. KAPLAN, Y., H. MÉCHOULAN & R.H. POPKIN (eds.). *Menasseh Ben Israel and His World*. 1989. ISBN 90 04 09114 9
16. BOS, A.P. *Cosmic and Meta-Cosmic Theology in Aristotle's Lost Dialogues*. 1989. ISBN 90 04 09155 6
17. KATZ, D.S. & J.I. ISRAEL (eds.). *Sceptics, Millenarians and Jews*. 1990. ISBN 90 04 09160 2
18. DALES, R.C. *Medieval Discussions of the Eternity of the World*. 1990. ISBN 90 04 09215 3
19. CRAIG, W.L. *Divine Foreknowledge and Human Freedom*. The Coherence of Theism: Omniscience. 1991. ISBN 90 04 09250 1
20. OTTEN, W. *The Anthropology of Johannes Scottus Eriugena*. 1991. ISBN 90 04 09302 8
21. ÅKERMAN, S. *Queen Christina of Sweden and Her Circle*. The Transformation of a Seventeenth-Century Philosophical Libertine. 1991. ISBN 90 04 09310 9
22. POPKIN, R.H. *The Third Force in Seventeenth-Century Thought*. 1992. ISBN 90 04 09324 9
23. DALES, R.C & O. ARGERAMI (eds.). *Medieval Latin Texts on the Eternity of the World*. 1990. ISBN 90 04 09376 1
24. STROLL, M. *Symbols as Power*. The Papacy Following the Investiture Contest. 1991. ISBN 90 04 09374 5
25. FARAGO, C.J. *Leonardo da Vinci's 'Paragone'*. A Critical Interpretation with a New Edition of the Text in the *Codex Urbinas*. 1992. ISBN 90 04 09415 6

26. JONES, R. *Learning Arabic in Renaissance Europe*. Forthcoming. ISBN 90 04 09451 2
27. DRIJVERS, J.W. *Helena Augusta*. The Mother of Constantine the Great and the Legend of Her Finding of the True Cross. 1992. ISBN 90 04 09435 0
28. BOUCHER, W.I. *Spinoza in English*. A Bibliography from the Seventeenth-Century to the Present. 1991. ISBN 90 04 09499 7
29. McINTOSH, C. *The Rose Cross and the Age of Reason*. Eighteenth-Century Rosicrucianism in Central Europe and its Relationship to the Enlightenment. 1992. ISBN 90 04 09502 0
30. CRAVEN, K. *Jonathan Swift and the Millennium of Madness*. The Information Age in Swift's *A Tale of a Tub*. 1992. ISBN 90 04 09524 1
31. BERKVENS-STEVELINCK, C., H. BOTS, P.G. HOFTIJZER & O.S. LANKHORST (eds.). *Le Magasin de l'Univers. The Dutch Republic as the Centre of the European Book Trade*. Papers Presented at the International Colloquium, held at Wassenaar, 5-7 July 1990. 1992. ISBN 90 04 09493 8
32. GRIFFIN, JR., M.I. J. *Latitudinarianism in the Seventeenth-Century Church of England*. Annotated by R.H. Popkin. Edited by L. Freedman. 1992. ISBN 90 04 09653 1
33. WES, M.A. *Classics in Russia 1700-1855*. Between two Bronze Horsemen. 1992. ISBN 90 04 09664 7
34. BULHOF, I.N. *The Language of Science*. A Study in the Relationship between Literature and Science in the Perspective of a Hermeneutical Ontology. With a Case Study in Darwin's *The Origin of Species*. 1992. ISBN 90 04 09644 2
35. LAURSEN, J.C. *The Politics of Skepticism in the Ancients, Montaigne, Hume and Kant*. 1992. ISBN 90 04 09459 8
36. COHEN, E. *The Crossroads of Justice*. Law and Culture in Late Medieval France. 1993. ISBN 90 04 09569 1
37. POPKIN, R.H. & A.J. VANDERJAGT (eds.). *Scepticism and Irreligion in the Seventeenth and Eighteenth Centuries*. 1993. ISBN 90 04 09596 9
38. MAZZOCCO, A. *Linguistic Theories in Dante and the Humanists*. Studies of Language and Intellectual History in Late Medieval and Early Renaissance Italy. 1993. ISBN 90 04 09702 3
39. KROOK, D. *John Sergeant and His Circle*. A Study of Three Seventeenth-Century English Aristotelians. Edited with an Introduction by B.C. Southgate. 1993. ISBN 90 04 09756 2
40. AKKERMAN, F., G.C. HUISMAN & A.J. VANDERJAGT (eds.). *Wessel Gansfort (1419-1489) and Northern Humanism*. 1993. ISBN 90 04 09857 7
41. COLISH, M.L. *Peter Lombard*. 2 volumes. 1994. ISBN 90 04 09859 3 (Vol. 1), ISBN 90 04 09860 7 (Vol. 2), ISBN 90 04 09861 5 (Set)
42. VAN STRIEN, C.D. *British Travellers in Holland During the Stuart Period*. Edward Browne and John Locke as Tourists in the United Provinces. 1993. ISBN 90 04 09482 2
43. MACK, P. *Renaissance Argument*. Valla and Agricola in the Traditions of Rhetoric and Dialectic. 1993. ISBN 90 04 09879 8
44. DA COSTA, U. *Examination of Pharisaic Traditions*. Supplemented by SEMUEL DA SILVA's *Treatise on the Immortality of the Soul*. Tratado da immortalidade da alma. Translation, Notes and Introduction by H.P. Salomon & I.S.D. Sassoon. 1993. ISBN 90 04 09923 9
45. MANNS, J.W. *Reid and His French Disciples*. Aesthetics and Metaphysics. 1994. ISBN 90 04 09942 5
46. SPRUNGER, K.L. *Trumpets from the Tower*. English Puritan Printing in the Netherlands, 1600-1640. 1994. ISBN 90 04 09935 2
47. RUSSELL, G.A. (ed.). *The 'Arabick' Interest of the Natural Philosophers in Seventeenth-Century England*. 1994. ISBN 90 04 09888 7
48. SPRUIT, L. Species intelligibilis: *From Perception to Knowledge*. Volume I: Classical Roots and Medieval Discussions. 1994. ISBN 90 04 09883 6
49. SPRUIT, L. Species intelligibilis: *From Perception to Knowledge*. Volume II: Renaissance Controversies, Later Scholasticism, and the Elimination of the Intelligible Species in Modern Philosophy. 1995. ISBN 90 04 10396 1
50. HYATTE, R. *The Arts of Friendship*. The Idealization of Friendship in Medieval and Early Renaissance Literature. 1994. ISBN 90 04 10018 0
51. CARRÉ, J. (ed.). *The Crisis of Courtesy*. Studies in the Conduct-Book in Britain, 1600-1900. 1994. ISBN 90 04 10005 9

52. BURMAN, T.E. *Religious Polemic and the Intellectual History of the Mozarabs, 1050-1200*. 1994. ISBN 90 04 09910 7
53. HORLICK, A.S. *Patricians, Professors, and Public Schools*. The Origins of Modern Educational Thought in America. 1994. ISBN 90 04 10054 7
54. MacDONALD, A.A., M. LYNCH & I.B. COWAN (eds.). *The Renaissance in Scotland*. Studies in Literature, Religion, History and Culture Offered to John Durkan. 1994. ISBN 90 04 10097 0
55. VON MARTELS, Z. (ed.). *Travel Fact and Travel Fiction*. Studies on Fiction, Literary Tradition, Scholarly Discovery and Observation in Travel Writing. 1994. ISBN 90 04 10112 8
56. PRANGER, M.B. *Bernard of Clairvaux and the Shape of Monastic Thought*. Broken Dreams. 1994. ISBN 90 04 10055 5
57. VAN DEUSEN, N. *Theology and Music at the Early University*. The Case of Robert Grosseteste and Anonymous IV. 1994. ISBN 90 04 10059 8
58. WARNEKE, S. *Images of the Educational Traveller in Early Modern England*. 1994. ISBN 90 04 10126 8
59. BIETENHOLZ, P.G. *Historia and Fabula*. Myths and Legends in Historical Thought from Antiquity to the Modern Age. 1994. ISBN 90 04 10063 6
60. LAURSEN, J.C. (ed.). *New Essays on the Political Thought of the Huguenots of the Refuge*. 1995. ISBN 90 04 09986 7
61. DRIJVERS, J.W. & A.A. MacDONALD (eds.). *Centres of Learning*. Learning and Location in Pre-Modern Europe and the Near East. 1995. ISBN 90 04 10193 4
62. JAUMANN, H. *Critica*. Untersuchungen zur Geschichte der Literaturkritik zwischen Quintilian und Thomasius. 1995. ISBN 90 04 10276 0
63. HEYD, M. *"Be Sober and Reasonable."* The Critique of Enthusiasm in the Seventeenth and Early Eighteenth Centuries. 1995. ISBN 90 04 10118 7
64. OKENFUSS, M.J. *The Rise and Fall of Latin Humanism in Early-Modern Russia*. Pagan Authors, Ukrainians, and the Resiliency of Muscovy. 1995. ISBN 90 04 10331 7
65. DALES, R.C. *The Problem of the Rational Soul in the Thirteenth Century*. 1995. ISBN 90 04 10296 5
66. VAN RULER, J.A. *The Crisis of Causality*. Voetius and Descartes on God, Nature and Change. 1995. ISBN 90 04 10371 6
67. SHEHADI, F. *Philosophies of Music in Medieval Islam*. 1995. ISBN 90 04 10128 4
68. GROSS-DIAZ, T. *The Psalms Commentary of Gilbert of Poitiers*. From *Lectio Divina* to the Lecture Room. 1996. ISBN 90 04 10211 6
69. VAN BUNGE, W. & W. KLEVER (eds.). *Disguised and Overt Spinozism around 1700*. Papers Presented at the International Colloquium, held at Rotterdam, 5-8 October, 1994. 1996. ISBN 90 04 10307 4
70. FLORIDI, L. *Scepticism and the Foundation of Epistemology*. A Study in the Meta-logical Fallacies. 1996. ISBN 90 04 10533 6
71. FOUKE, D. *The Enthusiastical Concerns of Dr. Henry More*. Religious Meaning and the Psychology of Delusion. 1997. ISBN 90 04 10600 6
72. RAMELOW, T. *Gott, Freiheit, Weltenwahl*. Der Ursprung des Begriffes der besten aller möglichen Welten in der Metaphysik der Willensfreiheit zwischen Antonio Perez S.J. (1599-1649) und G.W. Leibniz (1646-1716). 1997. ISBN 90 04 10641 3
73. STONE, H.S. *Vico's Cultural History*. The Production and Transmission of Ideas in Naples, 1685-1750. 1997. ISBN 90 04 10650 2
74. STROLL, M. *The Medieval Abbey of Farfa*. Target of Papal and Imperial Ambitions. 1997. ISBN 90 04 10704 5
75. HYATTE, R. *The Prophet of Islam in Old French:* The Romance of Muhammad *(1258) and* The Book of Muhammad's Ladder *(1264)*. English Translations, With an Introduction. 1997. ISBN 90 04 10709 2
76. JESTICE, P.G. *Wayward Monks and the Religious Revolution of the Eleventh Century*. 1997. ISBN 90 04 10722 3
77. VAN DER POEL, M. *Cornelius Agrippa, The Humanist Theologian and His Declamations*. 1997. ISBN 90 04 10756 8
78. SYLLA, E. & M. McVAUGH (eds.). *Texts and Contexts in Ancient and Medieval Science*. Studies on the Occasion of John E. Murdoch's Seventieth Birthday. 1997. ISBN 90 04 10823 8

79. BINKLEY, P. (ed.). *Pre-Modern Encyclopaedic Texts*. Proceedings of the Second COMERS Congress, Groningen, 1-4 July 1996. 1997. ISBN 90 04 10830 0
80. KLAVER, J.M.I. *Geology and Religious Sentiment*. The Effect of Geological Discoveries on English Society and Literature between 1829 and 1859. 1997. ISBN 90 04 10882 3
81. INGLIS, J. *Spheres of Philosophical Inquiry and the Historiography of Medieval Philosophy*. 1998. ISBN 90 04 10843 2
82. McCALLA, A. *A Romantic Historiosophy*. The Philosophy of History of Pierre-Simon Ballanche. 1998. ISBN 90 04 10967 6
83. VEENSTRA, J.R. *Magic and Divination at the Courts of Burgundy and France*. Text and Context of Laurens Pignon's *Contre les devineurs* (1411). 1998. ISBN 90 04 10925 0
84. WESTERMAN, P.C. *The Disintegration of Natural Law Theory*. Aquinas to Finnis. 1998. ISBN 90 04 10999 4
85. GOUWENS, K. *Remembering the Renaissance*. Humanist Narratives of the Sack of Rome. 1998. ISBN 90 04 10969 2
86. SCHOTT, H. & J. ZINGUER (Hrsg.). *Paracelsus und seine internationale Rezeption in der frühen Neuzeit*. Beiträge zur Geschichte des Paracelsismus. 1998. ISBN 90 04 10974 9
87. ÅKERMAN, S. *Rose Cross over the Baltic*. The Spread of Rosicrucianism in Northern Europe. 1998. ISBN 90 04 11030 5
88. DICKSON, D.R. *The Tessera of Antilia*. Utopian Brotherhoods & Secret Societies in the Early Seventeenth Century. 1998. ISBN 90 04 11032 1
89. NOUHUYS, T. VAN. *The Two-Faced Janus*. The Comets of 1577 and 1618 and the Decline of the Aristotelian World View in the Netherlands. 1998. ISBN 90 04 11204 9
90. MUESSIG, C. (ed.). *Medieval Monastic Preaching*. 1998. ISBN 90 04 10883 1
91. FORCE, J.E. & D.S. KATZ (eds.). *"Everything Connects": In Conference with Richard H. Popkin*. Essays in His Honor. 1999. ISBN 90 04 110984
92. DEKKER, K. *The Origins of Old Germanic Studies in the Low Countries*. 1999. ISBN 90 04 11031 3
93. ROUHI, L. *Mediation and Love*. A Study of the Medieval Go-Between in Key Romance and Near-Eastern Texts. 1999. ISBN 90 04 11268 5
94. AKKERMAN, F., A. VANDERJAGT & A. VAN DER LAAN (eds.). *Northern Humanism between 1469 and 1625*. 1999. ISBN 90 04 11314 2
95. TRUMAN, R.W. *Spanish Treatises on Government, Society and Religion in the Time of Philip II*. The 'de regimine principum' and Associated Traditions. 1999. ISBN 90 04 11379 7
96. NAUTA, L. & A. VANDERJAGT (eds.) *Demonstration and Imagination*. Essays in the History of Science and Philosophy Presented to John D. North. 1999. ISBN 90 04 11468 8
97. BRYSON, D. *Queen Jeanne and the Promised Land*. Dynasty, Homeland, Religion and Violence in Sixteenth-Century France. 1999. ISBN 90 04 11378 9
98. GOUDRIAAN, A. *Philosophische Gotteserkenntnis bei Suárez und Descartes im Zusammenhang mit der niederländischen reformierten* Theologie und Philosophie des 17. Jahrhunderts. 1999. ISBN 90 04 11627 3
99. HEITSCH, D.B. *Practising Reform in Montaigne's* Essais. 2000. ISBN 90 04 11630 3
100. KARDAUN, M. & J. SPRUYT (eds.). *The Winged Chariot*. Collected Essays on Plato and Platonism in Honour of L.M. de Rijk. 2000. ISBN 90 04 11480 7
101. WHITMAN, J. (ed.), *Interpretation and Allegory:* Antiquity to the Modern Period. 2000. ISBN 90 04 11039 9
102. JACQUETTE, D., *David Hume's Critique of Infinity*. 2000. ISBN 90 04 11649 4
103. BUNGE, W. VAN. *From Stevin to Spinoza*. An Essay on Philosophy in the Seventeenth-Century Dutch Republic. 2001. ISBN 90 04 12217 6
104. GIANOTTI, T., *Al-Ghazālī's Unspeakable Doctrine of the Soul*. Unveiling the esoteric psychology, of the Ihyā. 2001. ISBN 90 04 12083 1
105. SAYGIN, S., *Humphrey, Duke of Gloucester (1390-1447) and the Italian Humanists*. 2001. ISBN 90 04 12015 7
106. BEJCZY, I., *Erasmus and the Middle Ages*. The Historical Consciousness of a Christian Humanist. 2001. ISBN 90 04 12218 4